How to Make Money in Stocks

How to Make Money in Stocks

A Winning System in Good Times or Bad

William J. O'Neil

Second Edition

McGraw-Hill, Inc.

New York   San Francisco   Washington, D.C.   Auckland   Bogotá
Caracas   Lisbon   London   Madrid   Mexico City   Milan
Montreal   New Delhi   San Juan   Singapore
Sydney   Tokyo   Toronto

Library of Congress Cataloging-in-Publication Data

O'Neil, William J.
   How to make money in stocks : a winning system in good times or
bad / William J. O'Neil.—2nd ed.
         p.   cm.
   Includes index.
   ISBN 0-07-048059-1 (hc)   —ISBN 0-07-048017-6 (pb)
   1. Investments.   2. Stocks.   I. Title.
HG4521.0515   1995
332.63'22—dc20   94-28192
                                                                CIP

1 2 3 4 5 6 7 8 9 0   DOC/DOC   9 0 9 8 7 6 5 4   (HC)
    10 11 12 13 14 15   DOC/DOC   9 0 9 8   (PBK)
9 10 11 12 13 14 15   DOC/DOC   9 0 9 8   (PBK McGRAW)

ISBN 0-07-048059-1 (hc)
ISBN 0-07-048017-6 (pbk)
ISBN 0-07-048074-5 (pbk McGraw)

The sponsoring editor for this book was Philip Ruppel, the editing super-
visor was Fred Bernardi, and the production supervisor was Suzanne
Babeuf. It was set in Baskerville by McGraw-Hill's Professional Book
Group composition unit.

Printed and bound by R. R. Donnelley & Sons Company.

This book is printed on recycled, acid-free paper containing a
minimum of 50% recycled, de-inked fiber.

Success in a free country is simple.
Get a job, get an education, and
learn to save and invest wisely.
Anyone can do it.
You can do it.

Contents

Part 3 Investing like a Professional

Preface

America is the world's leader in successful new, entrepreneurial companies. Many are in the computer, communications, and technology sectors. Others are in the medical, retail, and leisure and entertainment industries. As an investor, you should develop the skills and acquire the knowledge necessary to recognize and invest in the fast-growing, innovative companies that comprise our New America.

But how do you pick which stocks to buy and how can you significantly minimize the risk you take in buying stocks? And, most importantly, when do you sell your stocks? This book will answer all of those questions for you.

How to Make Money in Stocks gives you a simple, easy-to-use system called *C-A-N S-L-I-M*. The *C-A-N S-L-I-M* method is based on an exhaustive, ongoing analysis of every big winning stock each year since 1953. Each letter in *C-A-N S-L-I-M* stands for one of the seven key factors that all of these past super winners had in common. So, this is not some theoretical or academic method. This is based on how the stock market actually works.

How well does the *C-A-N S-L-I-M* method work? It is the best method devised and available for individual investors, whether new or experienced. More than 200,000 people have attended our free investment seminars and all-day paid workshops where the method is explained in detail. At each session, many people tell us how they made 50% or 100% in the previous year using the *C-A-N S-L-I-M* system.

David Ryan was the first to use the method in the U.S. Investing Championship and won three years in a row. He invested his own money in an actual account that was monitored by CPAs. He averaged over 100% per year and is now the portfolio manager of the New USA Mutual Fund.

Ced Moses entered the contest in 1991 using the method and came in first with a record-setting 379%. Lee Freestone, one of our associates, came in second that year with a 279% increase using *C-A-N S-L-I-M*. In 1994, Lee won it with a 234% increase. The Dow Jones Industrials that year increased 13.7%. There are numerous other examples, such as Dan Running of the University of Baltimore, who won the *USA Today* championship with a 115% increase in 1994; and Jay Plisco of Cold Spring Harbor, N.Y., who won the 1995 Fidelity Investment Challenge by using *C-A-N S-L-I-M* for an impressive 135% gain.

You may want to read this book a couple of times to get it all down, but anyone can learn to invest more successfully if he or she is willing to work at it. Any why shouldn't you learn to capitalize on and benefit financially from the most successful entrepreneurial companies in America?

How to Make Money in Stocks took me many years to write, and I've now been in the battlefield of the financial marketplace for 40 years. So this book can and should help you avoid most of the pitfalls all investors face in this treacherous arena.

In the long run, the U.S. market always goes up because businesses create new products, new services, and new technological inventions. It is the companies with the best new products and services that serve the most people that are always the top stock market winners.

In the last 100 years, the stock market has had 25 bear market declines. These were natural corrections of the previous bull market advances. Every time the market recovered and ultimately soared back into new high ground. So don't get sidetracked by the vast number of gloom and doomers. They rarely have made money for anyone. Besides, I don't ever remember meeting a successful pessimist.

In the early 1960s, William O'Neil & Co. created the first daily computer database on the stock market in the United States. In 1970, we created *Datagraphs*, an institutional investors' service. Today, more than 600 top institutional investors take a wide variety of our research services. We also publish *Daily Graphs*, a daily charting service provided weekly and designed for individual investors.

In 1983, I created the basic format for a new national daily business and financial newspaper, *Investor's Business Daily*. *Investor's Business Daily* made major advances in the quality and availability of vital, relevant information for all public investors and people in business. Sold nationally in every city, the newspaper is the fastest-growing newspaper in the

United States. It has steadily taken share of market away from the centu-ry-old *Wall Street Journal.*

For those still uncertain if *C-A-N S-L-I-M* really works, William O'Neil & Co. was started solely with profits made in Syntex stock in 1963 and *Investor's Business Daily* was built and promoted with profits made in Pic N Save, Price Company, and Amgen.

My deepest appreciation and heartfelt thanks go out to those loyal hardworking souls who read, edited, worked on the graphics, criticized, typed, and retyped the endless changes made to this work. Some of those dedicated individuals are Anne Gerhard, Carolyn Hoffman, Jeannie Kihm, Jim Lan, Stanley Liu, Diane Marin, Milton Perrin, Kathy Russell, Lindee Shadrake, Kathy Sherman, Frank Spillers, and Susan Warfel. And, of course, a great amount of valuable assistance and numerous suggestions were provided by my wife, Fay, and Bill Sabin in the original edition and Philip Ruppel and the excellent McGraw-Hill staff in this second revised edition.

William J. O'Neil

How to Make Money in Stocks

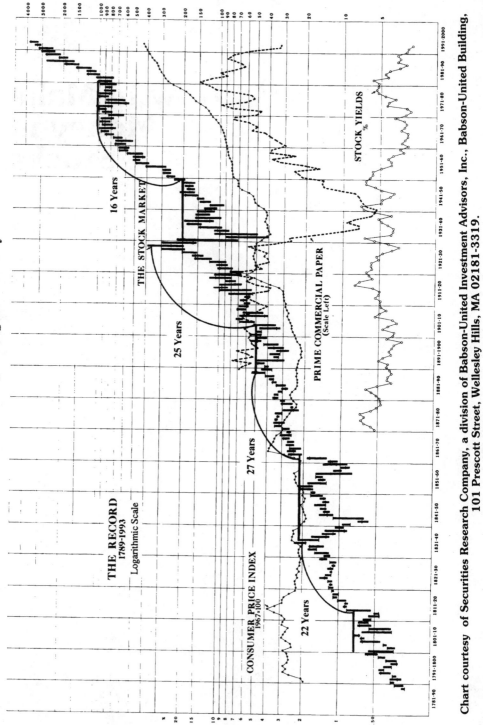

America's Great Continuing Growth Story

THE RECORD
1789-1993
Logarithmic Scale

THE STOCK MARKET

16 Years

25 Years

27 Years

22 Years

CONSUMER PRICE INDEX
1967=100

PRIME COMMERCIAL PAPER
(Scale Left)

STOCK YIELDS
%

Chart courtesy of Securities Research Company, a division of Babson-United Investment Advisors, Inc., Babson-United Building, 101 Prescott Street, Wellesley Hills, MA 02181-3319.

PART 1

A Winning System: C-A-N S-L-I-M

Introduction: Learning from the Greatest Winners

In the following chapters, I will show you exactly how to pick more big winners in the stock market and how to substantially reduce your losses and mistakes. I will examine and discuss other investments, as well.

In the past, most people who bought and sold stocks either had mediocre results or lost money because of their clear lack of knowledge. But no one has to lose money.

This book will provide you with most of the investment understanding, skills, and methods you need to become a more successful investor.

I believe that most people in this country and many others throughout the free world, young and old, regardless of profession, education, background, or economic position, can and definitely should own common stock. This book isn't written for an elite but for the millions of little guys and gals everywhere who want a chance to be better off.

YOU CAN START SMALL   If you are a typical working man or woman or a beginning investor, it doesn't take a lot of money to start. You can begin with as little as $500 to $1000 and add to it as you earn and save more money. I began with the purchase of just five shares of Procter & Gamble when I was only 21 and fresh out of school.

You live in a fantastic time of unlimited opportunity, an era of outstanding new ideas, emerging industries, and new frontiers. But you have to read to learn how to recognize and take advantage of these extraordinary situations.

The opportunities are out there for everyone. You are now witnessing a New America. We lead the world in high technology, medical advancements, computer software, military capabilities, and innovative new entrepreneurial companies. The communist socialist system was finally relegated to the ash heap of history under Ronald Reagan and our system of freedom and opportunity serves as a prime success model for the majority of countries in the world.

It is not enough today to just work and earn a salary. To do the things you want to do, to go the places you want to go, to have the things you want to have in your life, **you absolutely must save and invest intelligently.** The second income from your investments and the net profits you can make will help you reach your goals and provide real security.

SECRET TIP #1 The first step in learning to pick stock market winners is for you to examine leading winners of the past to learn all the characteristics of the most successful stocks. You will learn from this observation what type of price patterns these stocks developed just before their spectacular price advances.

Other key factors you will uncover include what kind of company quarterly-earnings reports were publicly known at the time, what the annual earnings histories of these organizations had been in the prior five years, what amount of stock trading volume was present, what degree of relative price strength occurred in the price of the stocks before their enormous success, how many shares of common stock were outstanding in the capitalization of each company, how many of the greatest winners had significant new products or new management, and how many were tied to strong industry group moves caused by important changes occurring in an entire industry.

It is easy to conduct this type of practical, commonsense analysis of past successful leaders. I have already completed such a comprehensive study. In our historical analysis, we selected the greatest winning stocks in the stock market each year (in terms of percentage increase for the year), spanning more than 40 years.

We call the study *The Record Book of Greatest Stock Market Winners.* It covers the period from 1953 through 1993 and analyzes in detail over 500 of the biggest winning companies in recent stock market history: super stocks such as Texas Instruments, whose price soared from $25 to $250 from January 1958 through May 1960; Xerox, which escalated from $160 to the equivalent of $1340 from March 1963 to June 1966;

Syntex, which leaped from $100 to $570 in only six months during the last half of 1963; Dome Petroleum and Prime Computer, which respectively advanced 1000% and 1595% in the 1978–1980 stock market; Limited Stores, which wildly excited lucky shareowners with a 3500% increase between 1982 and 1987; and Cisco Systems, which advanced from a split-adjusted $1.88 to $40.75 between October 1990 and March 1994. Home Depot and Microsoft both increased more than 20 times during the 1980s and early '90s. Home Depot was one of the all-time great performers jumping twentyfold in less than 2 years from its initial public offering in September of 1981 and then again climbing another 10 times from 1988 to 1992. All of these companies offered exciting new products and concepts.

Would you like to know the common characteristics and secret rules of success we discovered from this intensive study of all past glamorous stock market leaders?

It's all in the next few chapters and in a simple easy-to-remember formula we have named *C-A-N S-L-I-M*. Write the formula down, and repeat it several times so you won't forget it.

Each letter in the words *C-A-N S-L-I-M* stands for one of the seven chief characteristics of these great winning stocks at their early developing stages, just before they made huge profits for their shareholders.

You can learn how to pick winners in the stock market, and you can become part owner in the best companies in the world. So, let's get started right now. Here's a sneak preview of *C-A-N S-L-I-M*.

C   =   Current Quarterly Earnings Per Share: How Much Is Enough?

A   =   Annual Earnings Increases: Look for Meaningful Growth.

N   =   New Products, New Management, New Highs: Buying at the Right Time.

S   =   Supply and Demand: Small Capitalization Plus Volume Demand.

L   =   Leader or Laggard: Which Is Your Stock?

I   =   Institutional Sponsorship: A Little Goes a Long Way.

M   =   Market Direction: How to Determine It?

Please begin immediately with Chapter 1.

1

C = Current Quarterly Earnings Per Share: How Much Is Enough?

M/A-Com Inc.

Humana Inc.

Kirby Exploration Co.

What did shares of the above-mentioned microwave component manufacturer, hospital operator, and oil service company have in common? From 1977 to 1981, they all posted price run-ups surpassing 900%.

In scrutinizing these and other past stock market superstars, I've found a number of other similarities as well.

For example, trading volume in these sensational winners swelled substantially before their giant price moves began. The winning stocks also tended to shuffle around in price consolidation periods for a few months before they broke out and soared. But one key variable stood out from all the rest in importance: the profits of nearly every outstanding stock were booming.

The common stocks you select for purchase should show a major percentage increase in the current quarterly earnings per share (the most recently reported quarter) when compared to the prior year's same quarter.

Earnings per share are calculated by dividing a company's total after-tax profits by the company's number of common shares outstanding. The percentage increase in earnings per share is the single most important element in stock selection today.

The greater the percentage of increase, the better, as long as you aren't misled by comparing current earnings to nearly nonexistent earnings for the year earlier quarter, like 1 cent a share.

Ten cents per share versus one cent may be a 900% increase, but it is definitely distorted and not as meaningful as $1 versus $.50. The 100% increase of $1 versus $.50 is not overstated by comparison to an unusually low number in the year ago quarter.

I am continually amazed at how many professional pension fund managers, as well as individual investors, buy common stocks with the current reported quarter's earnings flat (no change), or even worse, down. There is absolutely no reason for a stock to go anywhere if the current earnings are poor.

Even if the present quarter's earnings are up 5% to 10%, that is simply not enough of an improvement to fuel any significant upward price movement in a stock. It is also easier for a corporation currently showing a mere increase of 7% or 8% to suddenly report lower earnings the next quarter.

Seek Stocks Showing Big Current Earnings Increases

In our models of the 500 best performing stocks in the 40 years from 1953 through 1993, three out of four of these securities showed earnings increases averaging more than 70% in the latest publicly reported quarter *before* the stocks began their major price advance. The one out of four that didn't show solid current quarter increases did so in the very next quarter, and those increases averaged 90%!

If the *best* stocks had profit increases of this magnitude *before* they advanced rapidly in price, why should you settle for mediocre or down earnings?

Our study showed that among all big gainers between 1970 and 1982, 86% reported higher earnings in their most recently published quarter, and 76% were up over 10%. The median earnings increase was 34% and the mean (average) was up 90%.

You may find that only about 2% of all stocks listed for trading on the New York or American stock exchanges will, at any one time, show increases of this proportion in current quarterly net income.

But, remember you want to find the exceptional stocks rather than the lackluster ones, so set your sights high and start looking for the superior stocks, the small number of real leaders. They are there.

Success is built on dreams and ideas; however, it helps to know exactly what you're looking for. Before you start your search for tomorrow's super stock market leader, let me tell you about a few of the traps and pitfalls.

Watch Out for Misleading Reports of Earnings

Have you ever read a corporation's quarterly earnings report that stated, "We had a terrible first three months. Prospects for our company are turning down due to inefficiencies in the home office. Our competition just came out with a better product, which will adversely affect our sales. Furthermore, we are losing our shirt on the new midwestern operation, which was a real blunder on management's part."

No! Here's what you see. "Greatshakes Corporation reports record sales of $7.2 million versus $6 million (+ 20%) for the quarter ended March 31." If you own their stock, this is wonderful news. You certainly are not going to be disappointed. You think this is a fine company (otherwise you wouldn't own its stock), and the report confirms your thinking.

Is this record-breaking sales announcement a good report? Let's suppose the company also had record earnings of $2.10 per share of stock for the quarter. Is it even better now?

What if the $2.10 was versus $2 (+ 5%) per share in the same quarter the previous year? Why were sales up 20% and earnings ahead only 5%? Something might be wrong—maybe the company's profit margins are crumbling. At any rate, if you own the stock, you should be concerned and evaluate the situation closely to see why the earnings increased only 5%.

Most investors are impressed with what they read, and companies love to put their best foot forward. Even though this corporation may have had all-time record sales, up 20%, it didn't mean much. You must be able to see through slanted published presentations if you want the vital facts.

The key factor for the winning investor must always be **how much the current quarter's earnings are up in percentage terms from the same quarter the year before!**

Let's say your company discloses that sales climbed 10% and net income advanced 12%. This sounds good, but you shouldn't be concerned with the company's total net income. You don't own the whole organization. You own shares of stock in the corporation. Perhaps the company issued additional shares or there was other dilution of the common stock. Just because sales and total net income for the company were up, the report still may not be favorable. Maybe earnings per share of common stock inched up only 2% or 3%.

Break Down Six or Nine Month Earnings into Quarterly Percentage Changes

Suppose your company announces that earnings for the six months that ended June 30 were $2.50 per share versus $2 for the same period a year earlier (+ 25%). Your "pet" stock must be in great shape. You couldn't ask for better results—or could you?

Beware. The company reported earnings for six months. What did the stock earn in the last quarter, the three months ended in June?

Maybe in the first quarter ended in March the stock earned $1.60 per share versus $1 (+ 60%). What does this leave for the last quarter ended June 30? Ninety cents versus one dollar. This is a terrible report, even though the way it was presented to you sounded terrific.

If you own common stock in a company whose earnings had been up 60% and they came out with a statement of $.90 versus $1 (down 10%), you had better wake up. The outfit might be deteriorating.

You can't always assume that because an earnings report appears to be rosy, everything is fine. You have to look deeper and not accept the reassuring manner of corporate news releases reported in your favorite newspaper.

Many times, earnings declarations are published for the most recent nine months. This tells you nothing, and all too often it masks serious weakness in the numbers that really count. The first quarter may have been up 30%, the second quarter up 10%, and the last quarter off 10%. By always breaking down the figures to show the quarter-by-quarter earnings, you will be able to see a completely different picture and trend.

Omit a Company's One-Time Extraordinary Gains

The last important trap the winning investor should sidestep is being influenced by nonrecurring profits.

If an organization that manufactures computers reports earnings for the last quarter that include profits from the sale of real estate or a plant, for example, that part of the earnings should be subtracted from the report. Those are one-time, nonrecurring earnings and are not representative of the true, ongoing profitability of corporate operations. Ignore them.

Set a Minimum Level for Current Earnings Increases

As a general guide for new or experienced investors, I would suggest you *not* buy any stock that doesn't show earnings per share up *at least 18% or 20%* in the most recent quarter versus the same quarter the year before. Many successful money-makers use 25% or 30% as their minimum earnings parameter. And make sure you calculate the percentage change; don't guess or assume. You will be even safer if you insist the last two quarters each show a significant percentage increase in earnings from year-ago quarters.

During bull markets, I prefer to concentrate in equities (common stocks) that show powerful current earnings leaping 40% or 50% up to 500%. Why not buy the very best merchandise available?

If you want to further sharpen your stock selection process, before you buy, look ahead to the next quarter or two and check the earnings that were reported for those same quarters the previous year. See if the company will be coming up against unusually large or small earnings achieved a year ago.

In some instances, where the unusual year-earlier earnings are not due to seasonal factors (the December quarter is always big for retailers, for example), this procedure may help you anticipate a strong or poor earnings report due ahead in the coming months.

Many individuals and institutions alike buy stocks with earnings down in the most recently reported quarter just because they like a company and think the stock's price is cheap. Usually they accept a story that earnings will rebound strongly in the near future.

While this may be true in some cases (it frequently isn't), the main point is that at any time in the market, you have the choice of investing in at least 5000 or more stocks. You don't have to accept promises of something that may never occur when alternative investments are actually showing current earnings advancing strongly.

The Debate on Overemphasis of Current Earnings

Recently it has been noted that Japanese firms concentrate more on longer-term profits rather than on trying to maximize current earnings per share.

This is a sound concept and one the better-managed organizations in the United States (a minority of companies) also follow. That is how well-managed entities create colossal quarterly earnings increases, by spending several years on research, developing superior new products, and cutting costs.

But don't be confused. You as an individual investor can afford to wait until the point in time when a company positively proves to you its efforts have been successful and are starting to actually show real earnings increases.

Requiring that current quarterly earnings be up a hefty amount is just another smart way the intelligent investor can reduce the risk of excessive mistakes in stock selection.

Many corporations have mediocre management that continually produces second-rate earnings results. I call them the "entrenched maintainers." These are the companies you want to avoid until someone has the courage to change top management. Ironically, these are generally the companies that strain to pump up their current earnings a dull 8% or 10%. True growth companies with outstanding new products do not have to maximize current results.

Look for Accelerating Quarterly Earnings Growth

My studies of thousands of the most successful concerns in America proved that virtually every corporate stock with an outstanding upward price move showed accelerated quarterly earnings increases some time in the previous ten quarters before the towering price advance began.

Therefore, what is crucial is not just that earnings are up or that a certain price-to-earnings ratio (a stock's price divided by its last twelve months' earnings per share) exists; it is the change and improvement from the stock's prior percentage rate of earning increases that causes a supreme price surge. Wall Street now calls these earnings surprises.

I once mentioned this concept of earnings acceleration to Peter Vermilye, the former head of Citicorp's Trust Investment Division in New York City. He liked the term and felt it was much more accurate and relevant than the phrase "earnings momentum" sometimes used by investment professionals.

If a company's earnings are up 15% a year and suddenly begin spurting 40% to 50% a year, it usually creates the basic conditions for important stock price improvement.

Two Quarters of Major Earnings Deceleration May Mean Trouble

Likewise, when the rate of earnings growth starts to slow and begins meaningful deceleration (for instance, a 50% rate of increase suddenly decreases to only 15% for a couple quarters), the security probably has either topped out permanently, regardless of what analysts and Wall Street may say, or the rate of upward progress will dwindle into a lengthy and unrewarding price consolidation period characterized by prolonged sideways movement.

I prefer to see two quarters of *material* slowdown before turning negative on a company's earnings since the best of organizations can periodically have one slow quarter.

Consult Log Scale Weekly Graphs

One reason that logarithmic scale graphs are of such great value in security analysis is that acceleration or deceleration in the percentage rate of quarterly earnings increases can be seen very clearly on a log graph.

Log graphs show percentage changes accurately, since one inch anywhere on the price or earnings scale represents the same percentage change. This is not true of arithmetically scaled charts.

For example, a 100% stock price increase from $10 to $20 a share would show the same space change as a 50% increase from $20 to $30 a share on an arithmetically scaled chart. A log graph, however, would show the 100% increase as twice as large as the 50% increase.

The principle of earnings acceleration or deceleration is essential to understand.

Fundamental security analysts who recommend stocks because of an absolute level of earnings expected for the following year could be looking at the wrong set of facts. A stock that earned $5 per share and expects to report $6 the next year can mislead you unless you know the previous trend in the percentage rate of earnings change.

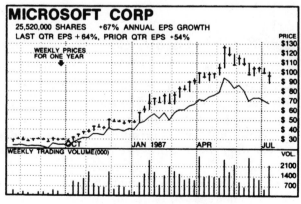

Arithmetic price scale

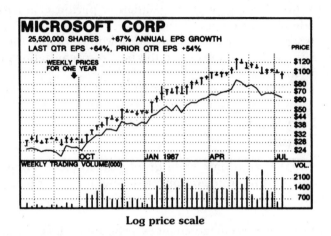

MICROSOFT CORP
25,520,000 SHARES   +67% ANNUAL EPS GROWTH
LAST QTR EPS +64%, PRIOR QTR EPS +54%

Log price scale

To say the security is undervalued just because it is selling at a certain price-earnings ratio or because it is in the low range of its historical P/E ratio is also usually nonsense unless primary consideration has first been given to whether the momentum and rate of change in earnings is substantially increasing or decreasing.

Perhaps this partially explains who so few public or institutional investors, such as banks and insurance companies, make worthwhile money following the buy-and-sell recommendations of most securities analysts.

You, as a do-it-yourself investor, can take the latest quarterly earnings per share, add them to the prior three quarters' earnings of a company, and plot the amounts on a logarithmic scale graph. The plotting of the most recent twelve-month earnings each quarter should, in the best companies, put the earnings per share close to or already at new highs.

Check Other Key Stocks in the Group

For added safety, it is wise to check the industry group of your stock. You should be able to find at least one other noteworthy stock in the industry also showing good current earnings. This acts as a confirming factor. If you cannot find any other impressive stock in the group displaying strong earnings, the chances are greater that you have selected the wrong investment.

Note the date when a company expects to report its next quarterly earnings. One to four weeks prior to the report's release, a stock frequently displays unusual price strength or weakness, or simply "hesitates" while the market and other equities in the same group advance. This could give you an early clue of an approaching good or bad report. You may also want to be aware and suspicious of stocks that have gone several weeks beyond estimated reporting time without the release of an earnings announcement.

Where to Find Current Corporate Earnings Reports

New quarterly corporate earnings statements are published every day in the financial section of your local paper, in *Investor's Business Daily,* and in *The Wall Street Journal. Investor's Business Daily* separates all new earnings reports into companies with "up" earnings and those disclosing "down" results so you can easily see who produced excellent gains.

AMERICAN TRAVELLERS CORP		ATVC 27%
Insurance-Acc & Health		Eps 99 Rel 99
Quar Mar 31:	1990	1989
Sales	$18,619,000	$10,018,000
Net Income	2,555,000	1,199,000
Avg shares	3,784,470	3,526,960
Share earns:		(OTC)
Net Income	0.68	0.34
% Change	+100% ★	

WAL-MART STORES		WMT 52
Retail-Discount&Variety		Eps 98 Rel 90
Quar Apr 30:	1990	1989
Sales	$6,819,227,000	$5,403,117,000
Net Income	253,443,000	198,289,000
Avg shares	567,743,000	567,356,000
Share earns:		(NYSE)
Net Income	0.45	0.35
% Change	+29% ★	

NORDSTRÖM INC		NOBE 27%
Retail-Apparel/Shoe		Eps 67 Rel 23
Quar Apr 30:	1990	1989
Sales	$555,038,000	$512,210,000
Net Income	13,169,000	22,973,000
Avg shares	81,617,436	81,504,205
Share earns:		(OTC)
Net Income	0.16	0.28
% Change	-43%	

Which earnings report do you think is best?

Chart services published weekly also show earnings reported during the prior week as well as the most recent earnings figures for every stock they chart.

One last point to clarify: **You should always compare a stock's percentage increase in earnings for the quarter ended December, to the December quarter a year earlier.** Never compare the December quarter to the immediately prior September quarter.

You now have the first critical rule for improving your stock selection: **Current quarterly earnings per share should be up a major percentage (at least 20% to 50% or more) over the same quarter last year.** The best ones might show earnings up 100% to 500%! A mediocre 8% or 10% isn't enough! In picking winning stocks, it's the bottom line that counts.

2

A = Annual Earnings Increases: Look for Meaningful Growth

If you want to own part of a business in your home town, do you choose a steadily growing, successful concern or one that is unsuccessful, not growing and highly cyclical?

Most of you would prefer a business that is showing profitable growth.

That's exactly what you should look for in common stocks. **Each year's annual earnings per share for the last five years should show an increase over the prior year's earnings.** You might accept one year being down in the last five as long as the following year's earnings quickly recover and move back to new high ground.

It is possible that a stock could earn $4 a share one year, $5 the next year, $6 the next, and the following year—$2. If the next annual earnings statement were $2.50 versus the prior year's $2 (+ 25%), that would not be a good report. The only reason it may seem attractive is that the previous year ($2) was so depressed any improvement would look good. In any case, the profit recovery is slow and is still substantially below the company's peak earnings of $6.

Select Stocks with 25% to 50% Annual Growth Rates

Owning common stock is just the same as being a part owner in a business. And who wants to own part of an establishment showing no growth? **The annual compounded growth rate of earnings in the superior firms you hand pick for purchasing stock in should be from 25% to 50%, or even 100% or more, per year over the last 4 or 5 years.**

Between 1970 and 1982, the average annual compounded earnings growth rate of all outstanding performing stocks at their early emerging stage was 24%. The median, or most common, growth rate was 21% per year, and three out of four of the prominent winners revealed at least some positive annual growth rate over the five years preceding the giant increase in the value of the stock. One out of four were turnarounds.

A typical successful yearly earnings per share growth progression for a company's latest five-year period might look something like $.70, $1.15, $1.85, $2.80, $4.

The earnings estimate for the next year should also be up a healthy percentage; the greater the percentage, the better. However, remember **estimates are opinions.** Opinions may be wrong whereas actual reported earnings are facts that are ordinarily more dependable.

What Is a Normal Stock Market Cycle?

Most bull (up) market cycles last two to four years and are followed by a recession or bear (down) market and eventually another bull market in common stocks.

In the beginning phase of a new bull market, growth stocks are usually the first sector to lead the market and make new price highs. Heavy basic industry groups such as steel, chemical, paper, rubber, and machinery are commonly more laggard followers.

Young growth stocks will usually dominate for at least two bull market cycles. Then the emphasis may change for the next cycle, or a short period, to turnaround or cyclical stocks or newly improved sectors of the market, such as consumer growth stocks, over-the-counter growth issues, or defense stocks that sat on the sidelines in the previous cycle.

Last year's bloody bums become next year's heroes. Chrysler and Ford were two such spirited turnaround plays in 1982. Cyclical and turnaround opportunities led in the market waves of 1953–1955, 1963–1965, and 1974–1975. Papers, aluminums, autos, chemicals, and plastics returned to the fore in 1987. Yet, even in these periods, there were some pretty dramatic young growth stocks available. Basic industry stocks in the United States frequently represent older, more inefficient industries, some of which are no longer internationally competitive and growing. This is perhaps not the area of America's future excellence.

Cyclical stocks' price moves tend to be more short-lived when they do occur, and these stocks are much more apt to suddenly falter and encounter disappointing quarterly earnings reports. Even in the stretch where you decide to buy strong turnaround situations, the annual compounded growth rate could, in many cases, be 5% to 10%.

Requiring a company to show two consecutive quarters of sharp earnings recovery should put the earnings for the latest twelve months into, or very near, new high ground. If the 12 months earnings line is shown on a chart, the sharper the upswing the better. This will make it possible in many cases for even the "old dog" about-face stock to show some annual growth rate for the prior five-year time period. Sometimes one quarter of earnings turnaround will suffice if the earnings upswing is so dramatic that it puts the 12 months ended earnings line into new highs.

Check the Stability of a Company's Five-Year Earnings Record

While the percentage rate of increase in earnings is most important, an additional factor of value, which we helped pioneer in the measurement and use of, is the stability and consistency of the past five years' earnings. We display the number differently than most statisticians do.

Our stability measurements are expressed on a scale from 1 to 99. The lower the figure, the more stable the past earnings record. The figures are calculated by plotting quarterly earnings for the last five years and fitting a trend line around the plot points to determine the degree of deviation from the basic earnings trend.

Growth stocks with good stability of earnings tend to show a stability figure below 20 or 25. Equities with a stability rating over 30 are more cyclical and a little less dependable in their growth. All other things being equal, you may want to choose the security showing a greater degree of consistency and stability in past earnings growth.

Earnings stability numbers are usually shown immediately after a company's five-year growth rate, although most analysts and investment services do not bother to make the calculation.

EARNINGS GROWTH RATE (STABILITY) RANK		
1983-87	+31%	(6)
1981-85	+19%	(8)
1979-83	+19%	(11)

Earnings stability rank

If you primarily restrict your selections to ventures with proven growth records, you avoid the hundreds of investments having erratic earnings histories or a cyclical recovery in profits that may top out as they approach earnings peaks of the prior cycle.

How to Weed Out the Losers in a Group

When you investigate a specific industry group, **using the five-year growth criteria will also help you weed out 80% of the stocks in an industry.** This is because the majority of companies in an industry have lackluster growth rates or no growth.

When Xerox was having its super performance of 700% growth from March 1963 to June 1966, its earnings growth rate averaged 32% per year. Wal-Mart Stores, a discount retailer, sported an annual growth rate from 1977 to 1990 of 43% and boomed in price an incredible 11,200%. Cisco Systems growth rate in October 1990 was an enormous 257% per year and Microsoft's was 99% in October 1986, both before their long advances.

The fact that an investment possesses a good five-year growth record doesn't necessarily cause it to be labeled a growth stock. Ironically, in fact, some companies called growth stocks are producing a substantially slower rate of growth than they did in several earlier market eras. These should usually be avoided. Their record is more like a fully matured or nearly senile growth stock. Older and larger organizations frequently show slow growth.

New Cycles Create New Leaders

Each soaring new cycle in the stock market will catapult fresh leadership stocks to the attention of the market, some of which will begin to be called growth stocks. The growth record in itself, however, is only a starting point for would-be victorious investors, and it should be the first of many earnings measurements you should check.

For example, companies with outstanding five-year growth records of 30% per year but whose current earnings in the last two quarters have slowed significantly to + 15% and + 10% should be avoided in most instances.

Insist on Both Annual and Current Quarterly Earnings Being Excellent

We prefer to see current quarterly earnings accelerating or at least maintaining the trend of several past quarters. **A standout stock needs a** sound growth record during recent years but also needs a strong current earnings record in the last few quarters. It is the unique combination of these two critical factors, rather than one or the other being outstanding, that creates a superb stock, or at least one that has a higher chance of true success.

Investor's Business Daily provides a relative earnings ranking (based on the latest five-year annual earnings record and recent quarterly earnings reports) for all common stocks shown in the daily NYSE, AMEX, and OTC stock price quotation tables.

More than 6000 stocks are compared against each other and ranked on a scale from 1 to 99. An 80 earnings per share rank means a company's current and five-year historical earnings record outclassed 80% of all other companies.

The earnings record of a corporation is the most critical, fundamental factor available for selecting potential winning stocks.

Are Price-Earnings Ratios Important?

Now that we've discussed the indispensable importance of a stock's current quarterly earnings record and annual earnings increases in the last five years, you may be wondering about a stock's price-to-earnings (P/E) ratio. How important is it in selecting stocks? Prepare yourself for a bubble-bursting surprise.

P/E ratios have been used for years by analysts as their basic measurement tool in deciding if a stock is undervalued (has a low P/E) and should be bought or is overvalued (has a high P/E) and should be sold.

Factual analysis of each cycle's winning stocks shows that P/E ratios have very little to do with whether a stock should be bought or not. A stock's P/E ratio is not normally an important cause of the most successful stock moves.

Our model book studies proved the percentage increase in earnings per share was substantially more crucial than the P/E ratio as a cause of impressive stock performance.

During the 33 years from 1953 through 1985 the average P/E for the best performing stocks at their early emerging stage was 20 (the Dow

FRANKLIN RES INC
3,494,000 SHARES   +97% ANNUAL EPS GROWTH
LAST QTR EPS +115%, PRIOR QTR EPS +150%

Profile of a standout stock

Jones Industrial's P/E at the same time averaged 15). While advancing, these stocks expanded their P/Es to approximately 45 (125% expansion of P/E ratio).

Why You Missed Some Fabulous Stocks!

While these figures are merely averages, they do strongly imply that **if you were not willing to pay an average of 20 to 30 times earnings for growth stocks in the 40 years through 1993, you automatically eliminated most of the best investments available!**

P/Es were higher on average from 1953 to 1970 and lower between 1970 and 1982. From 1974 through 1982, the average beginning P/E was 15 and expanded to 31 at the stock's top. P/Es of winning stocks during this period tended to be only slightly higher than the general market's P/E at the beginning of a stock's price advance.

High P/Es were found to occur because of bull markets. With the exception of cyclical stocks, low P/Es generally occurred because of bear markets. Some OTC growth stocks may also display lower P/Es if the stocks are not yet widely owned by institutional investors.

Don't buy a stock solely because the P/E ratio looks cheap. There usually are good reasons why it is cheap, and there is no golden rule in the marketplace that a stock which sells at eight or ten times earnings cannot eventually sell at four or five times earnings. Many years ago, when I was first beginning to study the market, I bought Northrop at four times earnings and in disbelief watched the outfit decline to two times earnings.

How Price-Earnings Ratios Are Misused

Many Wall Street analysts inspect the historical high and low price-earnings ratios of a stock and feel intoxicating magic in the air when a security sells in the low end of its historical P/E range. Stocks are frequently recommended by researchers when this occurs, or when the price starts to drop, because then the P/E declines and the stock appears to be a bargain.

Much of this kind of analysis is based on questionable personal opinions or theories handed down through the years by academicians and some analysts. Many "green" newcomers to the stock market use the faulty *method* of selecting stock investments based chiefly on low P/E ratios and go wrong more often than not.

This system of analysis often ignores far more basic trends. For example, the general market may have topped out, in which case all stocks are headed lower and it is ridiculous to say "Electronic Gizmo" is undervalued because it was 22 times earnings and can now be bought for 15 times earnings. The market break of 1987 hurt many value buyers.

The Wrong Way to Analyze Companies in an Industry

Another common, poor use of price-earnings ratios by both amateurs and professionals alike is to evaluate the stocks in an industry and conclude that the one selling at the cheapest P/E is always undervalued and is therefore, the most attractive purchase. This is usually the company with the most ghastly earnings record, and that's precisely why it sells at the lowest P/E.

The simple truth is that stocks at any one time usually sell near their current value. So the stock which sells at 20 times earnings is there for one set of reasons, and the stock that trades for 15 times earnings is there for other reasons the market already has analyzed. The one selling for seven times is at seven times because its overall record is more deficient. **Everything sells for about what it is worth** at the time.

If a company's price level and price-earnings ratio changes in the near future, it is because conditions, events, psychology, and earnings continue to improve or suddenly start to deteriorate as the weeks and months pass.

Eventually a stock's P/E will reach its ultimate high point, but this normally is because the general market averages are peaking and starting an important decline, or the stock definitely is beginning to lose its earnings growth.

High P/E stocks can be more volatile, particularly if they are in the high-tech area. The price of a high P/E stock can also get temporarily ahead of itself, but so can the price of low P/E stocks.

Some High P/Es That Were Cheap

It should be remembered that in a few captivating smaller-company growth situations that have revolutionary new product breakthroughs, high P/E ratios can actually be low. Xerox sold for 100 times earnings in 1960—before it advanced 3300% in price (from a split-adjusted price of $5 to $170). Syntex sold for 45 times earnings in July 1963, before it advanced 400%. Genentech was priced at 200 times earnings in the over-the-counter market in early November 1985, and it bolted 300% in the next five months. All had fantastic new products.

Don't Sell High P/E Stocks Short

When the stock market was at rock bottom in June 1962, a big, heavyset Beverly Hills investor barged into the office of a broker friend of mine and in a loud voice shouted Xerox was drastically overpriced because it was selling for 50 times earnings. He sold 2000 shares short at $88.

After he sold short this "obviously overpriced stock," it immediately started advancing and ultimately reached a price equal to $1300 before adjusting for stock splits. So much for amateur opinions about P/E ratios being too high. **Investors' personal opinions are generally wrong; markets seldom are.**

Some institutional research firms in recent years published services and analyses based on the principle of relative P/E ratios for companies, compared to individual company earnings growth rates. Our detailed research over many cycles has shown these types of studies to be misleading and of little practical value.

The conclusion we have reached from years of in-depth research into winning corporations is that the percentage increase and acceleration in earnings per share is more important than the level of the stock's P/E ratio. At any rate, it may be easier to spot emerging new trends than to accurately assess correct valuation levels.

In summary: **Concentrate on stocks with a proven record of significant annual earnings growth in the last five years.** Don't accept excuses; insist the annual earnings increases plus strong recent quarterly earnings improvements be there.

3

N = New Products,
New Management,
New Highs:
Buying at the Right Time

It takes something new to produce a startling advance in the price of a stock.

This something new can be an important new product or service, selling rapidly and causing earnings to accelerate above previous rates of increase. It could also be new top management in a company during the last couple of years. A new broom sweeps clean, or at least may bring inspiring ideas and vigor to the ball game.

Or the new event could be substantial changes within the company's industry. Industrywide shortages, price increases, or new technology could affect almost all members of the industry group in a positive way.

New Products That Created
Super Successes

1. Rexall's new Tupperware division, in 1958, helped push the company's stock to $50 a share, from $16.

2. Thiokol in 1957–1959 came out with new rocket fuels for missiles, propelling its stock from $48 to the equivalent of $355.

3. Syntex, in 1963, marketed the oral contraceptive pill. In six months the stock soared from $100 to $550.

4. McDonald's, in 1967–1971, with low-priced fast food franchising, snowballed into an 1100% profit for stockholders.

5. Levitz Furniture stock increased 660% in 1970–1971, with the popularity of their giant warehouse discount furniture centers.

6. Houston Oil & Gas, in 1972–1973, with a major new oil field ran up 968% in 61 weeks and later in 1976 picked up another 367%.

7. Computervision stock advanced 1235% in 1978–1980, with the introduction of new Cad-Cam factory automation equipment.

8. Wang Labs Class B stock grew 1350% in 1978–1980, due to the creation of their new word-processing office machines.

9. Price Company stock shot up more than 15 times in 1982–1986 with the opening of a southern California chain of innovative wholesale warehouse membership stores.

10. Amgen developed two successful new biotech drugs, Epogen and Neupogen, and the stock raced ahead from 60% in 1990 to the equivalent of 460% in January 1992.

11. Cisco Systems, another California company, created routers and networking equipment that allowed company links with geographically dispersed local area computer networks. The stock advanced over 2000% in $3\frac{1}{2}$ years.

12. International Game Technology rose an astounding 1600% in 1991–1993 with new microprocessor-based gaming products.

In our study of greatest stock market winners from 1953 through 1993, we discovered more than 95% of these stunning successes in American industry either had a major new product or service, new management, or an important change for the better in the conditions of their particular industry.

The Stock Market's Great Paradox

There is another fascinating phenomenon we found in the early stage of all winning stocks. We call it "the great paradox." Before I tell you what this last new observation is, I want you to look at three typical stocks shown on the next page. Which one looks like the best buy to you? Which stock would you probably avoid?

Among the thousands of individual investors attending my investment lectures in the 1970s, 1980s, and 1990s, 98% said they do not buy stocks that are making new highs in price.

The staggering majority of individual investors, whether new or experienced, feel delightful comfort in buying stocks that are down substantially from their peaks.

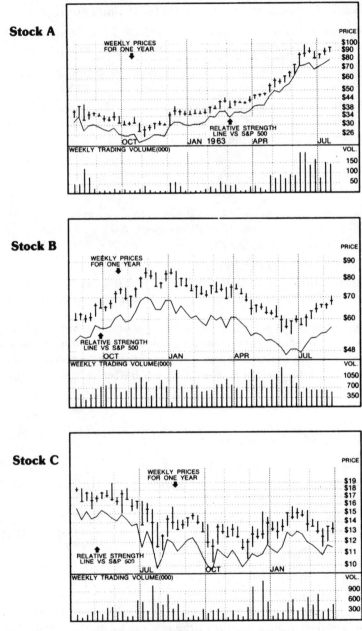

Stock A

WEEKLY PRICES
FOR ONE YEAR
↓

RELATIVE STRENGTH
LINE VS S&P 500

PRICE
$100
$90
$80
$70
$60
$50
$44
$38
$34
$30
$26

OCT   JAN 1963   APR   JUL

WEEKLY TRADING VOLUME(000)   VOL.
150
100
50

Stock B

WEEKLY PRICES
FOR ONE YEAR
↓

RELATIVE STRENGTH
LINE VS S&P 500

PRICE
$90
$80
$70
$60
$48

OCT   JAN   APR   JUL

WEEKLY TRADING VOLUME(000)   VOL.
1050
700
350

Stock C

WEEKLY PRICES
FOR ONE YEAR
↓

RELATIVE STRENGTH
LINE VS S&P 500

PRICE
$19
$18
$17
$16
$15
$14
$13
$12
$11
$10

JUL   OCT   JAN

WEEKLY TRADING VOLUME(000)   VOL.
900
600
300

Which stock looks like the best buy?

I have provided extensive research for over 600 institutional investors in the United States. It is my experience that most institutional money managers are also bottom buyers—they, too, feel safer buying stocks that look cheap because they're either down a lot in price or selling near their lows.

The hard-to-accept great paradox in the stock market is that **what seems too high and risky to the majority usually goes higher and what seems low and cheap usually goes lower.** Haven't you seen this happen before?

In case you find this supposed "high-altitude" method a little difficult to boldly act upon, let me cite another study we conducted. An analysis was made of the daily newspapers' new-high and new-low stock lists during several good, as well as poor, market periods.

Our findings were simple. Stocks on the new-high list tended to go higher, and those on the new-low list tended to go lower.

Put another way, a stock listed in the financial section's new-low list of common stocks is usually a pretty poor prospect, whereas **a stock making the new-high list the first time during a bull market and accompanied by a big increase in trading volume might be a red-hot prospect worth checking into. Decisive investors should be out of a stock long before it appears on the new-low list.**

You may have guessed by now what the last intriguing new realization is that I promised to disclose to you earlier. So here are the three stocks you had to choose among on the previous page, Stock A, Stock B, and Stock C. Which one did you pick? Stock A (Syntex Corp, see below) was the right one to buy. The small arrow pointing down above the weekly prices in July 1963 shows the same buy point at the end of Stock A in July on the previous page. Stock B and Stock C both declined.

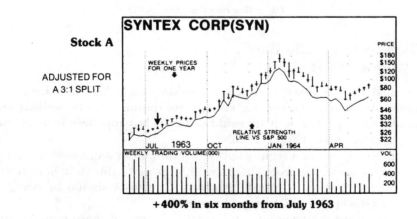

+400% in six months from July 1963

Stock B

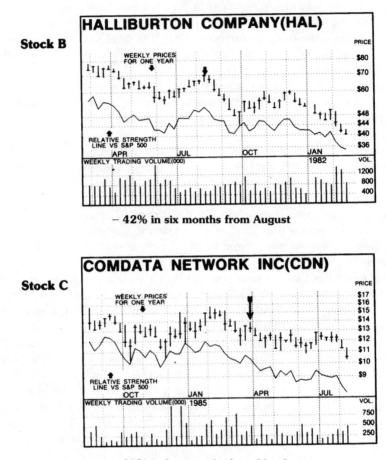

HALLIBURTON COMPANY(HAL)

PRICE

WEEKLY PRICES
FOR ONE YEAR

$80
$70
$60

$48
$44
$40
$36

RELATIVE STRENGTH
LINE VS S&P 500

APR   JUL   OCT   JAN
                                        1982

WEEKLY TRADING VOLUME(000)   VOL.
1200
800
400

– 42% in six months from August

Stock C

COMDATA NETWORK INC(CDN)

PRICE

WEEKLY PRICES
FOR ONE YEAR

$17
$16
$15
$14
$13
$12
$11
$10

$9

RELATIVE STRENGTH
LINE VS S&P 500

OCT   JAN   APR   JUL

WEEKLY TRADING VOLUME(000) 1985   VOL.
750
500
250

– 21% in five months from March

When to Correctly Begin
Buying a Stock

**A stock should be close to or actually making a new high in price after
undergoing a price correction and consolidation. The consolidation
(base-building period) in price could normally last anywhere from seven
or eight weeks up to fifteen months.**

As the stock emerges from its price adjustment phase, slowly resumes
an uptrend, and is approaching new high ground, this is, believe it or
not, the correct time to consider buying. The stock should be bought
just as it's starting to break out of its price base.

You must avoid buying once the stock is extended more than 5% or

10% from the exact buy point off the base. Here is an example of the proper time to have bought Reebok, at $29, in February 1986 before it zoomed 260%. The second graph shows the correct time to have bought Amgen at $60—in March 1990—before it jumped more than sixfold.

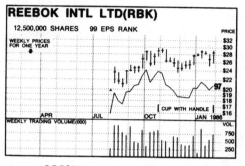

392% increase in 13 months

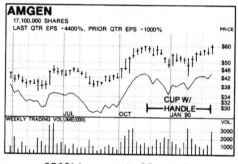

681% increase in 22 months

How Does a Stock Go from $50 to $100?

As a final appeal to your trusty common sense and judgment, it should be stated that if a security has traded between $40 and $50 a share over many months and is now selling at $50 and is going to double in price, it positively must first go through $51, $52, $53, $54, $55, and the like, before it can reach $100.

Therefore, **your job is to buy when a stock looks high to the majority of conventional investors and to sell after it moves substantially higher and finally begins to look attractive to some of those same investors.**

In conclusion: **Search for corporations that have a key new product or service, new management, or changes in conditions in their industry. And most importantly, companies whose stocks are emerging from price consolidation patterns and are close to, or actually touching, new highs in price are usually your best buy candidates.** There will always be something new occurring in America every year. In 1993 alone, there were nearly 1,000 initial public offerings. Dynamic, innovative new companies—a bundle of future, potential big winners.

4

S = Supply and Demand: Small Capitalization Plus Big Volume Demand

The law of supply and demand determines the price of almost everything in your daily life. When you go to the grocery store and buy fresh lettuce, tomatoes, eggs, or beef, supply and demand affects the price.

The law of supply and demand even impacted the price of food and consumer goods in former Communist, dictator-controlled countries where these state-owned items were always in short supply and frequently available only to the privileged class of higher officials in the bureaucracy or in the black market to comrades who could pay exorbitant prices.

The stock market does not escape this basic price principle. **The law of supply and demand is more important than all the analyst opinions on Wall Street.**

Big Is Not Always Better

The price of a common stock with 300 million shares outstanding is hard to budge up because of the large supply of stock available. A tremendous volume of buying (demand) is needed to create a rousing price increase.

On the other hand, if a company has only 2 or 3 million shares of common stock outstanding, a reasonable amount of buying can push the stock up rapidly because of the small available supply.

If you are choosing between two stocks to buy, one with 10 million shares outstanding and the other with 60 million, the smaller one will usually be the rip-roaring performer if other factors are equal.

The total number of shares of common stock outstanding in a company's capital structure represents the potential amount of stock available for purchase.

The stock's "floating supply" is also frequently considered by market professionals. It measures the number of common shares left for possible purchase after subtracting the quantity of stock that is closely held by company management. **Stocks that have a large percentage of ownership by top management are generally your best prospects.**

There is another fundamental reason, besides supply and demand, that companies with large capitalizations (number of shares outstanding) as a rule produce dreadful price appreciation results in the stock market. The companies themselves are simply too big and sluggish.

Pick Entrepreneurial Managements Rather Than Caretakers

Giant size may create seeming power and influence, but size in corporations can also produce lack of imagination from older, more conservative "caretaker managements" less willing to innovate, take risks, and keep up with the times.

In most cases, top management of large companies does not own a meaningful portion of the company's common stock. This is a serious defect large companies should attempt to correct.

Also, too many layers of management separate the senior executive from what's really going on out in the field at the customer level. And in the real world, the ultimate boss in a company is the customer.

Times are changing at a quickening pace. A corporation with a fast-selling, hot new product today will find sales slipping within three years if it doesn't continue to have important new products coming to market.

Most of today's inventions and exciting new products and services are created by hungry, innovative, small- and medium-sized young companies with entrepreneurial-type management. As a result, these organizations grow much faster and create most of the new jobs for all Americans. This is where the great future growth of America lies. Many of these companies will be in the services or technology industries.

If a mammoth-sized company occasionally creates an important new product, it still may not materially help the company's stock because the new product will probably only account for a small percentage of the gigantic company's sales and earnings. The product is simply a little drop in a bucket that's just too big.

Institutional Investors Have a Big Cap Handicap

Many large institutional investors create a serious disadvantage for themselves because they incorrectly believe that due to their size they can *only* buy large capitalization companies. This automatically eliminates from consideration most of the true growth companies. It also practically guarantees inadequate performance because these investors may restrict their selections mainly to slowly decaying, inefficient, fully matured companies. As an individual investor, you don't have this limitation.

If I were a large institutional investor, I would rather own 200 of the most outstanding, small- to medium-sized growth companies than 50 to 100 old, overgrown, large-capitalization stocks that appear on everyone's "favorite fifty" list.

If you desire clear-cut factual evidence, the 40 year study of the greatest stock market winners indicated **more than 95% of the companies had fewer than 25 million shares in their capitalization when they had their greatest period of earnings improvement and stock market performance. The average capitalization of top-performing listed stocks from 1970 through 1982 was 11.8 million shares. The median stock exhibited 4.6 million shares outstanding before advancing rapidly in price.**

Foolish Stock Splits Can Hurt

Corporate management at times makes the mistake of excessively splitting its company's stock. This is sometimes done based upon questionable advice from the company's Wall Street investment bankers.

In my opinion, it is usually better for a company to split its shares 2-for-1 or 3-for-2, rather than 3-for-1 or 5-for-1. (When a stock splits 2-for-1, you get two shares for each one previously held, but the new shares sell for half the price.)

Overabundant stock splits create a substantially larger supply and may put a company in the more lethargic performance, or "big cap," status sooner.

It is particularly foolish for a company whose stock has gone up in price for a year or two to have an extravagant stock split near the end of a bull market or in the early stage of a bear market. Yet this is exactly what most corporations do.

They think the stock will attract more buyers if it sells for a cheaper price per share. This may occur, but may have the opposite result the company wants, particularly if it's the second split in the last couple of years. Knowledgeable professionals and a few shrewd traders will probably use the oversized split as an opportunity to sell into the obvious "good news" and excitement, and take their profits.

Many times a stock's price will top around the second or third time it splits. However, in the year preceding great price advances of the leading stocks, in performance, only 18% had splits.

Large holders who are thinking of selling might feel it easier to sell some of their 100,000 shares before the split takes effect than to have to sell 300,000 shares after a 3-for-1 split. And smart short sellers (a rather infinitesimal group) pick on stocks that are beginning to falter after enormous price runups—three-, five-, and ten-fold increases—and which are heavily owned by funds. The funds could, after an unreasonable stock split, find the number of their shares tripled, thereby dramatically increasing the potential number of shares for sale.

Look for Companies Buying Their Own Stock in the Open Market

One fairly positive sign, particularly in small- to medium-sized companies, is for the concern to be acquiring its own stock in the open marketplace over a consistent period of time. This reduces the number of shares of common stock in the capital structure and implies the corporation expects improved sales and earnings in the future.

Total company earnings will, as a result, usually be divided among a smaller number of shares, which will automatically increase the earnings per share. And as we've discussed, **the percentage increase in earnings per share is one of the principal driving forces behind outstanding stocks.**

Tandy Corp., Teledyne, and Metromedia are three organizations that successfully repurchased their own stock during the era from the mid-1970s to the early 1980s. All three companies produced notable results in their earnings-per-share growth and in the price advance of their stock.

Tandy (split-adjusted) stock increased from $2¾ to $60 between 1973 and 1983. Teledyne stock zoomed from $8 to $190 in the thirteen years prior to June 1984, and Metromedia's stock price soared to $560 from $30 in the six years beginning in 1977. Teledyne shrunk its capitalization from 88 million shares in 1971 to 15 million shares and increased its earnings from $0.61 a share to nearly $20 per share with eight different buybacks.

Low Corporate Debt to Equity Is Usually Better

After you have picked a stock with a small or reasonable number of shares in its capitalization, it pays to **check the percentage of the firm's total capitalization represented by long-term debt or bonds. Usually the lower the debt ratio, the safer and better the company.**

Earnings per share of companies with high debt-to-equity ratios can be clobbered in difficult periods of high interest rates. These highly leveraged companies generally are deemed to be of poorer quality and higher risk.

A corporation that has been reducing its debt as a percent of equity over the last two or three years is well worth considering. If nothing else, the company's interest expense will be materially reduced and should result in increased earnings per share.

The presence of convertible bonds in a concern's capital structure could dilute corporate earnings if and when the bonds are converted into shares of common stock.

It should be understood that smaller capitalization stocks are less liquid, are substantially more volatile, and will tend to go up and down faster; therefore, they involve additional risk as well as greater opportunity. There are, however, definite ways of minimizing your risks, which will be discussed in Chapter 9.

Lower-priced stocks with thin (small) capitalization and no institutional sponsorship or ownership should be avoided, since they have poor liquidity and a lower-grade following.

A stock's daily trading volume is our best measure of its supply and demand. Trading volume should dry up on corrections and increase significantly on rallies. As a stock's price breaks out of a sound and proper base structure, its volume should increase at least 50% above normal. In many cases, it can increase 100% or more.

In summary, remember: **stocks with a small or reasonable number of shares outstanding will, other things being equal, usually outperform older, large capitalization companies.**

5

L = Leader or Laggard: Which Is Your Stock?

Most of the time, people buy stocks they like, stocks they feel good about, or stocks they feel comfortable with, like an old friend, old shoes, or an old dog. These securities are frequently sentimental, draggy slowpokes rather than leaping leaders in the overall exciting stock market.

Let's suppose you want to buy a stock in the computer industry. If you buy the *leading* security in the group and your timing is sound, you have a crack at real price appreciation.

If, on the other hand, you buy equities that haven't yet moved or are down the most in price, because you feel safer with them and think you're getting a real bargain, you're probably buying the sleepy losers of the group. Don't dabble in stocks. Dig in and do some detective work.

Buy among the Best Two or Three Stocks in a Group

The top two or three stocks actionwise in a strong industry group can have unbelievable growth, while others in the pack may hardly stir a point or two. Has this ever happened to you?

In 1979 and 1980, Wang Labs, Prime Computer, Datapoint, Rolm Corp., Tandem Computer, and other small computer companies had five-, six-, and seven-fold advances before topping and retreating, while grand old IBM just sat there and giants Burroughs, NCR, and Sperry Rand turned in lifeless price performances. In the next bull market cycle, IBM finally sprang to life and produced excellent results. Home

Depot advanced 10 times from 1988 to 1992, while Waban and Hechinger, the laggards, clearly underperformed.

Avoid Sympathy Stock Moves

There is very little that's really new in the stock market. History just keeps repeating itself. In the summer of 1963, I bought Syntex, which afterwards advanced 400%. Yet most people would not buy it then because it had just made a new high in price at $100 and its P/E ratio, at 45, seemed too high.

Several investment firms recommended G. D. Searle, a sympathy play, which at the same time looked much cheaper in price and had a similar product to Syntex's. But Searle failed to produce stock market results. Syntex was the leader, Searle the laggard.

Sympathy plays are stocks in the same group as a leading stock, but ones showing a more mediocre record and weaker price performance. They eventually attempt to move up and follow "in sympathy" the powerful price movement of the real group leader.

In 1970, Levitz Furniture became an electrifying stock market winner. Wickes Corp. copied Levitz and plunged into the warehouse furniture business.

Many people bought Wickes instead of Levitz because it was cheaper in price. Wickes never performed. It ultimately got into financial trouble, whereas Levitz increased 900% before it finally topped. As Andrew Carnegie, the steel industry pioneer, said in his autobiography, "The first man gets the oyster; the second, the shell."

Is the Stock's Relative Price Strength Below 70?

Here is a simple, easy-to-remember measure that will help tell you if a security is a leader or a laggard. If the stock's relative price strength, on a scale from 1 to 99, is below 70, it's lagging the better-performing stocks in the overall market. That doesn't mean it can't go up in price, it just means *if* it goes up, it will probably rise a more inconsequential amount.

Relative price strength normally compares a stock's price performance to the price action of a general market average like the Standard & Poor's (S&P) Index, or in some cases, all other stocks. A relative strength of 70, for example, means a stock outperformed 70% of the stocks in the comparison group during a given period, say, the last six or twelve months.

The 500 best-performing listed equities for each year from 1953 through 1993 averaged a relative price strength rating of 87 just before their major increase in price actually began. So the determined winner's rule is: Avoid laggard stocks and avoid sympathy movements. Look for the genuine leaders!

Most of the better investment services show both a relative strength line and a relative strength number and update these every week for a list of thousands of stocks.

Relative strength numbers are shown each day for all stocks listed in the *Investor's Business Daily* NYSE, AMEX, and NASDAQ price tables. Updated relative strength numbers are also shown in Daily Graphs charting service each week.

Pick 80s and 90s That Are in a Chart Base Pattern

If you want to upgrade your stock selection and concentrate on the best leaders, you could consider restricting your buys to companies showing a relative strength rank of 80 or higher. Establish some definite discipline and rules for yourself.

If you do this, make sure the stock is in a sound base-building zone (proper sideways price consolidation pattern) and that the stock is not extended (up) more than 5% or 10% above this base pattern. This will prevent you from chasing stocks that have raced up in price too rapidly above their chart base patterns. For example, in the Reebok chart shown at the end of Chapter 3, if the exact buy point was $29, the stock should not be purchased more than 5% or 10% above $29.

If a relative price strength line has been sinking for seven months or more, or if the line has an abnormally sharp decline for four months or more, the stock's behavior is questionable.

Why buy an equity whose relative performance is inferior and straggling drearily behind a large number of other, better-acting securities in the market? Yet most investors do, and many do it without ever looking at a relative strength line or number.

Some large institutional portfolios are riddled with stocks showing prolonged downtrends in relative strength. I do not like to buy stocks with a relative strength rating below 80, or with a relative strength line in an overall downtrend.

In fact, the really big money-making selections generally have a relative strength reading of 90 or higher just before breaking out of their first or second base structure. A potential winning stock's relative strength should be the same as a major league pitcher's fast ball. The average big league fast ball is clocked about 86 miles per hour and the outstanding pitchers throw "heat" in the 90s.

The complete lack of investor awareness, or at least unwillingness, in establishing and following minimum realistic standards for good stock selection reminds me that doctors many years ago were ignorant of the need to sterilize their instruments before each operation. So they kept killing off excessive numbers of their patients until surgeons finally and begrudgingly accepted studies by a young French chemist named Louis Pasteur on the need for sterilization.

It isn't very rewarding to make questionable decisions in any arena. And in evaluating the American economy, investors should zero in on sound new market leaders and avoid anemic-performance investments.

Always Sell Your Worst Stock First

If you own a portfolio of equities, you must learn to **sell your worst-performing stocks first and keep your best-acting investments a little longer.** In other words, sell your cats and dogs, your losers and mistakes, and try to turn your better selections into your big winners.

General market corrections, or price declines, can help you recognize new leaders if you know what to look for. The more desirable growth stocks normally correct $1\frac{1}{2}$ to $2\frac{1}{2}$ times the general market averages. However as a rule, growth stocks declining the least (percentagewise) in a bull market correction are your strongest and best investments, and stocks that plummet the most are your weakest choices.

For example, if the overall market suffers a 10% intermediate term falloff, three successful growth securities could drop 15%, 20%, and 30%. The ones down only 15% or 20% are likely to be your best investments after they recover. Of course, a stock sliding 35% to 40% in a general market decline of 10% could be flashing you a warning signal, and you should, in many cases, steer clear of such an uncertain actor.

Pros Make Mistakes Too

Many professional investment managers make the serious mistake of buying stocks that have just suffered unusually large price drops. In

June 1972, a normally capable, leading institutional investor in Maryland bought Levitz Furniture after its first abnormal price break in one week from $60 to around $40. The stock rallied for a few weeks, rolled over, and broke to $18.

Several institutional investors bought Memorex in October 1978, when it had its first unusual price break. It later plunged.

Certain money managers in New York bought Dome Petroleum in September 1981 after its sharp drop from $16 to $12, because it seemed cheap and there was a favorable story going around Wall Street on the stock. Months later Dome sold for $1, and the street talk was that the company might be in financial difficulties.

None of these professionals had recognized the difference between the normal price declines and the highly abnormal corrections that were a sign of potential disaster in this stock.

Of course, the real problem was that these expert investors all relied solely on fundamental analysis (and stories) and their personal opinion of value (lower P/E ratios), with a complete disregard for what market action could have told them was really going on. **Those who ignore what the marketplace is saying usually suffer some heavy losses.**

Once a general market decline is definitely over, the first stocks that bounce back to new price highs are almost always your authentic leaders.

This process continues to occur week by week for about three months or so, with many stocks recovering and making new highs. To be a truly astute professional or individual investor you must learn to recognize the difference between normal price action and abnormal activity. When you understand how to do this well, people will say you have "a good feel for the market."

Control Data—Abnormal Strength in a Weak Market

During a trip to New York in April 1967, I remember walking through a broker's office on one day when the Dow Jones Industrial Average was down over twelve points. When I looked up at the electronic ticker tape showing prices moving across the wall, Control Data was trading in heavy volume at $62, up $3\frac{1}{2}$ points for the day. I immediately bought the stock at the market, because I knew Control Data well, and this was abnormal strength in the face of a weak overall market. The stock subsequently reached $150.

In April 1981, just as the 1981 bear market was commencing, MCI Communications, a Washington, D.C.-based telecommunications stock trading in the over-the-counter market, broke out of a price base at $15. It advanced to the equivalent of $90 in the following 21 months.

MCI tripled in a declining market. This was a great example of abnormal strength during a weak market. Lorillard did the same thing in the 1957 bear market. Software Toolworks soared in January 1990.

So don't forget: **It seldom pays to invest in laggard performing stocks even if they look tantalizingly cheap. Look for the market leader.**

6

I = Institutional Sponsorship: A Little Goes A Long Way

It takes big demand to move supply up, and the largest source of demand for stocks is by far the institutional buyer. A stock certainly does not need a large number of institutional owners, but it should have at least a few such sponsors. Three to ten might be a minimum or reasonable number of mutual fund sponsors, although some stocks might have a good deal more.

The would-be winning investor should learn to sort through and recognize that certain institutional sponsors are more savvy, have a stronger performance record, and are better at choosing stocks than others are. I call it analyzing the quality of sponsorship.

What Is Institutional Sponsorship?

Sponsorship may take the form of mutual funds; corporate pension funds; insurance companies; large investment counselors; hedge funds; bank trust departments; or state, charitable, and educational institutions.

For measurement purposes, I do not consider brokerage firm research department reports as institutional sponsorship, although a few exert influence on certain securities. Investment advisory services and market letter writers are also not considered to be institutional or professional sponsorship in this definition.

Financial services such as Vickers and Arthur Weisenberger & Co. publish fund holdings and investment performance records of various institutions. In the past, mutual funds have tended to be slightly more aggressive in the market, but banks have managed larger amounts of money. More recently, numerous new "entrepreneurial type" investment counseling firms have been organized to manage institutional monies.

Performance figures for the latest 12 months plus the last three- to five-year period are usually the most relevant. However, results may change significantly as key portfolio managers leave one money management organization and go to another. The institutional leaders continually rotate and change.

For example, Security Pacific Bank (now merged into Bank America) had somewhat modest performance in its trust investment division up to 1981. But with the addition of new management and more realistic concepts in the investment area, it polished up its act to the point that it ranked at the very top in performance in 1982. In 1984, the top manager of Security Pacific left and formed his own company, Nicolas Applegate of San Diego.

If a stock has no professional sponsorship, chances are that its performance will be more run-of-the-mill. The odds are that at least several of the more than 1000 institutional investors have looked at the stock and passed it over. Even if they are wrong, it still takes large buying to stimulate an important price increase in a security.

Also, sponsorship provides buying support when you want to get out of your investment. If there is no sponsorship and you try to sell your stock in a poor market, you may have problems finding someone to buy it.

Daily marketability is one of the great advantages of owning stock. (Real estate is far less liquid and commissions and fees are much higher.) Institutional sponsorship helps provide continuous marketability and liquidity.

Is It "Overowned" by Institutions?

A stock can also have too much sponsorship and become "overowned." **Overowned** is a term we coined and began using in 1969 to describe a stock whose institutional ownership had become excessive. In any case, excessive sponsorship can be adverse since it merely represents large potential selling if anything goes wrong in the company or the general market. On the other hand, Snapple, in April 1993, was underowned.

The "favorite 50" and other lists of the most widely owned institutional stocks can be rather poor, and potentially risky, prospect lists. By the time performance is so obvious that almost all institutions own a stock, it is probably too late. The heart is already out of the watermelon.

An Unassailable Institutional Growth Stock Tops

In June 1974, we put Xerox on our institutional sell list at $115. We received unbelievable flack because Xerox was then one of the most widely held institutional stocks and had been amazingly successful up to that point. However, our research indicated it had topped and was headed down in price.

Institutions made Xerox their most widely purchased stock for that year. Of course that didn't stop it from tumbling in price. What it did prove was how sick the stock really was at that time, since it declined steadily in spite of such buying. The episode did bring us our first large insurance company account in New York City in 1974.

They had been buying Xerox on the way down in the $80s until we persuaded them they should be selling instead of buying.

Famous Last Words—"We'll Never Sell Avon Products"

We tried that same year to get another well-known eastern insurance company to sell Avon Products at $105, and I recall the head of their investment organization pounding the table and saying, "We'll never sell Avon Products; it's such an outstanding company." I wonder if they still have it?

Professionals, like the public, love to buy on declines. They also make mistakes and incur losses. In many ways, some institutions are like the public. Money management organizations have their experienced and realistic decision makers, as well as their less seasoned or unrealistic portfolio managers and analysts.

It is, therefore, not always as crucial to know how many institutions own a stock as it is to know which of the better ones own or have purchased a particular stock in the last quarter. The only important thing about the number of institutional owners is to note the recent quarterly trend. Is the number of sponsors increasing or decreasing?

Note New Stock Positions Bought in the Last Quarter

New institutional positions acquired in the last quarter are more relevant than are existing positions held for some time. Many investors feel disclosures of a fund's new commitments are published after the fact, too late to be of any real value. This is not true.

These reports are available publicly about six weeks after the end of a fund's quarter. The records are very helpful to those who can single out the wiser selections and understand correct timing and the proper use of charts.

Additionally, half of all institutional buying that shows up on the New York Stock Exchange ticker tape may be in humdrum stocks and much of the buying may be wrong. However, out of the other half you may have some truly phenomenal selections.

Your task, then, is to weed through and separate the intelligent, highly informed institutional buying from the poor, faulty buying. Though difficult, this will become easier as you learn to apply and follow the rules, guidelines, and principles presented in this book.

Institutional trades usually show up on the stock exchange ticker tape in most brokers' offices in transactions of 1000 shares up to 100,000 shares or more. Institutional buying and selling accounts for more than 70% of the activity in most leading companies. I estimate that close to 80% or 90% of the important price movements of stocks on the New York Stock Exchange are caused by institutional orders.

As background information, it may be valuable to find out the investment philosophy and techniques used by certain funds. For example, Pioneer Fund in Boston has always emphasized buying supposedly undervalued stocks selling at low P/E ratios, and its portfolio contains a larger number of OTC stocks. A chartist probably would not buy many of Pioneer's stocks. On the other hand, Keystone S-4 usually remains fully invested in the most aggressive growth stocks it can find. Evergreen Fund, run by Steve Lieber, does a fine job of uncovering fundamentally sound, small companies.

Jim Stower's Twentieth Century Ultra and his Growth Investors funds use computer screening to buy volatile, aggressive stocks that show the greatest percentage increase in recent sales and earnings.

Magellan and Contra Fund in Boston scours the country to get in early on every new concept or story in a stock. Some other managements worth tracking might be AIM Management, Nicolas Applegate, Thomson, Brandywine, Berger, and CGM. Some funds buy on new highs, others try to buy around lows and may sell on new highs.

In a capsule, **buy stocks that have at least a few institutional sponsors with better-than-average recent performance records.**

7

M = Market Direction: How to Determine It

You can be right on every one of the factors in the first six chapters; however, if you are wrong about the direction of the broad general market, three out of four of your stocks will slump with the market averages and you will lose money. Therefore, you need in your analytical tool kit a simple reliable method to determine if you're in a bull (up) market or a bear (down) market.

If you're in a bull market, are you in the early stage or in the latter stage? Most importantly, what is the general market doing right now? Is it weak and acting badly or is it merely going through a normal decline? Is the market doing just what it should be, based on current conditions in the country, or is it doing something abnormally strong or weak?

If you want to analyze the overall market correctly, you must start at the most logical point. **The best way to determine the direction of the market is to follow and understand _every day_ what the general market averages are doing.**

The Vital Importance of Daily General Market Averages

The daily Dow Jones Industrial Average is a simple convenient stock market average to study. The S&P 500 can also be used; however, it is no more reliable for determining trend or direction, even though it is a broader, more modern and representative average consisting of 500 companies. The most comprehensive average is the _Investor's Business Daily_ 6000 market value-weighted index, which covers all New York Stock Exchange, American Stock Exchange, and NASDAQ common stocks, over 6000 equities in the overall market.

A Harvard professor once asked his students to do a special report on fish. His scholars went to the library, read books about fish, and then wrote their expositions. The students were shocked when, after turning in their papers, the professor tore them up and threw them in the waste basket.

When they asked what was wrong with the reports, the professor said, "If you want to learn anything about fish, sit in front of a fish bowl and look at fish." He then made his students sit and look at fish for hours. The classmates rewrote their assignment solely from observing and studying the object itself.

The daily Dow Jones Industrial Average represents an average of thirty large, basic industry stocks in America. It is one of the objects you want to observe and study carefully.

The difficult-to-recognize but meaningful changes in the behavior of the market averages at important turning points are the best indicators of the condition of the whole market.

Study the General Market Chart Every Day

The general market should be studied closely every day, since reverses in trends can begin on any one day. I emphasize this practical method rather than that of interpreting other subsidiary indicators that are supposed to tell you exactly what the market should be doing or listening to the many stock market letter writers or technical analysts that pore over twenty indicators and tell you what they think the market should be doing. Market letters sometimes may create doubt, uncertainty, and confusion in an investor's mind. Markets tend to go up when people are skeptical and disbelieving.

Learn to interpret a daily price and volume chart of the general market averages. If you do, you can't get too far off the track. You really won't need much else unless you want to argue with the trend of the market.

Experience teaches you that continually arguing with the market can be very expensive. That's how people go broke!

How You Can Identify Stock Market Tops

When market indexes peak and begin major reversals, individual investors should take action immediately and raise 25% or more cash by selling stocks at the market prices (use of price limits on orders is not generally recommended). Lightning action is even more critical if your stock account is on margin. If your portfolio is 50% margined with half of the money in your stocks borrowed from your broker, a 20% decline in the price of your stocks will cause you to lose 40% of your money.

Don't wait around after the first few definite indications of a general market top. Sell quickly before real weakness develops.

Napoleon once wrote that he never hesitated in the battlefield and thereby gained an advantage over opponents. For many years he was undefeated in battle. Similarly, in the market battlefield there are the quick and there are the dead!

General market top reversals are usually late signals—the last straw before a cave-in. In most cases, distribution or selling in individual market leaders has, for days or even weeks, preceded the approaching market break. Use of individual stock selling rules, which we will discuss in the next two chapters, should lead you to sell one or two of your stocks on the way up just prior to the general market peak.

After the top, poor market rallies and rally failures in the averages will occur. Further selling is advisable when these weak rallies or rally failures are recognized.

If you miss the S&P or Dow Jones topping signals, which is exceedingly easy to do since they occur on only one or two days, you will be wrong on the direction of the market and wrong on almost everything you do.

Recognizing when the market has hit a top or bottomed out is 50% of the whole complicated ball game. It is also the key investing skill that all-too-many professional and amateur investors seem to lack.

You can also try to plan ahead and write down on charts, based on the market's historical precedent, where you expect the Dow to go and when the rally or decline might end. But it is best to watch the market, as it will eventually tell you when the correction or uptrend is finally completed.

To help anticipate possible market peaks, you should also determine when long-term capital gains selling will begin by those who bought stock in increased volume at original break-out buy points on individual stock graphs. Every four or five years, like in 1986, Congress makes purely political decisions to sometimes raise or do away with capital gains rates, so this factor can become unimportant.

Congress Lacks Real Economic Knowledge

It is unfortunate that many in Congress have a deficient understanding of how the American economy actually works. A lower capital gains rate is a powerful incentive for Americans to decide to start innovative new businesses. And of course, new businesses create millions of new jobs and new taxpayers to keep our economy growing. These basic facts most in Congress have not yet been able to figure out. They incorrectly view the capital gains tax solely as a plum to the rich. Some day, proven competence and professional understanding may become an important prerequisite for obtaining high political office. Both Presidents John F. Kennedy and Ronald Reagan believed in lowering everyone's tax rates. However most administrations and particularly Democratic Congresses usually try to raise your tax rates so they can have more money to spend for their inefficient programs.

Historical Tops for Further Study

Historically, intermediate term distribution tops and reversals in the general market averages occurred on the first week of August 1954, where there was increased New York Stock Exchange volume without further upward price progress on the Dow Jones Industrials, followed the next day by heavy volume without further price progress up and a wide price spread from high to low on the Dow; they also occurred in the first week of July 1955, which was characterized by a price climax with a wide price spread from the day's low to its high, followed the next day by increased volume, with the Dow Jones average closing down in price, and three days later, increased New York Stock Exchange volume again with the Dow Jones closing down.

(Other market tops to study occurred in the second week of September 1955, third week of November 1955, second week of April 1956, second week of August 1956, first week of January 1957, third week of July 1957, third week of November 1958, third week of January 1959, first week of May 1959, first week of June 1959, second week of July 1959, first week of January 1960, second week of June 1960, first week of April 1961, fourth week of May 1961, first week of September 1961, November and December 1961, fourth week of March 1962, first week of June 1963, last week of October 1963, second week of May 1965, second week of February 1966, last week of April 1966, fourth week of June 1966, second week of May 1967, last week of September 1967, December 1967, and the first week of December 1968.)

Displayed on the next two pages are daily market average graphs of several tops that happened between 1973 and 1994.

Market tops, whether intermediate (usually 8% to 12% declines) or primary bull market peaks, occasionally occur six to seven months after the last major buy point in leading stocks and in the averages.

Specific Top Signs to Look for

Most of the top reversals in the past occurred after the averages moved into new high ground and during their third to ninth day of rally. The new highs were off small chart bases. The conditions under which the tops occurred all appeared similar.

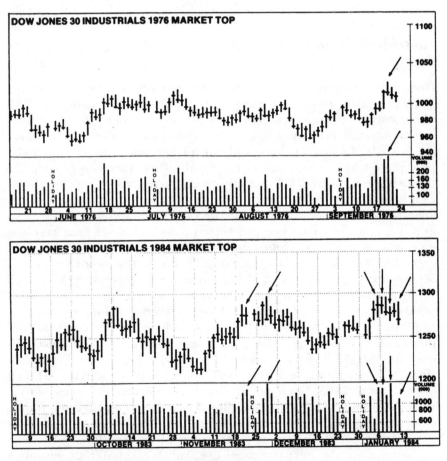

Market tops

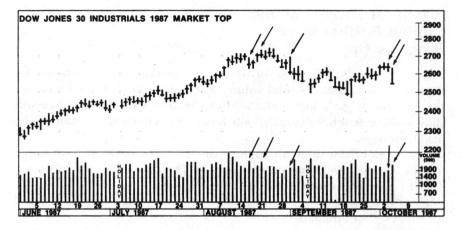

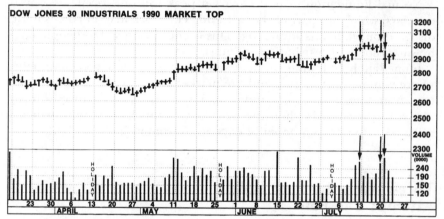

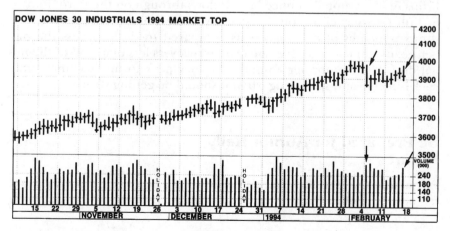

Market tops

49

Watch for Heavy Volume without Further Price Progress Up

What signs should you look for to detect a market top? **On one of the days in the uptrend, the total volume for the market will increase over the preceding day's high volume, but the Dow's closing average will show stalling action, or substantially less upward movement, than on the prior few days.**

The spread from the daily high to the daily low of the market index may be a little larger than on earlier days. The market average does not have to close down for the day, although in some instances it will do so, making it much easier to recognize the distribution as professional investors sell or liquidate stock.

Normal liquidation near the market peak will only occur on one or two days, which are part of the uptrend. The stock market comes under distribution while it is advancing! This is one reason so few people know how to recognize distribution (selling).

Immediately following the first selling near the top, a vacuum exists where volume may subside and the market averages will sell off for perhaps four days. The second and probably the last early chance to recognize a top reversal is when the market attempts its first rally, which it will always do after a number of days down from its highest point.

Three Ways the First Rally Attempt Can Fail

If this first attempted bounce back follows through on the third, fourth, or fifth rally day either on decreased volume from the day before, if it shows poor net price progress as compared to the progress the day before, or if the market average overall recovers less than half of the initial drop from its former absolute intraday peak to the low, the comeback is feeble and sputtering when it should be getting strong.

Be Prepared for Abrupt Rally Failures

Frequently, the first stock market rally during a beginning downtrend will fail abruptly. After the first day's resurgence, the second day will open strongly. But toward the end of the day, the market will suddenly close down. The abrupt failure of the market to follow through on its first recovery attempt should probably be met by further selling on your part.

The Initial Market Decline Can Be on Lower Volume

Most stock market technicians are fooled by the initial market decline off the top when they see volume contracting. They do not understand this is a normal occurrence after heavy distribution has occurred on the way up around the top.

Volume begins to pick up on the downside, days or weeks later, when it becomes obvious to more investors. But as in anything else, if you wait until it becomes obvious to most people, it is going to cost you more. You will be selling late.

Similar top indications can be seen on the S&P 500, New York Stock Exchange Composite, or even on occasion an index of the current cycle's speculative growth stock leaders. These averages should be followed together because sometimes one average may give a much clearer and more definite sell signal than another.

The speculative, or swinger-type, stock index is occasionally significant because market movements are almost always led by a few aggressive stocks. The leaders of the original move up may at times turn on their heels first. Therefore, a speculative index may highlight the one-day price reversal or stalling action on increased volume. I term this "heavy or increased volume without further price progress on the upside."

The Hourly Market Index and Volume Changes Give Hints Near Turning Points

At sensitive potential turning points, an active market operator can watch hour-by-hour market index price changes and hourly NYSE volume as compared with volume the same hour the prior day.

A good time to watch hourly volume figures is during the first attempted rally following the initial decline off the market peak. You should be able to see if volume is dull and dries up on the rally. Plus you can recognize the first hour that the rally starts to fade, with volume picking up on the downside.

HOURLY N.Y.S.E. VOLUME AND MARKET CHANGES					
NEW YORK TIME	TUE. VOLUME	MON. VOLUME	NET CHANGE	S&P 500	DJIA
9:30 TO 10:00	27,490,000	23,140,000	+ 4,350,000	+ 2.02	+14.51
10:00 TO 11:00	38,330,000	26,710,000	+11,620,000	+ 2.60	+21.36
11:00 TO 12:00	28,150,000	25,120,000	+ 3,030,000	+ 2.81	+24.39
12:00 TO 1:00	25,040,000	23,020,000	+ 2,020,000	+ 2.90	+23.44
1:00 TO 2:00	20,080,000	17,480,000	+ 2,600,000	+ 3.32	+26.78
2:00 TO 3:00	24,060,000	18,690,000	+ 5,370,000	+ 3.53	+28.70
3:00 TO 4:00	37,580,000	20,850,000	+16,730,000	+ 2.48	+20.25
TOTAL VOLUME	200,730,000	155,010,000	+45,720,000		

Another valuable period to observe hourly volume data is when the market averages reach an important prior low point and start breaking that support area. What you want to determine is the degree of pickup in selling that occurs as the market is collapsing into new low ground. Does the hourly volume pick up dramatically or only a small amount?

After a few days of undercutting of previous lows on only mildly increased volume, do you get one or two days of increased volume without further downside price progress? If so, you may be in a shakeout area ready for an upturn. This occurred on April 23 and 24, 1990.

Some institutional trading departments or technical chart rooms plot the market averages and volume on an hourly basis every day.

Look for Divergence of Key Averages at Major Turns

At possible market turning points, check several averages to see if there are significant divergences. For example, if the Dow Jones was up 10 and the S&P was up only the equivalent of two on the Dow for the day, the S&P, being a broader index, would indicate the rally was not as broad and strong as it would appear on the surface.

To easily compare the S&P change to the Dow, divide the S&P average into the Dow Jones Industrials'. This figure can then be multiplied by the change in the S&P to convert it into numbers comparable to the Dow Jones movement for the day.

As an illustration: if the Dow closed at 1000 and the S&P 500 finished at 125, the 1000 Dow would be eight times the S&P index of 125. Therefore, if the Dow, on a particular day, is up 10 points and the S&P is up .60, you can multiply the .60 by 8 and find that the S&P was only up the equivalent of 4.80 on the Dow Jones.

A 33% Drop Requires a 50% Rise to Break Even

The critical importance of recognizing the direction of the general market cannot be ignored, because a 33% loss in a portfolio of stocks requires a 50% gain just to recover to your break-even point.

For example, if a $10,000 portfolio is allowed to decline to $6666 (a 33% decline), the portfolio has to rise $3333 (or 50%), just to get you even. Therefore, it is essential to try to preserve as much of the profit you have built up as possible rather than to ride most investments up and down through difficult cycles like many people do.

I generally have not had much problem recognizing and acting upon the early signs of bear markets, such as those in 1962, 1966, 1969, 1973, 1976, and 1981. However, between 1962 and 1981, I twice made the sad mistake of buying back too early. When you make a mistake in the stock market, the only sound thing to do is correct it. Pride doesn't pay.

Most typical bear markets (some aren't typical) tend to have three separate phases, or legs, of decline interrupted by a couple of rallies that last just long enough to convince investors to begin buying. In 1969 and 1974 these phony, drawn out rallies lasted 15 weeks.

Many institutional investors love to "bottom fish." They will start buying stocks off the bottom and help make the rally convincing enough to draw you in. You will usually be better off staying on the sidelines in cash and avoiding short-term counterfeit rallies during the first few legs of a bear market.

FRB Discount Rate Changes Are Influential

The Federal Reserve Board discount rate and stock margin level changes by the Fed (as it is called) are valuable indicators to watch. They are perhaps the most important fundamental general market measurements, more so than the prime rate charged by leading banks.

Interest rates, as a rule, provide the best confirmation of changing basic conditions. Changes in the Federal Reserve Board's discount rate are by far the most reliable market measurement. The Alan Greenspan Federal Reserve Board discount rate increase to 6% in September 1987 led to the severe stock market break of October 1987.

In the past, it frequently marked the beginning of bear markets and impending recessions when the discount rate was increased three times

in succession, and it usually signaled the end of a bear market when the discount rate was finally lowered.

The Fed Kills the 1981 Economy

The bear market and the costly and protracted recession that began in 1981, for example, was created solely because the Federal Reserve Board increased the discount rate in rapid succession on September 26, 1980; November 17, 1980; and December 5, 1980.

Their fourth increase, on May 8, 1981, thrust the discount rate to an all-time high of 14%, which finally killed the American economy, our basic industries, and the stock market. This starkly documents and demonstrates how much our federal government controls and determines our economy, not Wall Street or business, as many people believe.

Discount rate changes should not be your primary indicator, however, because the stock market itself provides that function. Our detailed analysis of many market cycles shows there have been three separate important market turns that the discount rate did not help predict, one of the more noteworthy being in 1962.

Washington Causes the 1962 Stock Market Break

Nothing was wrong with the economy in the spring of 1962, but the market got skittish after the Securities and Exchange Commission (SEC) announced it planned a major investigation of the stock market. Then President Kennedy jumped on the steel companies. IBM dropped 50%. A new bull market sprang to life following the Cuban missile showdown with the Russians in October. All this happened with no change in the discount rate.

Also there are situations where the discount rate was lowered six months after the market bottom was reached. In this case, you could be late in the stock game if you waited to see the first drop in the discount rate. The Federal Reserve discount rate is the interest rate the Fed, acting as a wholesaler, charges member banks to borrow money from it.

Other Key Market Factors to Recognize and Use

During a bear market, stocks frequently open strong early in the morning and close weak by the end of the day. During bull markets, stocks tend to open down and come back later in the day to close up strongly. (The market opens at 9:30 a.m. and closes at 4:00 p.m. New York time, 6:30 a.m. and 1:00 p.m. California time. But it is subject to periodic change.)

Catch a shift with this easy test: see if you show a profit on any of your last four or five purchases. If you haven't made a dime on any of them, you might be witnessing a negative shift in the overall market.

Additionally, if stop-loss orders are used and either placed on the stock exchange specialist's book at specific prices or mentally recorded and acted upon, the market that is starting to top out will mechanically force you, robotlike, out of many of your stocks. A stop-loss order instructs the specialist in the stock on the exchange floor that once the stock drops to your specified price, it then becomes a market order and will be sold out on the next transaction.

In general, I think it is usually better to not enter stop-loss orders. Watch your stocks closely and know ahead of time the exact price at which you will immediately sell to cut a loss.

If, on the other hand, you can't watch your stocks closely or you are the vacillating-type investor who can't make decisions to sell and get out when you are losing, stop-loss orders might help protect you against your distance or indecisiveness.

If you use them, remember to cancel the stop-loss order if you change your mind and sell a stock before the stop-loss order is executed; otherwise, you could later accidentally sell a stock you no longer own. Such errors can cost you money.

One of the biggest faults investors have is that it takes time to reverse their positive views. If you sell and cut losses 7% or 8% below buying points, you will automatically be forced into selling as a general market correction starts to develop. This should make you begin to shift into a questioning, defensive line of thinking sooner.

A sophisticated investor who uses charts and understands market action will also find there are very few leading stocks that are correct to buy at a market-topping juncture. There is also a great tendency for laggard stocks to show strength at this stage. Seeing a number of sluggish or low-priced, lower-quality stocks becoming strong is a loud signal to

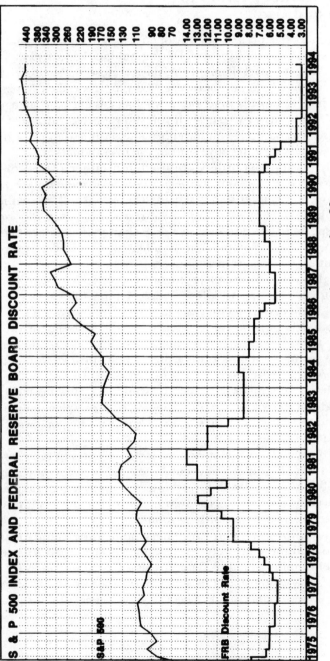

Federal Reserve discount rate changes for more than 20 years

56

the experienced market operator that the upward market move may be near its end. Even turkeys can try to fly in a windstorm.

A peculiar tendency during a bear market is for certain leading stocks to resist the decline and hold up in price, creating the impression of true strength. This is almost always false and simply postpones the inevitable collapse. When they raid the house, they usually get everyone.

How to Interpret the Advance-Decline Line

Some technical analysts religiously follow advance-decline line data, which are cumulative statistics on the total number of New York Stock Exchange stocks advancing each day versus the number declining. However, this measure is imprecise because the advance-decline line sometimes may veer down substantially before the actual top in a bull market. In other words, a market keeps advancing toward higher ground but is being led by fewer stocks.

There is one way an advance-decline can be an effective aid. During a **bear market** you will have several rallies. It is of value to know how the advance-decline line rallies during these intermediate recovery movements. In September 1987, the line lagged the Dow rally to 2662.

Frequently, the advance-decline line will lag the market averages and fail to break through prior resistance areas on the upside. This, in effect, gives you an internal indication that although the Dow may seem to be rallying strongly, the broad cross section of the market remains frail, suggesting the rally will fizzle. In other words, it takes more than just a few leaders to make a new bull market.

Forecasting the Powerful January 1985 Rally

On the positive side, the powerful resumption of the bull market in the second week of January 1985 was clearly and easily forecast by the advance-decline line three weeks earlier. The NYSE advance-decline line broke above immediately prior peaks three times while the *Investor's Business Daily* stock index moved sideways and the Dow Jones Industrials actually took a nosedive.

Market tops usually occur with odd lot (less than 100-share transactions), short-interest, relatively low (1% or less of total odd-lot selling activity), and, at a peak, in short-term, overbought, oversold indexes (a popular but overrated index) or, as is most often the case, on the way down from a peak in the index reached four to eight weeks earlier. These are only secondary indicators and should be used only as confirmation of the market environment after daily Dow distribution is spotted.

Following the one or two top signal days and the first decline off the top, there will be either a poor rally in the market averages, rally failure, or both. You should learn in detail exactly what signals you are looking for, and you should remain unbiased with no opinion about the market. Let the daily Dow tell you what the market has been doing and is doing.

You do not need to know what the market is going to do! All you need to know is what the market has actually done! This is the key! Think about it for a minute. There is a fortune in this paragraph.

Follow the Leaders for Market Clues

After the daily general market averages, I would say the second most important indicator of primary changes in stock market direction is simply the way leading stocks act.

After an advance in stocks for a couple of years or more, if the majority of the original price leaders top, you can be fairly sure the overall market is going to get into trouble. Of course, if you don't know how to recognize when the more aggressive market leaders are making tops and behaving in an abnormal fashion, this method of market analysis won't help you very much.

There are numerous indications of tops in individual stock leaders. Many of these securities will break out of their third or fourth price base formation on the way up. Most of these base structures will appear wider and looser in their price fluctuations and volatility and have definite faulty characteristics in their price patterns. A faulty base can best be recognized and analyzed by studying charts of a stock's daily or weekly price and volume history.

Some stocks will have climax tops with rapid price runups for two or three consecutive weeks. A few will have their first abnormal price break off the top and display an inability to rally more than a trivial amount from the lows of their correction. Still others will show a serious loss of upward momentum in their most recent quarterly earnings reports. The subject of when to sell individual stocks will be presented in great detail in the next two chapters.

How You Can Spot Stock Market Bottoms

Once you've recognized a bear market and scaled back your stock holdings, the big question is how long you should remain on the sidelines. If you plunge back in the market too soon, the apparent rally may fade and you'll lose money. But if you hesitate at the brink of a roaring recovery, opportunities will pass you by.

Again, the daily general market averages provide the best clues. **Watch for the first time an attempted short-term rally follows through on anywhere from its third to tenth day of recovery. The first and second days of an attempted improvement can't tell you if the market has really turned, so I ignore them and concentrate on the follow-through days of the rally. The type of action to be looked for after the first few days of revival is an increase in total market volume from the day before, with substantial net price progress for the day up 1% or more on the Dow Jones or S&P Index.**

There will be some scarce cases where whipsaws may occur; however, in almost every situation where the rally has a valid follow-through and then abruptly fails, the market will very quickly come crashing down on furious volume, normally the next day.

Just because the market corrects the day after a follow-through, however, does not mean the upward follow-through was false. When the general market bottoms, it frequently backs and fills (testing) near the lows made during the previous few weeks. It is usually more constructive if these pullbacks or tests hold up at least a little above the absolute intraday lows made recently in the market averages.

Wait for a Second Confirmation at Market Bottoms

At stock market lows, the individual investor is safer to wait for a second confirmation of the turn before buying heavily. The bottom day in the Dow Jones or the first strong day up after a major decline is usually the first indication of a possible bottom. A good follow-through, with the Dow Jones up 18 or 20 points or more (if the Dow is in the 1800 area) and accompanied by an increase in daily volume from the day before, will usually be on the fourth, fifth, sixth, or seventh day of the attempted rally. This is your second confirmation and main buy signal. Follow-throughs after the tenth day indicate weakness.

Occasionally, you may have a follow-through as early as the third day if the first, second, and third day are all very powerful, for example, each day being up 15 or 20 points on the Dow with large increased volume. A follow-through day should give the feeling of an explosive rally that is strong, decisive, and conclusive, not begrudging and on the fence, up only a marginal eight or nine points. Following are examples of several important bottoms in the stock market between 1974 to 1990.

Is the Dow Theory Useful?

The Dow Theory is another method used by some to predict the beginning of a new bull market. I do not recommend its use because it is just

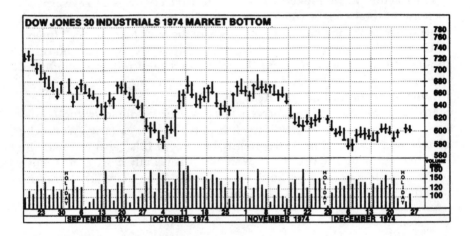

Market bottoms

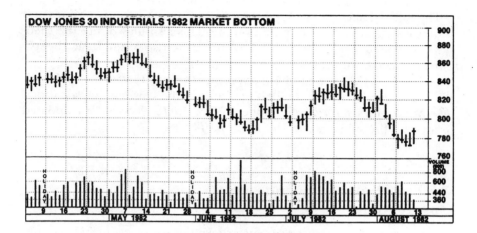

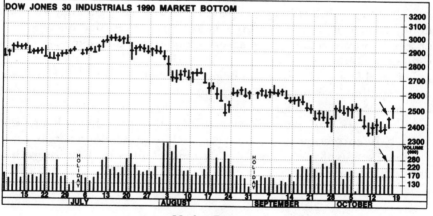

Market Bottoms

too late and obsolete to be of practical use in today's modern market. The Dow Theory, it must be remembered, was created around the turn of the century when the railroad industry was a booming growth sector of the American economy.

The theory simply states that you must always analyze the industrial and railroad averages together. If, after a prolonged bear market, the industrial average breaks out into new territory, you must wait for the rails to also blast out and confirm the movement of the industrials before you can safely turn bullish and begin buying.

The rail average was changed several years ago to include airlines and is now called the transportation average. This also may dilute the theory's original concept, which was to confirm the rise of the basic (heavy) industrial sector of the economy.

For investors interested in pursuing the matter in more detail, William Peter Hamilton, in 1922, published the classical work entitled *The Stock Market Barometer.* Robert Rhea, in 1932, wrote an updated treatise on the subject, entitled *The Dow Theory.*

General Philosophy and Observations

To many people, it seems prudent or fashionable to say or believe they are long-term investors. Their policy is to stay fully invested through thick and thin. Indeed, some institutions follow this philosophy. This inflexible strategy can at times bring tragic results, particularly for individual investors. Individuals and institutions alike may get away with this nonmovement in several relatively mild bear markets that decline 20% or less. However, many bear markets are not mild, and some are downright devastating.

The problem is always at the beginning when you first start to sense an impending bear market. You cannot, in every case, project how bad economic conditions might become or how long they could linger.

For example, Vietnam, inflation, and tight money helped turn the 1969–1970 correction into a two-year decline of 36.9%, whereas prior bear markets typically averaged only nine months in duration with a 26% market downturn.

1973–1974: The Worst Market Plunge Since 1929

Watergate hearings and the 1974 oil embargo by OPEC combined to make 1973–1974 the worst stock market catastrophe since the 1929–1933 depression. While the 1973–1974 bear market saw the Dow correct 50%, the average stock plummeted over 70%. This was a complete disaster for stockholders and was almost as severe as the approximately 90% correction the average stock showed from 1929 to 1933. (However, in 1933, industrial production was only 56% of the 1929 level and more than 13 million of that period's population were unemployed.)

The markets were so demoralized in 1973–1974 that most members on the floor of the New York Stock Exchange were afraid the stock exchange might not survive as a viable institution.

At that time, the head of a large brokerage firm lobbied two years in Washington to get negotiated commission rates approved allowing brokers to provide markets in NYSE stocks upstairs within their own organizations and among their own customers.

This seemingly altruistic ploy might have limited the New York Stock Exchange's ability to conduct an auction market and could have resulted in the industry leaders' sharply cutting prices and driving many smaller competitors out of business. Thereafter, the leader could theoretically more easily dominate markets in stocks and set the price markups it might desire. Of course, this is not what was told members of Congress.

Delegations of other New York Stock Exchange members went to Washington to plead their case, which mainly fell on deaf ears because the powers in Washington at the time didn't trust the self-serving nature of the pleas. Fortunately, I had known Harold Williams, then chairman of the SEC, when he was the dean of the University of California-Los Angeles Business School. My firm had provided a few scholarships to students, so we used to go to lunch on occasion, where we usually discussed the economy.

So I made a trip to Washington and discussed what I believed was going on. A few days later the SEC began a policy change away from abruptly switching from fixed to negotiated rates and allowing big firms to make upstairs markets with their listed stock customers. It slowed down the breakneck pace it had been following toward possibly decapitating the New York Stock Exchange market making function, putting smaller organizations out of business and maybe opening the door to more monopolistic control for the industry's largest firm.

So much for the effectiveness of self-serving industry groups, at least in this one instance!

As an interesting postscript, the SEC was shortly after lambasted in the press by a particular senator for dragging its feet on vitally needed changes in the structure of the financial markets. The senator's name was Harrison Williams, later convicted in the Abscam investigations.

Industry Action That Led to the Creation of Discount Firms

Some constructive changes were brought about several years later, after a more thorough and proper period of analysis and testing. However, it

should be noted that when negotiated commissions were finally adopted to replace fixed rates, the end result was as follows: Many smaller
research firms were put out of business or forced into mergers with
industry giants, commissions to institutions were immediately cut in
half, and commission rates to individual investors were actually raised
several times, thereby laying the foundation for the successful development of numerous discount brokerage firms.

Other Bear Market Warnings

**Another sure sign of the beginning of a bear market, as mentioned ear-
lier, is when the original bull market leaders falter and a number of
lower-quality, low-priced speculative stocks begin to move up.** When the
forgotten old dogs begin to bark and raise up out of the grave and
spearhead the market's advance, the stock market is on its last feeble
leg. Watch out.

Many times this will show up in the form of poor-quality stocks domi-
nating the most active stock list on "up" days in the market. It is simply
a matter of weak leadership trying to command the market. **If the best
ones can't lead the market, the worst ones certainly aren't going to for
very long.**

At other times, when the market begins an important top, it will recover for a couple of months to a point near its high or actually go into new
high ground for a few days before it breaks down in earnest. This characteristic occurred in December 1976 and January 1981 and again in
January 1984. This happens for a very important psychological reason.
The majority of people in the market can never be exactly right at exactly the right time. In 1994 the NASDAQ topped weeks after the Dow.

In the stock market, the majority will be fooled first. This goes for
professionals as well as amateurs. If you were smart enough to sell or
sell short in January 1981, the powerful rebound in February and March
probably forced you to cover your short sales at a loss or buy some
stocks back during the strong rally. This is an example of how tricky and
difficult the stock market really is.

The new high by the Dow in January 1984 was accompanied by a divergence in the broader-based and more significant S&P 500. It did not hit a
new high. This is the reason most professionals plot the indexes together—to facilitate spotting the nonconfirmations at key turning points.

Bull markets do not end easily; neither do bear markets. You generally get at least two or three pullbacks to fake out or shake out the few
remaining tenacious, but emotional, speculators. After everyone that
can be run in or run out throws in the towel and acts, there isn't anyone

left to take action in the same direction, so the market will finally turn and begin a whole new trend.

Experts, Education, and Egos

On Wall Street, wise men, as well as fools, can be easily drawn into booby traps. In fact, in my experience a person's years and quality of education have very little to do with making big money investing in the market.

The more intelligent people are, the more they tend to think they know what they are doing—and the more they will have to learn the hard way how little they really know about outsmarting the stock market. The few people I have known over the years who have been unquestionably successful making money in stocks were decisive, decision-making individuals without huge egos.

The market has a simple way of whittling all excessive pride and overblown egos down to size. After all, the whole idea is to be completely objective and recognize what the marketplace is telling you, rather than try to prove that the thing you said or did yesterday or six weeks ago was right. The fastest way to take a bath in the stock market or go broke is to try to prove that you are right and the market is wrong.

In the final analysis, there is only one thing you can really do when a new bear market begins. That is to have the sense to sell and get out or go short. When you get out, you should stay out until the bear market is over. This usually means nine months, and in the prolonged, problem-ridden 1969–1970 and 1973–1974 periods, it meant two years.

Selling short can be profitable, but it is a difficult, highly specialized subject and short selling should only be attempted during bear markets. Chapter 11 discusses short selling in more detail.

Psychological Market Indicators Can Help

There are several other indicators which may provide further data about the trend of the general market. The percentage of investment advisors that are bearish is an interesting measure of investment psychology. Near bear market bottoms, the great majority of advisory letters will be bearish, and near market tops, the majority will be bullish. In other words, the majority is almost always wrong when it is most important to be right.

The issue here is a question of degree. You cannot blindly assume that because the last time the general market hit bottom and 65% of investment advisors were bearish that the next time the advisors' index reaches the same point, a major market decline will be over.

One of the great problems with indexes that move counter to the trend is that you always have the question of how bad it can get before everything finally turns. In this line, most amateurs in the market follow and believe almost religiously in overbought/oversold indicators.

Overbought/Oversold: Two Risky Words

The **short-term overbought/oversold indicator,** which is avidly followed by some public investors, is a 10-day moving average of advances and declines in the market. Caution: Sometimes in the beginning of a new bull market the index will become substantially overbought because it has just come out of a long decline. This should not be taken as a sign to sell stocks. A similar occurrence can happen in the early stage or first leg of a major bear market when the index becomes unusually oversold. This event is really telling you that an eminent bear market may be beginning.

I once hired a well-respected professional who relied on such technical indicators. During the 1969 market break, at the very point when everything told me the market was beginning to get into serious trouble and I was aggressively trying to get several portfolio managers to liquidate stocks and raise large amounts of cash, he was telling them that it was too late to sell because his overbought/oversold indicator said the market was already very oversold.

You guessed it, the market split wide open after the index was oversold and really started to decline.

Needless to say, I rarely pay attention to overbought/oversold indicators. What you learn from years of trying experience is generally more important than the opinions and theories of experts using their favorite indicator. Sometimes, the more widely quoted and accepted the market or economic expert, the more trouble you might, on occasion, get yourself into.

Who can forget the expert who in the spring and summer of 1982 insisted that government borrowing was going to crowd out the private sector and interest rates and inflation would soar back to new highs? The exact opposite happened; inflation broke and interest rates came crashing down. Conventional wisdom is rarely right in the market.

Stages of a Stock Market Cycle

The winning investor should understand how a normal business cycle unfolds and the duration of these periods, paying particular attention to recent cycles. There is no foolproof guarantee that stock market cycles will last three or four years because it happened that way in the past.

Dedicated market students who desire to learn more about cycles and the longer-term history of U.S. economic growth may want to write to Securities Research Company, 101 Prescott Street, Wellesley Hills, MA 02181 and purchase one of their excellent long-term wall charts.

The stock market ordinarily bottoms out while business is still on a downtrend, anticipating economic events months in advance. Analysts refer to this phenomenon as "discounting of the future." In like manner, bull markets frequently top out and turn down before economic recession begins.

Therefore, using economic indicators to tell you when to buy or sell the stock market is generally an exceedingly poor procedure. Yet some firms have people trying to do this very thing.

It's a somewhat ridiculous approach, but it does seem to make those who don't understand the stock market very well feel better.

Ironically, economists also have a rather faulty record of predicting the economy. A few of our U.S. presidents, themselves lacking sufficient understanding of the American economy, have had to learn this lesson the slow, hard way. Around the beginning of 1983, just as the economy was in its first few months of recovery, the head of President Reagan's Council of Economic Advisors was a little concerned because the capital goods sector was not very strong. This was the first possible hint that this particular advisor might not be as thoroughly sound as he should be, because capital goods demand is never good at the early stage of economic recovery, and particularly so in the first quarter of 1983, when American plants were operating at a low percentage of capacity.

You should check earlier cycles to learn the sequence of industry group moves at various stages of the market. For example, railroad equipment, machinery, and other capital goods industries are late movers in a business or stock market cycle. This knowledge can help you determine what stage of the current market period you are in. When these groups start running up, you know you're near the tail end.

The Big Money Is in the First Two Years

Almost always, the really big money is made in the first one or two years of a normal new bull market's upward movement. This, then, is the point in time you must recognize as soon as possible and fully capitalize upon while the golden opportunity is there.

The remainder of the up cycle usually consists of back and forth movement in the market averages, followed by a bear market. The year 1965 was one of the few exceptions, but this strong market in the third year of a new cycle was caused by the advent of the Vietnam war.

In the first or second year of a bull market, you should have a few intermediate-term declines in the market averages, usually lasting a couple of months, with the market indexes dropping 8% to occasionally 15%. After several sharp downward adjustments of this nature, and once two years of a bull market have passed, heavy volume without further upside progress in the daily market averages could indicate the beginning of the next bear market.

Since the market is made up of supply and demand, you can decipher a chart of the general market averages almost the same as you read the chart of an individual stock. The better publications display the Dow Jones Industrial Average and S&P 500 in the front of their periodicals. They should show the high and low and close of the market averages day by day for the prior year, together with the daily New York Stock Exchange volume in millions of shares traded.

Bear markets normally show three legs of price movement down; however, there is no rule that says you cannot have two or even five "down" phases or more. You have to objectively evaluate overall conditions and events in the country and **let the general market tell its own story.** And you should learn to recognize the story the market is attempting to tell you.

The Effect of News Events on the Market

Some charts of market averages list major news events that occurred at specific times during the last 12 months. This information can be extremely valuable, particularly if you retain and review old back copies. You then have a history over many years of the market averages, together with important news events that may have influenced the market's direction in the past.

History can repeat itself. If you have solid information about how markets behaved during certain past incidents, then you can develop better judgment for the future.

It is valuable to know, for example, how the market reacted in the past to a change of administration in Washington, rumors of war, wage and price controls, discount rate changes by the Federal Reserve Board, or "panic" news circumstances.

The chart on the next page of the general market averages shows several past cycles.

Other General Market Indicators

The **upside/downside volume** is a short-term index plotted on a 10-day moving average which relates trading volume in stocks that close up in price for the day to volume in stocks that close down. This index may show divergence at some intermediate turning points in the market.

For example, following a 10% to 12% dip in the general market averages, the averages may continue to penetrate into new low ground for one or two more weeks. Yet the upside/downside volume may suddenly shift and show there is steadily increasing upside volume while the downside volume may be subsiding.

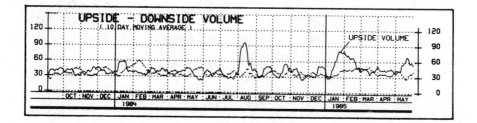

This switch usually signals an impending intermediate-term upturn in the market. Of course, if you follow carefully the daily Dow Jones price changes, together with daily volume on the NYSE, you'll pick up these same indications, so the upside/downside index is really not necessary.

The **short-interest ratio** is the total amount of short selling on the New York Stock Exchange, expressed as a percentage of total NYSE trading volume. It can reflect the degree of bearishness shown by speculators in the market. The May–June 1994 rally was a short squeeze rally.

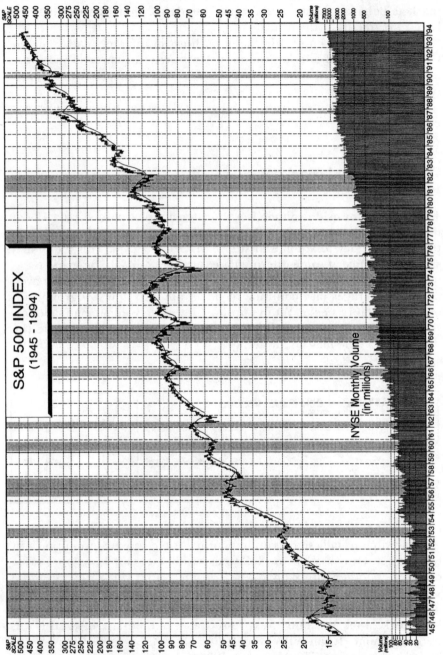

S&P 500 INDEX
(1945 – 1994)

NYSE Monthly Volume
(in millions)

Chart courtesy of William O'Neil & Co., Los Angeles, CA.

Historically, you will see two or three major peaks (measuring greatly increased short selling) in this index along bear market bottoms. There is no positive rule governing how high the index should go, but you can study past general market bottoms to review what has happened to the short-interest ratio in former periods.

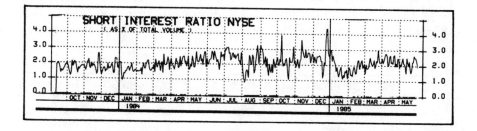

The **odd-lot-balance index** is a ratio between the total buying and selling of odd lotters. Odd lotters are individual investors that buy or sell in less than round lots (100 shares). The theory behind this index is that the less-informed crowd tends to be wrong at important turning points.

Odd-lot indexes have been of value in the past, yet often have been misunderstood and misinterpreted. It is not critical that the index show net buying or net selling. What is important is the trend of activity. If odd lotters have been buying, on balance, and trend toward buying less, it means they are becoming more cautious. Odd-lot theory suggests their caution could turn out to be wrong.

If odd lotters have been selling steadily, the point to watch for is when a shift in this trend occurs, in other words, when they begin to sell less or transition toward buying. If they are beginning to sell less, the suggestion is that they are less worried—and the market could be near a significant top.

Caution: There is confusing distortion in the odd-lot figures in December and January brought about by changes in investors' portfolios for year-end tax benefits. Odd-lot figures also have seemed to be of less importance in recent periods.

The **odd-lot, short-sales index,** which measures the percent of total odd-lot sales that are short sales, is one constructive measurement of crowd psychology and often has signaled the bottoms of bear markets. When you reach a point where numerous small investors conclude the only way to make money is to sell short, you are very late in the down cycle. Caution: Do not jump to a conclusion the first time the odd-lot, short-sales index increases. It can build up to a series of peaks over several months.

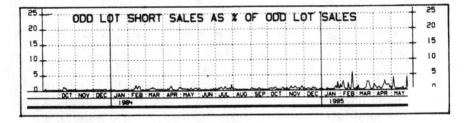

Although not watched as frequently at tops, this index is usually around its low point at major bull market tops. Researchers can note the extreme low point reached at the peak at the end of December 1976.

Of all the many general market indicators, the odd-lot, short-sales index historically has been one of the more reliable confirming indexes. Odd-lot figures are shown in the financial section of most daily newspapers. If you will compare the bottoms of all prior bear markets, you will see that in almost every case there was a substantial increase in emotional odd-lot short selling.

The odd-lot, short-sales index is valid because it tends to represent crowd psychology. Garfield Drew's book, *New Methods for Profits in the Stock Market,* written in 1948, provides statistics on odd-lot sales over many earlier eras.

Some people feel odd-lot studies have no validity in today's world of option buying and selling by small investors. However, it was valuable in the past, and human nature and mass psychology haven't changed much.

Now that speculation in put and call options is the get-rich-quick scheme for impatient new investors, you can also plot and analyze the **ratio of calls purchased to puts bought** for another valuable view of crowd temperament.

Another favorite indicator many investors watch is **the specialist short-selling index.** Investors believe that when a stock exchange specialist is short, he is very bearish and is likely to be correct.

Professionals are generally more correct than are most investors; however, the specialists' heavy short selling can result from an overpowering rally in the market that places huge demands upon their market-making capacity and which they fulfill by supplying stock short. I think this index is overused, overrated, not properly understood, and frequently misinterpreted.

You cannot assume future market rounds will exactly mirror past cycles and the relationship of the index to those tops and bottoms. Market conditions change, and influences upon the market change as well. Option trading, for example, has put a new twist into the action of specialists as well as other speculators.

The specialist short-selling index may, on occasion, be valuable as long as you survey it with common sense and don't try to build your case for the market around its implications. You can have an illuminating perspective if you plot the specialist short-selling index, the member firms short selling, and odd-lot or public short selling side by side for comparison.

Mutual fund sales and redemptions (excluding money market funds) are important indicators because mutual funds, although not as large as banks, are active investors and impact the stock market. If mutual fund redemptions have been steadily increasing, while fund cash positions are at a historical low point, mutual funds cannot provide much buying support for the market.

The **cash and equivalent position of mutual funds** (excluding money market funds) and the **cash position of pension funds** is an important indicator of future market trends.

Ironically, major bull markets begin when institutional cash positions are higher than normal, and bull markets usually top out when cash positions are lower than normal.

MUTUAL FUNDS CASH POSITION – HIGH(6/82)12.2%, LOW(1/84)8.0%					
OCTOBER 1988	10.0%	APRIL 1989	8.8%	OCTOBER 1989	10.6%
NOVEMBER 1988	9.7%	MAY 1989	9.2%	NOVEMBER 1989	11.1%
DECEMBER 1988	9.4%	JUNE 1989	9.8%	DECEMBER 1989	10.4%
JANUARY 1989	9.4%	JULY 1989	9.9%	JANUARY 1990	11.5%
FEBRUARY 1989	9.0%	AUGUST 1989	10.2%	FEBRUARY 1990	11.6%
MARCH 1989	8.7%	SEPTEMBER 1989	10.2%	**MARCH 1990**	**11.9%**

Mutual funds cash position

This occurred again at the bottom in August 1982 and was one of the reasons for the unbelievable bull market stampede on the upside that followed. A record number of mutual funds had 30% to 50% cash positions at the 1982 bottom, and they were dead wrong.

When you are wrong in the market, sooner or later you are forced back into the market to correct your untenable position.

Some services measure the percentage of new money flowing into corporate pension funds that is invested in common stocks and the amount invested in cash equivalents or bonds. This, too, provides a measure of institutional investor psychology.

For many years the composite strategy of institutional investors near market tops and bottoms invariably has been wrong. As did the odd lotters of old, when the majority of institutions decide it is time to keep more of their investments in cash or bonds, it is generally time for a roaring advance in the prices of common stocks.

In the stock market, majority (crowdlike) thinking is rarely right even if it is among institutions and supposed professionals. Wall Street every year or two does seem to adopt a one-track mind, with everyone following each other like a herd of cattle.

A decline in the average price of the most active stocks daily is an indicator of downgrading in quality and an increase in speculative buying. This, at times, occurs as a market is beginning to top out in its later phase.

Two indices frequently used to measure the degree of speculative activity are **OTC volume as a percent of NYSE volume, and AMEX volume compared to NYSE volume.** Volume on the over-the-counter market should be measured relative to activity on the Big Board (NYSE). This measure provided a helpful tip-off of impending trouble during the summer of 1983 when OTC volume reached the level of NYSE volume. When a trend persists, indicating wild, **rampant** speculation, you're close to a general market correction.

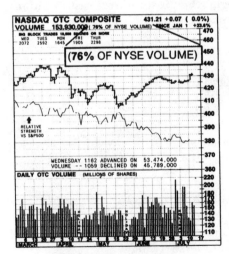

OTC volume as a percent of NYSE volume

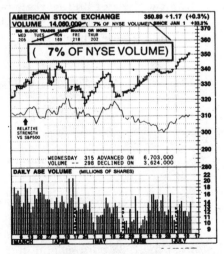

AMEX volume as a percent of NYSE volume

Some publications show a **long-term, inflation-adjusted market index.** This is an academic economist's concoction and is of no real value to decision makers or analysts in the market.

A **defensive stock index** is composed of defensive (more stable and supposedly safer) stocks, such as utilities, tobaccos, foods, and soaps. Increased strength in such stocks after a couple of years of bull market conditions may indicate "smart money" slipping into defensive positions and a weaker general market ahead.

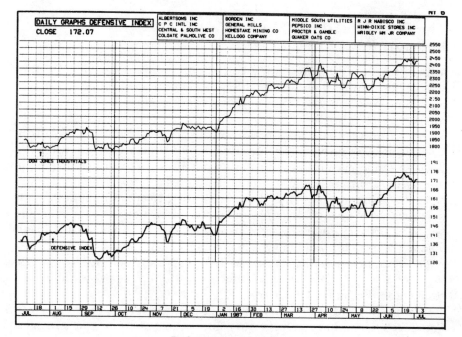

Defensive stock index

The **unweighted stock index** shows the true picture of the average stock. The unweighted index attempts to measure the market strength as a whole by eliminating any possible bias due to weighting of individual companies. In some markets, the weighted averages such as the S&P 500 may overstate the actual strength of the market.

The **glamour index** is composed of speculative or aggressive-type stocks. This index attempts to measure the demand for such stocks, thereby indicating investor sentiment toward the market. A strong upturn in this swinger-type index should indicate new or renewed speculative interest in the market and favorable conditions ahead.

Another possible indicator you should be aware of in evaluating the stage of a market cycle is the percentage of stocks on the daily new-high list that could be categorized as either defensive, low-priced, laggard, or preferred stocks. In pre-1983 cycles, some technicians stated their lack of concern with weakness in the market because of the number of new highs being made. Yet, a detailed analysis of the stocks that make the new-high list has shown that when a high number of preferred or defensive stocks appear, it has frequently signaled a bear market environment. A little surface knowledge can hurt you in the stock market.

The Best Monetary (Money) Indicators

Money market indicators mirror general economic activity. I follow selected government and Federal Reserve Board measurements, including 10 indicators of the supply and demand for money and indicators of interest rate levels.

History proves that the direction of the general market, as well as of several industry groups, is often affected by changes in interest rates. Because the level of interest rates is usually tied to Federal Reserve tight-or-easy monetary policy, you may want to be aware of measures such as reserve requirements for member banks, the M1 and M2 money supply percent rate of change, federal funds rate, consumer price index, member bank reserves, ratio of government securities holdings to bank loans, 90-day Treasury Bill yields, and U.S. Treasury Bond prices.

These monetary indicators might help you anticipate future government policy decisions and their effects on the stock market, individual stocks, and the American economy.

Changes in 90-day Treasury Bill rates and the erratic and tricky Fed Funds rate sometimes help predict impending discount rate changes. The **monetary base** and the **velocity of money** are other important measures used by professionals. The Fed also watches economic data such as unemployment figures and Gross National Product (GNP) changes.

Don't be discouraged if the subject of monetary indicators seems complex; it is. Few economists, few presidents, virtually no one in Congress, and even few people at the Federal Reserve, including some heads of the Fed, understand it as well as they should.

This is just one of the many reasons why the Fed should probably remain relatively independent and not subject to political control or extreme pressure from the Congress. It might, however, be constructive to let the term of office for the head of the Fed coincide with the president's term.

For the investor, the simplest and most relevant monetary indicator to follow and understand is the changes in the Federal Reserve Board discount rate. With the advent of program trading and various hedging devices, some funds use such techniques to hedge portions of their portfolio in an attempt to provide some downside protection during risky markets. The degree to which these are successful again depends greatly on skill and timing, but one possible effect for some managers may be to lessen the pressure to have to dump portfolio securities on the market.

More and more funds operate under a plan of very wide diversification and a fully or near fully invested policy at all times. This is because most managers have difficulty in getting out and into cash at the right time and, most importantly, then getting back in fast enough to participate in the initial powerful rebound off the ultimate bottom.

Is *C-A-N S-L-I-M* Momentum Investing?

No, *C-A-N S-L-I-M* has absolutely nothing to do with momentum investing. In fact, I'm not even sure what momentum investing is. Some analysts and reporters, who have no idea at all how we invest, have referred to what we're suggesting as momentum investing and have said that it's buying the stocks that have gone up the most and that have the strongest relative price strength. No one in their right mind invests that way.

That is not what we're doing. We're buying companies with strong fundamentals, large sales and earnings increases resulting from unique new products or services and trying to time the purchases at a correct point as the company emerges from consolidation periods and before the stock runs up dramatically in price.

To summarize this vitally important and rather complex subject, **learn to interpret the daily general market indexes and action of the individual market leaders.** Once you know how to do this correctly, you can stop listening to all the uninformed, costly, personal market opinions from amateurs and professionals alike.

How to Remember and Use What You've Read So Far

It isn't enough just to read; you need to remember by association and apply a simple-two word phrase—C-A-N S-L-I-M.

Most people seem to have as much trouble controlling weight as they do selecting winning stocks. So each letter in the C-A-N S-L-I-M slogan stands for one of the seven basic fundamentals of selecting outstanding stocks. If most successful stocks exhibit these seven common characteristics at early emerging growth stages, these basics are worth learning. Here is the formula. Repeat it several times until you can recall and use it easily.

C   =   Current quarterly earnings per share. They must be up at least 18% or 20%.

A   =   Annual earnings per share. They should show meaningful growth for the last five years.

N   =   New. Buy companies with new products, new management, or significant new changes in their industry conditions. And most important, buy stocks as they initially make new highs in price. (Forget cheap stocks; they are usually cheap for a very good reason.)

S   =   Supply and Demand. There should be a small or reasonable number of shares outstanding, not large capitalization, older companies. And look for volume increases when a stock begins to move up.

L   =   Leaders. Buy market leaders, avoid laggards.

I   =   Institutional sponsorship. Buy stocks with at least a few institutional sponsors with better than average recent performance records.

M   =   The general market. It will determine whether you win or lose, so learn to interpret the daily general market indexes (price and volume changes) and action of the individual market leaders to determine the overall market's current direction.

PART 2
Be Smart from the Start

8

Finding a Broker,
Opening an Account,
and What It Costs
to Buy Stocks

Branch offices of most New York Stock Exchange firms have a broker of the day. He or she will probably be called a **registered representative** (RR), an **account executive** (AE), or an **investment consultant** (IC). This is the person you will likely talk to if you visit a broker's office looking for information or to open an account.

How do you find a competent stockbroker? I suggest you follow a slightly different procedure.

Go to the office of the firm you choose and ask to see the office manager or vice president in charge of the office. Introduce yourself to the manager. Say you are considering opening a new account but would like to deal with a broker that has definitely been successful at making money in his or her own personal account and for most customers' accounts.

This person should have already been a broker for two or three years or more and possibly be 27 or older. But don't be too impressed with age. The registered representative you're looking for could be young, middle-aged, or older. Age or years of experience is certainly no sign that a broker is a very successful student of the stock market.

Did you ever hear the story about the schoolteacher who had 25 years' experience but was turned down for a job by a new principal? The principal felt the teacher didn't have 25 years' experience, but just one year's experience 25 times over.

Ask Questions....It's Your Money

When you meet the broker recommended to you, ask how he or she gets stock ideas and research information. Don't be afraid to ask a lot of questions. It's your money.

You could ask about the broker's investment philosophies, beliefs, and methods. What are two or three of the best stock market books he or she has read? If the broker can't easily name a few, then maybe you should be a little cautious.

If the broker relies solely on his or her own firm's research department for ideas, information, and reports, you may be better off visiting with a few other brokerage firms before you decide where to open your account.

The better brokers will show more initiative, perhaps by subscribing to a chart service or *Investor's Business Daily* on their own, and will probably have several other sources of information, ideas, and research.

Following brokerage firm research department reports is not necessarily an outstanding way to find money-making investment ideas. When I was a broker with a major New York Stock Exchange firm years ago, I never followed any of the firm's research because it wasn't too astute. Brokers that have attended *Investor's Business Daily* all-day workshops certainly should be far more knowledgeable than those who haven't.

Should You Have Several Brokerage Accounts?

Some customers have accounts with two or three different brokers. In most cases such a practice is silly, since your account won't be as important to any one broker. You may also receive conflicting advice, which will be confusing and costly.

Money is made in the stock market by concentrating, not scattering. The same should go for your brokerage account. Concentrate your activity with the best stockbroker you can find. If this doesn't work well after a year or two, change and find another broker.

If you are more accomplished and make your own buy-and-sell decisions, you might want to consider a discount broker. You could save as much as 50% on the cost of commissions. Discount brokerage firms have grown and increased their share of the retail securities business ever since the advent of negotiated commissions in May 1975.

If you don't know the name or location of a stock brokerage firm that is a member of the New York Stock Exchange, look in the yellow pages of your local telephone book. The reason I suggest a New York Stock Exchange firm is that NYSE membership in the securities industry is a little like the Good Housekeeping seal of approval. It certainly doesn't guarantee you will make money; however, you will be dealing with a more substantial organization. Members usually pay several hundred thousand dollars or much more just to buy a seat on the New York Stock Exchange.

Stock exchange firms also have many rules and regulations to which they must adhere. And they are subject to surprise audits and annual examinations from the stock exchange.

Conversely, some firms that are only members of the NASD, the National Association of Securities Dealers, and perhaps a local or regional exchange, may have too easily gained entrance into the securities business. They may not be backed up with as substantial a capital base.

If you've never opened an account with a brokerage firm, don't be timid or reluctant to visit one. It's simple and easy, just like opening an account with your local bank or savings and loan. You will have to fill out and sign new account papers before you will be able to buy or sell any stock. You may open a single account or, if you're married, you may want to open a joint account. The broker will also ask for credit references, such as your bank. All brokerage firms have a regular commission schedule which they should be able to show you. The commission generally averages from 1% to 2% to buy or sell a stock.

When you buy or sell stock, you will receive a confirmation in the mail (a small slip of paper) which will show what stock you bought or sold, the price paid or received, the commission paid, and the total dollar amount you owe or will receive if you sold a stock. It will also show the settlement date by which the transaction must be settled.

It's best to pay these bills immediately on receipt since they will be due in a few days. Stock certificates must be delivered to your broker properly endorsed without delay when you wish to sell a stock, otherwise the transaction can't be settled on time. Sometimes stock powers (legal endorsements) can be signed and mailed separately to your broker.

It is usually more convenient for both you and the NYSE firm to hold your stock certificates in street name (the brokerage company name), where they are held in safekeeping for you by the brokerage firm. All accounts are insured to $500,000 by the Securities Investor Protection Corporation, and additional insurance is carried by most firms. Certificates are kept in a vault, so they should be safer than if you try to take care of them yourself.

The largest retail brokerage firms in the United States are: Merrill Lynch, Pierce, Fenner & Smith; Dean Witter Reynolds; Prudential

Securities; Paine Webber; A.G. Edwards & Sons; Kidder, Peabody & Co.; Smith Barney Shearson, Inc.; Bear, Stearns & Co.; First Boston; Goldman, Sachs & Co.; Morgan Stanley & Co.; and Salomon Brothers. Charles Schwab, Fidelity Brokerage Services, and Quick & Reilly are a few of the larger discount firms.

All of the above brokerage organizations are substantial and experienced. Merrill Lynch has approximately 6 million customers, and Prudential is a member of the giant Prudential Insurance Company family. There are also many capable medium-sized, regional retail, or discount retail brokerage firms that are New York Stock Exchange members.

An exceptionally able broker can be almost as important to you as a good doctor, so choose wisely.

Why You Should Have an Individual Retirement Account (IRA)

Why are so many people investing in IRA accounts, as they are commonly known?

U.S. law allows working individuals to invest any amount up to $2000 every year in a tax-deferred IRA account if the company they work for does not have a qualified retirement plan. This can be an enormous tax advantage, and every American should consider taking advantage of it.

First, you may be able to deduct the $2000 investment from your taxable income and not have to pay income tax on that part of your earnings. And you can do this every year that you invest in an IRA, until you are 70 years old. If married and both of you are working, you can invest any amount up to $4000 every year.

The second advantage of an IRA is that the profits, dividends, or interest you earn from the investments you make in the IRA account are *tax-deferred*. These earnings compound tax-free for the many years until you retire and begin taking distributions.

Do you have any idea what $4000 invested tax-free every year, earning and compounding at an average rate of 12% per year, would be worth after 30 years? Your account would be worth $965,332!

IRA plans allow you to begin withdrawals (of course subject to regular income tax rates at the time of withdrawal) at age $59\frac{1}{2}$, but you must begin by age $70\frac{1}{2}$. If you are disabled, you can withdraw early; otherwise early withdrawal is subject to a 10% penalty plus the regular income tax.

You don't have to wait till age $59\frac{1}{2}$ to benefit from the plan, however; if you withdraw funds after five or six years and pay the penalty, you are still better off than if you had been in similar investments with no IRA tax benefit. You should, though, view your IRA as a long-term plan for deferring taxes and saving for your retirement. Be determined and stick with it.

Withdrawal, after age 59½, can be in a lump sum or spread in installments over a period of years. You will pay ordinary tax rates on your withdrawals, which should be lower once you retire.

Most families in America should budget carefully their monthly and annual expenses and make sure they save enough of their hard-earned income to invest in their own Individual Retirement Account each year. You can open an IRA account at any bank or stock brokerage firm. IRA accounts cannot be margined.

The most favored vehicles for investment of your IRA money have been interest-bearing money market funds, savings accounts, certificates of deposits, mutual funds, or self-directed accounts in common stocks through a NYSE stock brokerage firm. However, fixed-income savings accounts and money market funds are not likely to provide the maximum hedge against inflation.

Keogh plans are similar to IRAs except they are only for self-employed workers. Keoghs, however, allow a higher maximum contribution: a defined contribution Keogh has a maximum contribution limit of up to 20% of a person's annual salary or up to $30,000. Another form of a Keogh, known as a defined Benefit Keogh, may allow even greater annual contributions.

Many companies offer 401(k) salary-reduction plans which allow you to invest, on a tax-deferred basis, larger amounts than are allowable in IRAs, but under different rules and restrictions.

401(k) plans have several other advantages and if your company has a 401(k) plan you should definitely investigate participating.

In 1982, approximately 60 million American households were eligible to open one or more IRA plans. In time, IRAs could become more important than Social Security. This will mean a large increase in the number of savers and investors in America in the future.

If you only have $500 or $1000 to invest each year, that's okay. You don't have to invest the maximum allowed each year. There is no minimum dollar amount required to begin an IRA.

If you opt for an IRA, then you had better start learning about investments in a serious and planned way. Keep this book and read it two or three times until you understand everything in it. And then reread it every few years to help you keep on target. Why? Because, if you invest $2000 each year, in only four or five years you are going to have $10,000 or more—and that is an important sum for anyone. You owe it to yourself and your future to learn how to manage your important investments properly.

9

When to Sell
if Your Selection or Timing
Might Be Wrong

Sometimes the best offense is a great defense. Now that you've learned the basic rules of buying stocks, our emphasis will switch to when to sell them. In sports, a team that is all offense and no defense seldom wins the league. Since the days of Branch Rickey, the Los Angeles Dodgers, and before that the Brooklyn Dodgers, have generally had good pitching. The pitching staff and defense is probably 70% of the game of baseball. It's just impossible to win without it.

In the stock market, you absolutely can't win either unless you have a strong predetermined defense to protect yourself against large losses. This may surprise you, but if you invest in stocks, you are going to make a never-ending number of mistakes in your selection and timing of purchases.

These poor decisions will lead to losses, some of which can become quite awful. No matter how smart you may think you are or how good you believe your information or analysis is, you simply are not going to be right all of the time. In fact, you will probably be right only half the time!

Bernard Baruch's Secret
Market Method

Bernard Baruch, a famous market operator on Wall Street and trusted advisor to U.S. presidents said, "If a speculator is correct half of the time, he is hitting a good average. Even being right three or four times out of 10 should yield a person a fortune if he has the sense to cut his losses quickly on the ventures where he has been wrong."

This point of Baruch's was proven to my satisfaction in the case of an account I managed many years ago. In 1962, the general market took a 29% nosedive and we were right in only 33% of the commitments made in this particular account. Yet, the account was ahead at the end of the year because the average profit on the 33% correct decisions was over twice the size of the average small losses taken when we were off target.

The whole secret to winning in the stock market is to lose the least amount possible when you're not right. In other words, in order to win you've got to recognize when you may be wrong and sell without hesitation to cut short your loss.

But how can you tell when you may be wrong? That's easy. The price of the stock will drop below your purchase price! Each point your favorite brainchild descends below your cost increases both the probability that you are mistaken, as well as the price you are going to pay for being incorrect.

Are Successful People Lucky or Always Right?

People think a successful person is either lucky or right most of the time. This is not so. Successful people make many mistakes. Their successes are a result of hard work rather than their being lucky. They succeed in spite of their mistakes because they try much harder and more often than the average person does. There just aren't many overnight successes. Success takes time.

In search of a filament for his electric lamp, Edison carbonized and tried 6000 different specimens of bamboo. Three of them worked. Before that, he tried thousands of other items from cotton thread to chicken feathers.

Babe Ruth tried so hard that he holds the lifetime record for strike-outs. And Irving Berlin said, "Out of more than 600 songs I have written, no more than 50 have been hits. I missed 11 times for every time I succeeded." The Beatles were turned down by every record company in England before they finally made it.

I have found over the years that only one or two stocks out of every 10 I bought turned out to be truly outstanding and capable of making substantial profits. This means in order to get the one or two, you have to look for and buy 10 different stocks.

If we find the two extraordinary investments, what should we do with the other eight average or poor choices? Sit with them and hope, like most people do, or keep trying until we come up with a few more formidable successes.

It takes a lot of tries and many misses before you can own and nail down substantial gains in stocks like Brunswick and Great Western Financial when they doubled in 1961, Chrysler and Syntex in 1963, Fairchild Camera and Polaroid in 1965, Control Data in 1967, Levitz Furniture in 1970–1972, Prime Computer and Humana in 1977–1981, MCI Communications in 1981–1982, Price Company in 1982–1983, Microsoft in 1986–1992, Amgen in 1990–1991, and International Game Technology in 1991–1993. These stocks dazzled the market with gains ranging from 100% to more than 1000%.

Are You a Speculator or an Investor?

Before we delve further into the intriguing shell game of when to sell, let's define two misunderstood words. These words are *speculator* and *investor.*

Bernard Baruch interpreted *speculator* as follows: "The word speculator comes from the Latin 'speculari' which means to spy and observe. A speculator, therefore, is a person who observes and acts before it occurs."

Jesse Livermore, another old-time stock market legend, defined *investor* this way: "Investors are the big gamblers. They make a bet, stay with it, and if it goes wrong, they lose it all."

These definitions are a bit different than those you will read in *Webster's Dictionary.* But we know Baruch and Livermore on occasion made millions of dollars in the stock market. We're not sure about Webster.

One of my primary goals is to convince you to question many of the investment ideas, beliefs, and methods you have heard about or used in the past.

The amount of erroneous information and ignorance about how the stock market really works and how to succeed in the market is downright unbelievable.

How the Normal Investor Thinks

Let's examine how the normal investor thinks and makes decisions. If you are a typical investor, you probably keep records of your transactions in the market, perhaps in the following manner:

Buys	Cost	Current price
100 Navistar	$27	$23
100 Luby's Cafeterias	20	30
50 SmithKline Beckman	76	74
100 Toys R Us	30	48
100 Storage Technology	22	15
100 H. J. Heinz	31	37
60 Wal-Mart Stores	55	61

When you think about selling a stock, you likely look at your records to see what price you paid for the stock, don't you? If you have a profit, you may sell; if you have a loss, you will wait rather than take the loss. After all, you didn't invest in the market to lose money.

So, in this example, you may decide to sell your Luby's Cafeterias or Wal-Mart Stores stock because they show a profit. But these are the stocks you should consider keeping. Instead, you should probably sell one of the stocks showing a loss, like Navistar or Storage Technology.

If you're the type of person who would have been inclined to sell Luby's, the entire basis of your sell decision is unwise, resulting from the "price-paid bias" which 95% of investors have.

Suppose you paid $30 for a stock two years ago. Today it is $34. You may sell it because you've made a profit. But what does the price you paid for that stock two years ago have to do with its worth today—or whether it should be held or sold now?

Suppose you paid $40 for the same stock six months earlier and, therefore, have a loss today. Does this change its future potential? Probably not! What you paid for a stock years ago or whether you have a profit or loss may have little to do with future potential.

When Does a Loss Become a Loss?

When you say, "I can't sell a stock because I don't want to take a loss," you assume that what you want has some bearing on the situation. **Yet the stock does not know who you are, and it doesn't care what you hope or want.**

Furthermore, you may believe that if you sell the stock you will be taking the loss, but selling doesn't give you the loss; you already have it. If you think a loss is not incurred until you sell the stock, you may be kidding yourself. The larger the paper loss, the more real it will become.

For example, if you paid $40 per share for 100 shares of Ace Chemical, and it's currently worth $28 per share, you have $2800 worth of stock that cost you $4000. You have a $1200 loss. Whether you convert it to cash or hold the stock, it is only worth $2800.

You took your loss as this stock dropped in price even though you didn't sell; now you will probably be better off selling the stock and going back to a cash position. You can think more objectively with cash in your stock account than you can if you're worrying about a stock that has lost money for you. Anyway, there are other securities where your chance of recouping your loss could be far greater.

Here's another suggestion that may help you decide whether or not to sell. Pretend you don't own the stock and you have $2800 in the bank. Then ask yourself this question, "Do I really want to buy this stock now?" If your answer is "no," then why are you holding it?

A Unique Way to Keep Your Records

To help avoid the price-paid bias, I suggest you use a completely different method of keeping records. At the end of each quarter, figure the value of each stock position you own by multiplying the current market price of the stock by the number of shares you own.

Compute the percentage change in price of each stock from the last date you did this type of analysis. Now list your investments in order of their relative price performance since your previous evaluation period. Let's say your Tektronix is down 8%, your Exxon is unchanged, and Polaroid is up 10%. Your list would start with Polaroid on top, then Exxon and Tektronix.

At the end of the following quarter, do the same thing. After a few reviews, you will easily recognize the holdings that are not doing well. They will be at the bottom of the list, and the ones that performed best will be at the top.

This method, while not foolproof, does force you to focus your attention not on what you paid for stocks, but on the relative performance of your investments in the market. It will help you maintain a clearer perspective. Of course, you have to keep records of your costs for tax reasons, but you should use this more realistic method in the management of your portfolio.

Eliminating the price-paid bias can be profitable and rewarding. If you base your sell decisions on your cost and hold stocks that are down in price because you do not want to accept the fact you have made an imprudent selection and lost money, you are making decisions exactly the opposite of those you would make if you were running your own business.

The Red Dress Story

The stock market is really no different from your own business. Investing is a business and should be operated just like a business.

Assume you own a small retail women's clothing store. You have bought and stocked women's dresses in three colors—yellow, green, and red. The red dresses are quickly sold out, the green ones are half sold, and the yellow ones have not sold at all. What do you do about it?

Do you go to your buyer and say, "The red dresses are all sold out. The yellow ones don't seem to have any demand, but I still think they're good and besides, yellow is my favorite color, so let's buy some more of them anyway"?

Certainly not!

The clever merchandiser who survives in the retail business eyes this predicament objectively and says, "We sure made a mistake. We'd better eliminate the yellow dresses. Mark them down 10%. Let's have a sale. If they don't sell at that price, mark them down 20%. Get our money out of those 'old dogs,' and put it in more of the hot-moving red dresses that are in demand." This is common sense in a retail business. Do you do this with your investments? Why not?

Everyone will make buying errors. The buyers for department stores are professional buyers and even they make mistakes. When you do slip up, as soon as you recognize it, sell and go on to the next thing. You do not have to be correct on all your investment decisions to make a net profit.

Anytime a commitment in a security is made, you should define the potential profit and the possible loss. This is only logical: you would not buy a stock if there were a potential profit of 20% and a potential loss of 80%, would you? But how do you know this is not the situation when you buy a stock if you do not attempt to define these factors and operate according to well-thought-out selling rules? Do you have any specific selling rules, or are you flying blindly?

I suggest you **consider writing down the price at which you expect to sell if you have a loss, as well as the expected profit potential of all the securities you purchase.** By writing it down, you will focus your attention later on the fact that the stock has reached one of these levels.

Limit Your Losses to 7% or 8% of Your Cost

Individual investors should **consider adopting a firm plan to try to limit the loss on initial invested capital in each stock to an absolute maximum of 7% or 8%.** Because of position size problems and broad diversification which lessen risk, most institutional investors do not usually follow such a quick loss-cutting plan. This is a terrific advantage you, the individual investor, have over the institution, so use it.

I am talking about cutting your loss when it is 7% or 8% below the price you paid. Once you are ahead and have a good profit, you can afford to, and should, allow the stock more than 7% or 8% room for normal fluctuations in price. Do *not* sell a stock just because it's off 7% to 8% from its peak price.

When the late Gerald M. Loeb of E. F. Hutton was writing his last book on the stock market, I had the pleasure of discussing this issue with him in my office. In his first work, *The Battle for Investment Survival,* Loeb advocated cutting all losses at 10%. I was curious and asked him if he followed the 10% loss policy himself. He said, "I would hope to be out long before they ever reach 10%."

Bill Astrop, president of Astrop Advisory Corporation in Atlanta, Georgia, suggests a minor revision of the 10% loss-cutting plan. He feels individual investors should sell half of their position in a stock if it is down 5% from their cost and the other half once it is down 10% below the price paid.

To preserve your hard-earned money, I think 7% or 8% should be the limit. Your overall *average* of all losses should be less, perhaps 5% or 6% if you are strict and fast on your feet.

There is no rule that says you have to wait until every single loss reaches 7% to 8% before you take it. On occasion, you can sense that the market or your stock isn't acting right or that you are starting off amiss. Then you can cut the loss sooner, when a stock may be down only one or two points.

ALSO, 7% TO 8% BELOW YOUR PURCHASE PRICE IS THE ABSOLUTE LIMIT. Once you get to that point, you can no longer hesitate. You can't think about it or wait a few more days to see what might happen. It now becomes automatic—no more vacillating—sell, and sell immediately at the market. The fact that you are down 7% or 8% below your cost is the reason you are selling. You don't need any other reason. At this time nothing else should have a bearing on the situation.

Cutting Losses Is like Buying an Insurance Policy

This policy of limiting losses is similar to paying insurance premiums. You reduce your risk to exactly the amount you are willing to take. Granted, many, many times the stock you sell will immediately turn around and go up. You will probably get very perturbed and think you made the wrong decision if the stock afterwards rebounds in price.

If you bought insurance on your car last year and didn't have an accident, did you waste your money? Are you going to buy the same insurance this year? Of course you are!

Did you buy fire insurance on your home or business last year? If your home did not burn down last year, are you upset because you made a bad financial decision?

You don't buy fire insurance because you know your house is going to burn down. You buy insurance just in case, to protect you from the remote possibility of a serious loss. It is the same for the winning investor who cuts losses quickly and closely; he or she wants to protect against the possible chance of a larger potentially devastating loss from which it may not be possible to recover.

Some people have even damaged their health agonizing over declining stocks they were holding. In this situation, it is best to sell and stop worrying.

I know a stockbroker who bought Brunswick in 1961 at $60. When it dropped to $50, he bought more, and when it dropped to $40, he added again. When it dropped to $30, he dropped dead on the golf course. Never argue with the market—your health and peace of mind are always more important than any stock!

Small losses are cheap insurance and the only kind of insurance you can buy on your investments. Even if a number of the stocks move up after you sell, which many of them surely will, you have accomplished your critical objective of keeping all your losses small. And you still have your money to try again for a winner in another stock.

If you can keep the average of all your mistakes and losses to 5% or 6%, you will be like the professional football team that opponents can never score yardage on. If you don't give up many first downs, how can they ever beat you?

Take Your Losses Quickly and Your Profits Slowly

There is an old investment saying that the first loss in the market is the smallest loss. In my view, the way to make investment decisions is to take your losses quickly and your profits slowly. Yet most investors get emotionally confused and take their profits quickly and their losses slowly.

Even after all this explanation, most investors will still ask, "Shouldn't we sit with stocks rather than selling and taking a loss? How about unusual situations where some bad news suddenly hits and causes price declines? Does this loss-cutting procedure apply all the time, or are there exceptions—like a company has a good, new product?" It doesn't change the situation one bit. You must protect your hard-earned pool of capital.

Letting your losses run is the most serious mistake made by almost all investors! You positively must accept that mistakes in either timing or selection of stocks are going to be made by even the most professional investors. In fact, I would go so far as to say if you aren't willing to cut short and take your losses, then you probably should not buy stocks. Would you drive your car down the street without brakes?

All Common Stocks Are Speculative

There is considerable speculation in all common stocks, regardless of their name, quality, or purported blue chip status.

Every 50% loss began as a 10% or 20% loss. Having the raw courage to sell and cheerfully take your loss is the only way you can protect yourself against the possibility of greater losses. Decision and action should be instantaneous and simultaneous. To be a winner, you have to learn to make decisions.

If a stock gets away from you and the loss becomes larger than 10% or 15%, which can occasionally happen to anyone, the stock normally should be sold anyway.

In fact, in my experience the ones that get away from you for larger than normal losses are usually the really awful selections that must be sold. It is wise to remind yourself, "If I let a stock drop 50%, I must make a 100% gain on the next stock just to get even, and how often do I buy stocks that double?"

It is a dangerous fallacy to assume that because a stock goes down, it has to come back up. Many don't, and some take years to recover. American Telephone and Telegraph hit a high of $75 in 1964 and took 20 years to come back.

"I'm A Long-Term Investor; I'm Not Worried; I'm Still Getting My Dividends"

Another risky statement is to say to yourself, "I'm not worried about my stocks being down because they are good stocks, and I'm still getting my dividends." This is naive because good stocks can go down as much as poor stocks if you buy them at the wrong time, and it is possible they might not be good stocks in the first place. It may be just your personal opinion that they are good stocks.

Furthermore, if your stocks are down 25% in value, isn't it rather absurd to say you're all right because you are getting a 4% yield? A 25% loss plus a 4% income gain makes a big fat 21% net loss.

If you aspire to be a successful investor, you must face facts—most of the reactions you have about taking losses are rationalizations, because no one wants to take losses. You have to do many things you don't want to do to increase your chances of success in the stock market. You must develop exact rules and tough-minded selling disciplines.

Should You Average Down in Price?

One of the worst mistakes I have seen some stockbrokers make is to be reluctant to call customers whose stocks are down in price from what they paid for them. That is the very time a client is unsure and may need some help and reassurance. To shirk duty in the difficult periods is not very professional and shows a lack of courage, or "guts," under pressure.

About the only sin that is worse is for brokers to take themselves off the hook by advising customers to average down and buy more of the stock that already shows a loss. If a broker advised me to do this, I would close my account and look for a smarter broker.

Everyone loves to buy stocks; no one loves to sell stocks. As long as you hold a stock, you still have hope it might come back up at least enough to get you out even. Once you sell, you abandon all hope and accept the cold reality of defeat. Investors are always hoping rather than being realistic. You just can't afford to have a love affair with any stock.

Let's see where the real problem lies. Does the fact that you want a stock to go up so you can at least get out even have anything to do with the action of the stock market?

The stock market only obeys the law of supply and demand. So try to overcome this harmful emotion because it has absolutely nothing to do with the action of your stocks.

A great trader once said, "There are only two emotions in the market—hope and fear. The only problem is we hope when we should fear and we fear when we should hope."

The Turkey Story

Many years ago, I heard a story by Fred C. Kelly, the author of *Why You Win or Lose,* that illustrates perfectly how the conventional investor thinks when the time comes to make a selling decision.

A little boy was walking down the road when he came upon an old man trying to catch wild turkeys. The man had a turkey trap, a crude contrivance consisting of a big box with the door hinged at the top.

This door was kept open by a prop to which was tied a piece of twine leading back a hundred feet or more to the operator. A thin trail of corn scattered along a path lured turkeys to the box. Once inside the turkeys found an even more plentiful supply of corn. When enough turkeys had wandered inside the box, the old man would jerk away the prop and let the door fall shut. Having once shut the door, he couldn't open it again without going up to the box and this would scare away any turkeys lurking outside. The time to pull away the prop was when as many turkeys were inside as one could reasonably expect.

One day he had a dozen turkeys in his box. Then one sauntered out, leaving 11. "Gosh, I wish I had pulled the string when all 12 were there," said the old man. "I'll wait a minute and maybe the other one will go back."

But while he waited for the twelfth turkey to return, two more walked out on him. "I should have been satisfied with 11," the trapper said. "Just as soon as I get one more back, I'll pull the string."

But three more walked out. Still the man waited. Having once had 12 turkeys, he disliked going home with less than eight. **He couldn't give up the idea that some of the original number would return.** When finally only one turkey was left in the trap, he said, "I'll wait until he walks out or another goes in, and then I'll quit." The solitary turkey went to join the others, and the man returned empty-handed.

The analogy to the psychology of the normal investor is amazingly close.

Now you know the real secret to reducing stock market risk...STOP COUNTING TURKEYS AND GET RID OF YOUR YELLOW DRESSES!

Never Lose Your Confidence

One last critical reason for taking losses before they have a chance to genuinely hurt you is that you must never lose your self-confidence and courage to make future decisions.

If you don't sell to curtail your losses when you begin to get into trouble, you can easily lose your confidence to act and make buy decisions in the future. In my book, the first and most important rule for beginners or experienced investors in the stock market is to trim all losses quickly. There was ample time to sell and cut short losses during September and early October 1987 before Black Monday's 500-point break in mid-October 1987. The market's correction actually began on August 26.

Wall Street is human nature on daily display. Buying and selling stocks properly and making a net profit is always a complicated affair.

And human nature being what it is, 90% of the people in the stock market, professionals and amateurs alike, simply haven't done enough homework.

They haven't really studied the problem to find out what they are doing right and wrong, and they haven't studied in enough detail to understand what makes a successful stock go up and down. There is no luck to it, it's not a total mystery, and it's certainly not a matter of random walk, like some inexperienced university professors believe.

There aren't too many people who are good at stock selection, but there are probably more than you realize. They are hard to find because they are certainly in the minority, perhaps one out of every twenty or thirty people in the market.

The fascinating point is that investors can be good at stock selection because they've studied, worked, and acquired the right understanding and experience, but they can also be ignorant about how and why and when to sell their stocks.

Very few people sell well. Selling a stock correctly is the toughest job and the one least understood by everyone. The next chapter will discuss when to sell and take your profits.

In short, if you want to make money in the stock market, **you need a specific defensive plan for cutting your losses quickly and you need to develop the decisiveness and discipline to make these tough, hard-headed business decisions without wavering.**

Remember, there are no good stocks—they are all bad...unless they go up.

10

When to Sell
and Take Your Profit

Common stock is just like merchandise that is bought and sold for a profit. You, as the merchant, must sell your merchandise in order to realize a profit. It is best to learn to sell on the way up while your stock is still advancing and looks strong to everyone else. By doing this, you will avoid getting caught in the 20% to 40% corrections which occur periodically in market leaders and cause great downside portfolio volatility.

It is far better to sell early. If you are not early, you will be late; you'll never sell at the exact top, so stop kicking yourself when a stock goes higher after you sell. The object is to make and take worthwhile gains and not get excited, optimistic, or greedy as a stock's price advance gets stronger! The old saying is, "Bulls make money and bears make money, but pigs don't."

Bernard Baruch, the financier who built a fortune in the stock market, said, "Repeatedly...I have sold a stock while it still was rising—and that has been one reason why I have held onto my fortune. Many a time, I might have made a good deal more by holding a stock, but I would also have been caught in the fall when the price of the stock collapsed."

Rothschild's Rule for Success

When asked if there was a technique for making money on the stock exchange, Nathan Rothschild said, "There certainly is. **I never buy at the bottom and I always sell too soon.**"

Joe Kennedy's Stock Market Secret

"Only a fool holds out for the top dollar," said Joe Kennedy, one-time Wall Street speculator and the father of former President John F. Kennedy. The object is to get out while a stock is up, before it has a chance to break. Gerald M. Loeb states, "Once the price has risen into estimated normal or overvaluation areas, the amount held should be reduced steadily as quotations advance." (At this point it's all right to ask yourself, "Why didn't I sell when it was going up and looked so strong?")

One simply must get out while the getting is good. The secret is to hop off the elevator on one of the floors on the way up. In the stock market one good profit in hand is worth two on paper.

The basic objective of every account should be to first show a net profit. To retain profits, you must sell and take them.

Develop a Profit-and-Loss Plan

If you want to be a big success investing or trading in the stock market, I believe you must operate with a set of rules and a profit-and-loss plan. I'm going to share with you the rules and plan I devised when I was between 26 and 28 years old and had been a stockbroker with Hayden, Stone for less than three years. These rules helped me to buy a seat on the New York Stock Exchange at the end of 1963 and start my own firm.

The buy rules were initially developed in January of 1960 after analyzing in depth the three best-performing mutual funds of the prior two years. The Dreyfus Fund, from 1957–1959, led in performance and in many cases had results twice as good as its competitors.

So I got copies of every Dreyfus quarterly report and prospectus for that time period and calculated the average cost of each new stock position they purchased. Next I obtained a chart book of stocks, and for each new stock Dreyfus had bought, I marked in red ink on the chart the average price they paid during the quarter the new position was purchased.

After looking at over 100 new stocks the then tiny Dreyfus Fund had bought over several years, I made quite a stunning surprise discovery. **Every single new stock was purchased at the highest price the stock had sold for in the past year. In other words, if a stock bounced from $40 to $50 for many months, Dreyfus bought as soon as it made a new high in price and traded between $50 and $51. The stocks also formed**

certain types of recognizable chart-price patterns prior to going into new high ground.

Jack Dreyfus Was a Chartist

Jack Dreyfus was a chartist and a tape reader. He bought all his stocks based on market action, and he only bought when the price broke into new high ground. He was also beating the pants off every one of his competitors that depended solely on fundamental analytical opinions and ignored the market behavior of stocks.

Jack's research department in those early big-performance days prior to his retirement consisted primarily of three young turks in their 20s. They posted to large oversized charts the day's price and volume action on hundreds of listed stocks.

Shortly after that, two small funds run by Fidelity in Boston began doing the same thing. They also produced superior results. Almost all the stocks these three funds bought also had strong increases in their quarterly earnings reports.

My first rules were as follows:

1. Concentrate on listed stocks that sell for over $20 a share and that have at least some institutional acceptance.
2. The company's earnings per share should have increased in each of the past five years, and the current quarterly earnings must be up at least 20%.
3. Timing-wise, the stock should be about to make a new high in price after emerging from a sound correction and price consolidation period. This should be accompanied by a volume increase of at least 50% above the stock's average daily volume.

The first stock I bought under this set of rules was Universal Match in February 1960, and it was fantastic. It doubled in only 16 weeks, but I failed to make much because I didn't have much money to invest then. I also got nervous and sold it too quickly.

Later that year, following my well-defined game plan, I selected Procter & Gamble, Reynolds Tobacco, and MGM, all of which over the next year had outstanding moves. However, my problem was still that I was relatively young, just getting started, didn't have many customers, and had very little money of my own to invest.

About this time, I was accepted to the Harvard Business School via the first Program for Management Development (PMD). I was plain lucky since I was a year below their minimum age requirement.

Jesse Livermore and Pyramiding

At the business school, in my extra time, I read a number of business and investment books in the library. The best one was called *How to Trade in Stocks* by J. Livermore. From his book, I learned that your objective in the market was not to be right but to make big money when you were right.

I adopted his method of averaging up, or pyramiding, when a stock moved up after purchase. This helped to concentrate my buying when I seemed to be right. If I was wrong and the stock dropped a certain amount below my cost, I sold the stock to cut short the loss.

In the first half of 1961 my rules and plan worked great. Some of the top winners I bought that year were Great Western Financial, Brunswick, Kerr-McGee, Crown Cork & Seal, AMF, and Certain-teed. But by summer, all was not well.

I had bought exactly the right stocks at the right time and had pyramided with additional buys so I had good positions and profits. But when the stocks finally topped, I held on too long and watched my profits vanish. When you snooze, you lose.

It was hard to swallow: I had been dead right on my stock selections for over a year and just broke even.

Learning by Post-Analysis of My Failures

I was so mad that I spent the last six months of 1961 carefully analyzing every transaction made during the prior year. Much like the medical profession and the Civil Aeronautics Board conduct postmortem operations and postcrash investigations, I marked with a red pen on charts exactly where each buy and sell decision was made and overlaid the general market averages on each chart.

Eventually the answer to the problem became crystal clear. I definitely knew how to select leading stocks but I had no selling plan. I simply had no rules, no plans, and no idea about when to sell and take a profit.

Like the majority of people's, my stocks went up and then down like a yo-yo and my paper profits were wiped out.

My Mistakes in Certain-teed

There was one stock I handled particularly poorly. I bought Certainteed in the low $20s and sold it for a two- or three-point gain because I was scared out during a weak moment in the market. Certain-teed then proceeded to triple in price. I was right at the right time but didn't recognize what I had and failed to capitalize on this phenomenal situation.

This in-depth postanalysis of my several failures was the key turning point to getting totally on the right track and succeeding in the future. Have you ever analyzed your failures to try and learn from them? Most people don't.

A Revised Profit-and-Loss Plan

I found that successful stocks, after breaking out, tend to move up 20% to 25% and then decline, build a new base, and in some cases resume their advance. Therefore, I created a rule that I would buy exactly at the pivot buy point, not pyramid more than 5% past the buy point and would sell each stock when it was up 20% from the breakout point.

The Certain-teed case had been so powerful, however, that it had increased 20% in just two weeks' time. This was the type of big winner I was hoping to find and capitalize on the next time around.

Therefore, one important exception was made in the "sell at + 20% rule." If the stock was so strong that it vaulted 20% in less than eight weeks, the stock had to be held at least eight weeks. Then it would be analyzed to see if the stock should be held for a possible six-month, long-term capital gain (six months was the capital gains period at that time). If stocks declined below their purchase price by 8%, they would be sold and the loss taken.

In summary, here was the revised profit-and-loss plan: **Take 20% profits when you have them (except with the most powerful of all stocks) and cut losses at 8%.**

The plan had several enormous advantages. You could be wrong twice and right once and still not get into financial trouble. When you were right and wanted to follow up with another buy in the same stock a few points higher, you were frequently forced into a decision to sell one of your weakest-performing holdings. The questionable money continually was force-fed into the best investments.

Also, you were utilizing your money in a far more efficient manner. You could make two or three 20% plays in a good year, and you did not have to sit through so many prolonged, unproductive corrections in price while a stock built a whole new base for many months.

A 20% gain in three to six months was substantially more productive than a 20% gain that took 12 months to achieve. Two 20% gains in one year equaled a 40% annual rate of return, and if you were using 50% margin, your return would be a whopping 80%.

How I Discovered the General Market System

I made one other profitable observation from analyzing all of my dumb mistakes. Most stocks that topped had done so because the general market started into a decline of 10% or more.

This conclusion led to my system of interpreting the daily general market averages to establish the true trend and crucial changes in direction of the overall market.

Three months later, by April 1, 1962, my selling rules forced me out of every stock. I was 100% in cash, with no idea the market was headed for a real crash.

About that time I had just finished reading *Reminiscences of a Stock Operator* by LeFevre and was struck by the parallel between the 1907 stock market panic, which was discussed in detail, and what seemed to be happening in April 1962.

Since I was 100% in cash and my daily Dow analysis said the market was weak at that point, I began to sell short stocks like Certain-teed and Alside (an earlier sympathy play to Certain-teed). For this, I got into trouble with Hayden, Stone's home office on Wall Street because it had just recommended Certain-teed as a buy, and I was going around telling everyone it was a short sale.

Later in the year Korvette was sold short over $40. The profits from the short sales were fairly substantial.

By October 1962 and the Cuban crisis, I was again in cash. A day or two after the Russians backed down from President Kennedy's naval blockade, on the first follow-through day in the Dow Jones, I bought the first stock of the new bull market—Chrysler—at $58.

Throughout all of 1963 my rules were strictly applied, and they worked so well that the worst performing account I managed in 1963 was up 115%. It was a cash account. Other accounts were up several hundred percent. There were many individual stock losses, but they were usually small, averaging 5% to 6%, and the profits were awesome when we were right because of the concentrated position sizes from pyramiding.

Starting with only $4000 or $5000 which I had earned and saved from salary, plus some borrowed money and use of full margin, I had three back-to-back big winners—Korvette on the short side in late 1962, Chrysler on the buy side, and Syntex, which was bought at $100 with the Chrysler profit in June 1963. By the end of eight weeks Syntex was up 40%, short-term gains were building, and I decided to play this powerful stock out for a six-month capital gain.

By the fall of 1963, the profits were over $200,000 and I decided to buy a seat on the New York Stock Exchange. So don't ever let anyone tell you it can't be done!

Many long evenings of study at last led to rules, disciplines, and a plan that finally worked. Luck had nothing to do with it; it was persistence and hard work. You cannot expect to watch television or drink beer every evening and find the answers to something as complex as the stock market or the American economy.

Anyone can do anything in America by working at it. If you at times get discouraged, go back and put in some detailed "extra effort" and don't give up. It's the time you put in after 9 to 5 Monday through Friday that ultimately makes the difference.

Other Prime Selling Pointers

There are a number of additional selling guidelines I developed as a result of the six-month intensive analysis of my past ignorant selling mistakes. Following is a list and explanation of many of them:

1. Buying right solves half of your selling problem. If you buy exactly at the right time off a proper base structure in the first place and do not chase or pyramid a stock when it is extended in price too far past a buy point, you will be in a position to sit through most normal corrections in the price of your stock. Winning stocks seldom drop 8% below a correct pivot-point buying price.

2. Beware of the big-block selling you see on the ticker tape just after you have bought a stock during a bull market. The selling might be emotional, uninformed, temporary, or not as large, relative to past volume, as it appears. The best of stocks can have sharp sell-offs for a few days or a week. You should refer to a chart of the stock for

overall perspective to avoid getting scared or shaken out in what may just be a normal pullback.

3. If after a stock's price is extended from a proper base, its price closes for a larger increase than on any previous up days, watch out! This move usually occurs at or very close to a stock's peak.

4. The ultimate top may occur on the heaviest volume day since the beginning of the advance.

5. Sell if a stock advance gets so active that it has a rapid price runup for two or three weeks (eight to twelve days). This is called climax (blow-off) top activity.

6. Sell if a stock runs up on a stock split for one or two weeks (usually + 25% or + 30% and, in a few rare instances, + 50%). If a stock's price is extended from its base and a stock split is announced, in many instances the stock should be sold.

7. Big investors must sell when they have buyers to absorb their stock; therefore, consider selling if a stock runs up and then good news or major publicity (a cover article in *Business Week,* for example) is released.

8. New highs on decreased or poor volume means there is temporarily no demand for the stock at that level and selling may soon overcome the stock.

9. After an advance, heavy volume without further upside price progress signals distribution.

10. Tops will show arrows pointing down on a stock's daily chart (closing at lows of the daily price range on several days—in other words, full retracement of a day's advance).

11. When it's exciting and obvious to everyone that a stock is going higher, sell, because it is too late! Jack Dreyfus said, "Sell when there is an *overabundance* of optimism. When everyone is bubbling optimism and running around trying to get everyone else to buy, they are fully invested. At this point, all they can do is talk. They can't push the market up anymore. It takes buying power to do that." Buy when you are scared to death and others are unsure. Wait until you are happy and tickled to death to sell.

12. If a stock that has been advancing rapidly is extended from its base and opens on a gap up in price, the advance is probably near its peak. A two-point gap in a stock's price would occur if it closed at its high of $50 for the day and the next morning opened at $52 and held above $52 during the day.

13. Sell if a stock's price breaks badly for several days and does not rally.

14. Consider selling if a stock takes off for a good advance over several weeks and then retraces all of that advance.

15. When quarterly earnings increases slow materially or earnings actually decline for two consecutive quarters, in most cases sell.

16. Consider selling if there is no confirming price strength by another important member of the same group.

17. Be careful of selling on bad news or rumors; they are usually of temporary influence. Rumors are sometimes started to catch the little fish off balance.

18. Try to avoid selling on shakeouts (below major price-support areas).

19. If you didn't sell early while the stock was still advancing, sell on the way down from the peak. After the first break, some stocks may once pull back up in price.

20. After a stock declines 8% or so from its peak, in some cases examination of the previous runup, the top, and the decline may help determine if the advance may be over or if a normal 8% to 12% correction is in progress. You may occasionally want to sell if a decline from peak exceeds 12% or 15%.

21. If a stock already has made an extended advance and suddenly makes its greatest one-day price drop since the beginning of the move, consider selling, but only if confirmed by other signals.

22. When you see initial heavy selling near the top, the next recovery will either follow through weaker in volume, show poor price recovery, or last a shorter number of days. Sell on the second or third day of poor rally; it will be the last good chance to sell before trend lines and support areas are broken.

23. Sell if a stock closes the end of the week below a major long-term uptrend line or breaks a key price-support area on overwhelming volume.

24. The number of down days in price versus up days in price will change after a stock starts down.

25. Wait for a second confirmation of major changes in the general market, and don't buy back stocks you sold just because they can be bought cheaper.

26. Learn from your past selling mistakes. Do your own post-analysis by plotting on charts your past buy-and-sell points.

27. Sell quickly before it becomes completely clear that a stock should be sold. Selling after a stock has broken an obvious support level could be a poor decision because the stock could pull back after touching off stop orders and attracting short sellers.

28. Always project the week you can expect capital-gains selling by those who bought in volume at the original breakout point from a base. (This applies only if current tax laws favor capital gains.)

29. In a few cases, you should sell if a stock hits its upper channel line. (Channel lines are drawn to connect the lows and connect the highs on a stock's price chart.) Stocks surging above their upper channel lines should normally be sold.

30. Sell when your stock makes a new high in price if it's off a third- or fourth-stage base. The third chance is seldom a charm in the market. It has become too obvious and almost everyone sees it.

31. Sell on new price highs off a wide-and-loose, erratic chart price formation.

32. Sell on new highs if a stock has a weak base with much of the price work in the lower half of the base or below its 200-day moving average price line.

33. In some cases, sell if a stock breaks down on the largest weekly volume in its prior five years.

34. Some stocks can be sold when they are 70% to 100% above their 200-day moving average price line.

35. After a prolonged upswing, if a stock's 200-day moving average line of its price turns into a downtrend, consider selling the stock.

36. Poor relative price strength can be a reason for selling. Consider selling when a stock's relative strength on a scale from 1 to 99 drops below 70.

Before going to the next subject, a few words or rules should be suggested on the question of when to be patient and hold a stock. The decision to sit tight is important and closely related to making selling decisions.

When to Be Patient and Hold a Stock

1. After a new purchase, draw a red defensive sell line on a daily or weekly graph at the precise price level where you will sell and cut

your loss. In the first 1½ to 2 years of a new bull market, you may want to give stocks this much room on the downside and hold until the price touches the sell line before taking defensive action.

The defensive, loss-cutting sell line may in some instances be raised but kept below the low of the first normal correction after your initial purchase. If you raise your sell point, don't move it up too close to the current price, because any normal little weakness will shake you out of your stock. If your stock increases 15% or more after a correct purchase, move the defensive sell line up to less than 5% below the pivot purchase price.

I do not think you should continue to follow a stock up by raising stop-loss orders because you will be forced out near the low of an inevitable, natural correction. Once your stock is 15% above your purchase price, you can begin to concentrate on the definite price where you will sell on the way up to nail down your short-term profit.

2. Your objective is to buy the best stock with the best earnings at exactly the right time and have the patience to hold it until you have been proven right or wrong. You should give securities 13 weeks after your first purchase week before you conclude that a stock that hasn't moved is a dull, faulty selection. This, of course, applies only if the stock did not reach your defensive sell price first.

3. Any stock that rises close to 20% should never be allowed to drop back into the loss column. For example, if you buy a stock at $50 and it shoots up to $60 (+20%) and you don't take the profit when you have it, there is no intelligent reason to ever let it drop all the way back to $50 or below and create a loss. You may feel embarrassed, ridiculous, and not too bright buying at $50, watching it hit $60, and then selling at $50 to $51, but you've already made the mistake of not taking your profit. Avoid making a second mistake and letting it develop into a loss.

4. Always pay attention to the general market. If you initiate new purchases when the market averages are topping and beginning to reverse direction, you will likely have trouble holding the stocks bought. (Most breakouts will fail.)

5. Major advances require time to complete. Don't take profits during the first eight weeks of a move unless the stock gets into serious trouble or is having a two- or three-week "climax" rapid runup on a stock split. Stocks that show a 20% profit in less than eight weeks should be held through the eight weeks unless they are of poor quality without institutional sponsorship or strong group action. In certain cases, dramatic stocks advancing 20% or more in only four or five

weeks are the most powerful stocks of all, capable of increases of 100%, 200%, or more. You can try for long-term moves in many of them, once your account shows a good profit and you are ahead for the year.

6. If you own a dynamic leader or a stock belonging to a leading group, you may want to hold it at least until its weekly close is below its 10-week moving-average price line on increased volume. Some outstanding leaders go an amazing distance before this occurs.

7. If possible, try to hold through the stock's first short-term correction once you already have a profit.

8. Holding for a long-term gain during the early stage of a new bull market, in many cases, may force you to stick to your position long enough to make a big gain. Remember, the object is not to be right, but to make big money when you are right.

According to Livermore, **"It never is your thinking that makes big money, it's the sitting."** Investors who can be right and sit tight are uncommon. It takes time for a stock to make a large gain. The first two years of a new bull market typically provide your best and safest period for courage, patience, and profitable sitting. If you really know a company and its products well, you will have the additional confidence required to sit tight through several inevitable normal corrections. Achieving giant profits in a stock usually takes one to three years time and patience.

You've just read one of the most valuable chapters in this book. It should be worth several hundred times what you paid for *How to Make Money in Stocks*—if you will review and understand what you've read and adopt a disciplined profit-and-loss plan for your own investments. It might even be a good idea to reread this chapter once every year.

11

Should You Diversify, Invest for the Long Pull, Buy on Margin, Sell Short?

Do you remember when Mobil diversified into the retail business by buying Montgomery Ward? It never worked. Neither have hundreds of other corporate diversification attempts.

For years you have been told "Don't put all your eggs in one basket," haven't you? However, my experience is that few people do more than one or two things exceedingly well. The jack-of-all-trades and master of none is seldom a dramatic success in any field.

The best example of diversification in the corporate world is the conglomerate. Most are not real winners. They are too big, too inefficient, too spread out, and are involved in so many businesses they have trouble concentrating and creating profitable growth.

Would you like to go to a dentist who spent part of his time doing engineering on the side, wrote music, did a little cabinetmaking, and worked as an auto mechanic, plumber, and accountant on the weekends?

The more you diversify, the less you know about any one area. Many investors overdiversify. The best results are achieved through concentration: putting all your eggs in just a few baskets that you know a great deal about and continuing to watch those baskets very carefully. The more stocks you own, the slower you may be to react and take selling action to raise sufficient cash when the next serious bear market begins.

How Many Stocks Should You Own?

An individual investor with even a large portfolio of a million dollars need not own more than six or seven well-selected securities. Broad diversification is a hedge for lack of knowledge, or ignorance.

Most people with $20,000 to $100,000 to invest should consider limiting themselves to four or five carefully chosen stocks. Once you own five stocks and a tempting situation comes along that you want to buy, you should muster up the discipline to sell off your least attractive investment. If you have a total of $5000 to $20,000 to invest, three stocks might be a reasonable maximum. A $3000 account could be confined to two equities. Keep things manageable!

The more stocks you own, the harder it is to maintain proper track of them. It's a little like the starry-eyed fellow who made money in his pizza stand but decided to expand and open 20 pizza stands. He had quite a bit more to handle and found the additional outlets caused more problems and losses than he had anticipated.

You can also diversify your purchases over a period of time. When I owned Amgen during 1990 and 1991, the position was purchased on more than 100 different days. It was spread out over a period of time and add-on buys were only made when there was a significant cushion or gain on earlier buys. If the market price was 20 points over my average cost and a new buy point occurred, additional buys were made. This is not a method newcomers to the market should attempt because it needs to be done correctly and you also have to be willing to sell if things aren't working out as expected.

The winning investor's objective should be to have one or two big winners rather than dozens of very small profits. It is much better to have a number of small losses and a few very big profits.

One way to maneuver your portfolio toward concentrated positions is to follow up and make one or two smaller additional buys in stocks that have advanced 2% to 3% or so above your original or last purchase price. At the same time, sell and eliminate those that start to show losses, before they become big losses.

Have you ever bought a stock that had a giant price increase, but you owned a smaller number of shares of it than you had in other more uneventfully performing stocks? Using this follow-up purchasing procedure, in time, should result in your having more of your money stashed in just a few of your best stock investments. While no system is perfect, this method is more realistic and has a better chance of eventually achieving important results than does a haphazardly diversified portfolio.

Should You Invest for the Long Pull, or Trade?

If you decide to concentrate, should you invest for the long pull, or trade? The time period is not the main issue. Buying the right stock—the very best stock—at precisely the right time is the imperative issue. Sell this stock whenever the market or your various sell rules tell you it is time to sell. This time period could either be short-term or long-term. Let your rules and the market decide and determine how long to hold each stock.

If you do this, some of your winners will be held for three months, some for six months and a few for one, two, three years or even more. Most of your losses will be held for a shorter time period, normally from a few weeks up to three months.

No well-run portfolio should ever have losses that have been carried for six months or more. Keep your portfolio clean and in touch with the times. Good gardeners always weed the flower patch.

Do Not Day Trade

One type of stock trading you definitely do not want to engage in is day trading, or day-to-day trading, where you try to buy and sell a stock on the same day. The reason is simple. You are dealing with minor daily fluctuations which are much harder to determine than are basic trends.

There is not enough profit potential in daily trading to offset the commissions you generate and the inevitable losses that occur. As mentioned before, you also should not follow a program of taking short, two-point profits, because again your margin of profit is too small to offset larger losses, which in time must happen. Don't try to make money so fast. You can't build Rome in a day.

Should You Use Margin?

Is it safe or wise to invest on margin (borrowed money)? Or should you buy stocks on a cash basis only?

In the first year or two while an investor is learning, it is much safer to restrict activities to a cash basis. However, with a few years' experience, a sound plan, and a set of rules, you could consider buying on margin (using borrowed money from your stockbrokerage firm), particularly if you are young and still working.

It is absolutely essential that you understand that when the general market declines and your stocks start sinking in price, you will lose your capital twice as fast on 50% margin as you would if you were invested on a cash basis. This dictates that you cut losses quickly and get yourself off of margin when major general market deterioration begins.

A margin account should not be fully margined all the time. At times you will have large cash reserves and no margin, and at other times you will be invested on a cash basis. At other points you will be using a small part of your margin buying power, and in a few instances, where you are making genuine progress in a bull market, you may be fully invested on margin.

The margin interest expense, depending on current laws which constantly change, might be tax deductible. However, in certain periods, margin interest rates can become so high that the probability of substantial success may be more restricted.

The best time to use margin is usually during the first two years of a new bull market. Once you recognize a new bear market, you should get off margin immediately and raise as much cash as possible. If you are unquestionably active and more seasoned, you may consider limited short selling.

What to Do about a Margin Call

One last bit of wisdom. **Never answer a margin call.** If the stocks you have in your margin account collapse in value to a point where your stockbroker issues a margin call for you to put up money or sell stock, don't put up money—think about selling stock. Nine times out of ten you will be better off, because the marketplace is telling you that you are on the wrong path and things aren't working. So sell and cut back your risk level. Why put good money after bad?

To buy on margin you will need to sign a margin agreement with your stockbrokerage firm and have your stock certificates held in street name (the brokerage company name). As long as you're dealing with an established New York Stock Exchange firm, this should not create risk for you.

There is a great advantage in having stock held in street name, as it avoids tremendous paperwork and time on your part that would otherwise be spent keeping up with stock certificates, dividends, and stock splits. It also eliminates time and trouble taking securities back and forth to your broker each time you conduct a transaction. And it averts problems and notorious delays with transfer agents, whose work it is to collect, register, transfer, and mail certificates. The itemized monthly statements of your account, provided by most brokers, will also give you complete records for tax purposes.

Should You Sell Short?

In 1976, I wrote a booklet on short selling. Not much has changed over the years on the subject of short selling. It is a topic few investors understand, and in which even fewer succeed.

Why would you ever want to sell short? If you think the market is going to decline substantially or a certain stock is ready to cave in, you could sell the stock short even though you don't own it by borrowing the stock from your broker. If the stock falls in price as you expected, you can buy it at a lower price (this is called covering your short position) and pocket the difference in price as your profit.

Of course, it seldom works out so well. Usually the stock you sell short expecting a colossal price break will do the most unexpected thing—it will immediately begin creeping up in price.

When it goes up you will lose money; therefore, my first rule is don't sell anything short during a bull market. Why fight the general tide? Remember this, because sooner or later you may try it and will have to find out the hard way, just like you learned that signs saying "wet paint" usually mean what they say. Save the short selling for bear markets. Your odds will be a little better.

The second rule is never sell short a thinly capitalized (small number of shares outstanding) stock; it's too easy for the stock to be run up on you (that's called a short squeeze, and it doesn't feel very good when you are in one).

To be effective at short selling, you have to be in gear with the start of a general market decline and short off the behavior of the daily market averages. This requires the ability to interpret accurately the daily Dow Jones Industrials or S&P Index, as discussed in the chapter on determining general market direction, and the ability to select stocks that have had a tremendous runup and have definitely topped out.

Flawless timing is the whole game. You can be right but too early and be forced to cover at a loss. Don't kid yourself, you have to take and cut losses when you sell short just the same as you have a loss-cutting policy when you buy stocks. Otherwise, the sky is the limit, and a short-selling mistake could cause sickening losses.

The two best chart price patterns for selling short are:

1. The head and shoulders top. The right shoulder should be slightly lower than the left, and the best time to short is after the second or third upward pullback in price in the right shoulder is about over. In former big leaders, the several upward pullbacks can be 20% or more from the stock's low point in right shoulder. It also helps if the stock's quarterly earnings are showing substantial deceleration in its

rate of increase or have turned down. Furthermore, the stock's relative strength line should be on a clear downtrend over at least 3 or 4 months or longer so you can be more confident that the security has definitely topped. (Most short selling is done at the wrong time.)

2. Third or fourth stage cup with handle or other similar patterns that have definitely failed after an attempted breakout. The stock should be just picking up trading volume and starting to break down below the handle area. How to recognize chart patterns is discussed in Chapter 14.

There are a few other fine points to mention. If you short additional stock, make sure you are ahead on your first short position before you follow up with more short sales. And don't short larger amounts as the stocks drop. If you begin by shorting 200 shares, any follow-up at lower prices should be in smaller quantities and you should carefully limit how far down in price you will continue to sell short.

Since you have to get an uptick from the previous trade before your short-selling order is executed, orders should normally be entered either at the market or with a limit of $\frac{1}{4}$ point or so *below* the last price. A weak stock could trade down a point or more without having an uptick.

You'll have to short in a margin account, and you had better check with your broker first to see if you can borrow the stock you want to sell short. Also, if the stock pays a dividend while you are short, you will have to make good and pay the dividend to the person who bought the stock you sold. (So don't short big dividend paying stocks.)

As a possible alternative you may want to consider buying put options; at least you don't need an uptick to receive an executed trade. As mentioned, you can now buy puts on the S&P Market Index.

The whole matter of short selling is quite treacherous, even for professionals, and only the more able, daring, and successful investors should probably venture into this puzzling territory. One last absolute warning: Don't short an advancing stock just because its price seems too high to you. You could be "taken to the cleaners."

To summarize: **Don't overdiversify. Concentrate on a small list of well-selected stocks, and let the market help determine how long stocks should be held. Using margins is okay if you are experienced, but it involves extra risk.**

12

Should You Buy Options, OTC Stocks, New Issues...?

I do not think most investors should buy or sell options. Options are very speculative and involve substantially greater risks and price volatility than do common stocks. Winning investors should first learn how to minimize the investment risks they take, not increase them. After a person has proven he or she is able to make money in common stocks and has sufficient investment understanding and actual experience, then the *limited* use of options might be intelligently considered.

Limit Your Dollar Commitment to Options

When and if you do consider options, you should positively limit the percentage of your total investable money committed to options; 10% to 15% is a prudent limit.

Options are like making all or nothing bets. If you buy a three-month call option on General Motors, that gives you the right to purchase 100 shares of General Motors at a certain price anytime over the next three months; the option could expire worthless at the end of three months if General Motors common stock does not perform as expected.

Short-Term Options Are More Risky

If you buy options, you are better off buying longer time period options—six months, or so. This will minimize the chance your option will run out of time before your stock has had a chance to perform. Now that I've told you this, what do you think most investors do?

They buy shorter-term options, 30 days to 90 days, because these options are cheaper and move faster in both directions, up and down!

The problem with short-term options is that you could be right on your stock but the general market may slip into an intermediate correction, and all stocks will be down at the end of the short time period. You will then lose on all your options because of the general market. This is also a reason why you want to spread your option buying and option expiration dates over several different months.

I also prefer buying options on the most aggressive and outstanding stocks, ones where the premium you have to pay for the option is higher. Once again, you want options on the best stocks, not the cheapest.

You should also adopt some rule about where you intend to cut and limit your losses. The percentage will naturally have to be more than 8% since options are much more volatile than stocks. If an option fluctuates three times as rapidly as its underlying stock, then perhaps 20% or 25% might be a possible absolute limit. On the profit side, you might consider adopting a rule that you'll take many of your gains when they hit 50% to 75%.

Keep Option Trading Simple

Another intelligent rule is to always keep the investment problem as simple as possible. Don't let someone talk you into getting fancy and speculating in strips, straddles, and spreads.

A **strip** is a form of conventional option that couples one call and two puts on the same security at the same exercise price with the same expiration date. The premium is less than it would be if the option were purchased separately.

A **straddle** is either long or short. A long straddle is a long call and a long put on the same underlying security at the same exercise price and with the same expiration month. A short straddle is a short call and a short put on the same security at the same exercise price and with the same expiration month.

A **spread** is a purchase and sale of options of the same class (class refers to time).

It is difficult enough to just pick a stock or an option that is going up. If you confuse the issue and start hedging (being both long and short at the same time), you could, believe it or not, wind up losing on both sides.

If you think a stock is going up and it is the right time to buy, buy it or purchase a long-term option and put your order in at the market. If it's time to sell, sell at the market. Option markets are usually thinner and not as good as markets for a stock on the New York Stock Exchange. The way orders on the options exchanges are executed is even different.

Most amateur option traders constantly place price limits on their orders. Once they form the bad habit of placing limits, they are forever changing their price restraints as prices edge away from their limits. It is difficult to maintain sound judgment and perspective when you worry about changing your limits by $\frac{1}{8}$, $\frac{1}{4}$, and $\frac{1}{2}$ points. In the end, you'll get two or three executions after tremendous excess effort and frustration. When you finally pick the big winner for the year, the one that will triple in price, you'll lose out because you put in your order with a $\frac{1}{4}$-point limit below the actual market price.

You never make big money in the stock market by eighths and quarters. You could also lose your shirt when your security is in trouble and you fail to sell and get out because you put a price limit on your sell order. Your objective is to be right on the big moves, not on the minor fluctuations.

The secret to making money in options doesn't have much to do with options. You have to analyze and be right on the selection and timing of the underlying stock. Therefore, you should apply your C-A-N S-L-I-M formula and select the best possible stock at the best possible time. If you do this and are right, the option will go up along with the stock, except the option should move up much faster due to the leverage.

In a major bear market, you might consider buying put options on certain individual stocks or on the S&P index, along with selling short shares of common stock. You don't have to get an uptick in the trading of the stock when you buy put options. Sometimes the uptick rule for short-selling stocks listed on an exchange or the inability of your broker to borrow stock may make selling short more difficult than buying a put.

It will generally not be wise to buy puts during a bull market. Why be a fish trying to swim upstream? Put and call options are quoted daily in most local newspapers, as well as *Investor's Business Daily,* which also shows the volume for each option.

Should You Write Options?

Writing options is a completely different story from buying options. I am not overly impressed with the strategy of writing options on stocks.

A person that writes a call option receives a small fee in return for giving someone else (the buyer) the right to "call" away and buy the stock from the writer at a specified price, up to a certain date. In a bull market, I would rather be a buyer of calls than a writer of calls. In bad markets, just stay out or go short.

The writer of calls pockets a small fee and is, in effect, locked in for the time period of the call. What if the stock gets into trouble and plummets? The small fee won't cover the loss. Of course, there are maneuvers the writer can take, such as buying a put to hedge and cover oneself, but then the problem gets too complicated and the writer could get whipsawed back and forth.

What happens if the stock doubles? The writer gets the stock called away, and for a scrubby fee loses all chance for a worthwhile profit. Why take risks in stocks for only skimpy gains and no chance for large gains? The reasoning I'm giving you is not the reasoning you will hear from most investors or brokers. But then again, what most people are saying and doing in the stock market isn't worth knowing, is it?

Writing naked calls is even more foolish, in my opinion. Naked writers receive a fee for writing a call on a stock they do not own, so they are unprotected if the stock moves against them.

It is possible that large investors that have trouble making decent returns on their portfolio may find some minor added value in writing, on part of their investment position, short-term options in stocks that they feel are overpriced. However, I am always somewhat skeptical of new methods of making money that seem so easy. There are few free lunches in the stock market.

Great Opportunities in NASDAQ Stocks

NASDAQ stocks are not traded on a listed stock exchange but are traded through over-the-counter dealers. The over-the-counter market is a specialized field, usually of younger, less-established companies.

There are hundreds of intriguing new growth stocks in the NASDAQ market; however, you may want to learn to first make money buying and selling outstanding listed stocks. After you have been in the listed market and have a record of some success, then the exploration of the over-the-counter stock market should positively be considered.

If you buy over-the-counter securities, they should possibly be limited to no more than 25% to 50% of your total stock portfolio. For maximum flexibility and safety, it is vital to maintain marketability in all your investments.

Sometimes over-the-counter securities may prove to be less liquid in very poor markets. In truly terrible markets, some over-the-counter dealers may just stop making markets or be very slow to answer their telephone when you want out.

There is a considerable amount of information available today on the thousands of over-the-counter stocks. You can obtain charts that show volume figures, as well as price movement and most of the other necessary investment data. So don't overlook the NASDAQ market.

Many NASDAQ stocks are frequently available at lower P/E ratios because they may not have received wide recognition and strong institutional acceptance. In selecting over-the-counter stocks, you should apply the C-A-N S-L-I-M formula and steer clear of low-priced stocks ($5 and $10) that have no institutional sponsorship.

The over-the-counter market is a very large marketplace. There were days in the 1990s when trading volume on the OTC market was larger than that on the New York Stock Exchange. *Value Line, Standard & Poor's, Daily Graphs, Long Term Values, Quote Digest,* and *Mansfield* all provide services that trace OTC stocks.

In 1983 and again in 1993, more than 800 companies went public by selling stock in their enterprises. Almost all of these youthful and innovative organizations are traded in the NASDAQ market. Many of them are definitely outstanding companies, more than have been seen in generations, and many will emerge as leaders in future market cycles.

Winners on the American Stock Exchange

The AMEX, as it is referred to, lists companies that are typically younger or smaller in size than those on the NYSE. Trading on the AMEX is therefore much more speculative and volatile.

However, for skillful investors who follow a sound plan of operation, the American Exchange companies in certain market cycles may offer tremendous possibilities. Following is a list of some of the unbelievable price moves with all stock splits considered that occurred on the American (curb) Exchange in the past.

Amrep Corporation—March 1968 to May 1969, $14 to $62

Bergen Brunswig—June 1980 to May 1983, $15 to $94

Champion Home Builders—February 1968 to May 1969, $28 to $152

Chilton Corporation—July 1982 to September 1983, $10 to $78

Commodore Int'l. Ltd.—June 1978 to July 1983, $22 to $1215

Community Psychiatric—March 1977 to April 1987, $11 to $590

Crown Crafts—June 1986 to September 1987, $13 to $120

Deltona Corp.—April 1968 to October 1969, $26 to $150

Dome Petroleum—November 1977 to February 1980, $40 to $296

Fairchild Camera—February 1959 to June 1960, $16 to $200

Falcon Seaboard Inc.—October 1974 to December 1977, $14 to $142

Flightsafety Int'l. Inc.—August 1977 to May 1981, $9 to $100

General Cinema Corp.—July 1967 to December 1968, $21 to $125

Gerber Scientific Inc.—March 1979 to November 1980, $18 to $116

Hasbro Inc.—July 1982 to September 1983, $22 to $95

Houston Oil & Mine—October 1972 to November 1973, $15 to $186

Key Pharmaceuticals—August 1980 to June 1983, $25 to $132

Kirby Exploration Co.—September 1979 to August 1981, $30 to $450

La Quinta Motor Inns—November 1977 to January 1982, $11 to $104

Levitz Furniture—September 1970 to May 1972, $47 to $348

National Video—March 1965 to April 1966, $58 to $240

Paddington Corp.—January 1962 to November 1961, $68 to $138

Pall Corporation—November 1977 to January 1981, $35 to $203

Parvin Dohrmann—April 1968 to May 1969, $27 to $140

Petrie Stores Corp.—September 1970 to January 1973, $30 to $120

Petro Lewis Corp.—November 1976 to February 1980, $13 to $150

Prentice-Hall Inc.—July 1958 to February 1961, $35 to $225

Pulte Home Corp.—June 1982 to June 1983, $18 to $152

Resorts International—March 1978 to September 1978, $24 to $205

Syntex Corp.—May 1963 to January 1964, $45 to $570

T I E Communications—October 1982 to July 1983, $22 to $80

Topps Chewing Gum—June 1982 to June 1983, $7 to $45

Veeco Instruments Inc.—January 1978 to November 1980, $10 to $94

Wang Labs Inc., Class B—March 1978 to November 1980, $12 to $180

Wards Co. (now Circuit City)—November 1982 to July 1987, $14 to $360

Whitehall Corp.—August 1980 to June 1983, $11 to $132

There will be other giant winners in the future.

Should You Own Convertible Bonds?

I do not recommend that the average investor buy convertible bonds. Sometimes investors are attracted to this medium because they can borrow heavily and leverage their commitment. This simply increases your risk. Excessive leverage can be dangerous.

The theory goes that a convertible bond will almost rise as fast as the common stock rises, but the convertible bond will decline less during downturns. As it goes with most theories, the reality may be quite different. There is also a liquidity question to consider, since many convertible bond markets may dry up in extremely difficult periods.

How about Tax-Free Securities and Tax Shelters?

Should you consider tax-free securities and tax shelters? No, I don't think the average investor should use these investment vehicles.

People seeking too many tax benefits frequently end up investing in questionable or risky ventures. **The investment decision should always be considered first and tax considerations made a distant second.**

This is particularly true in today's environment of a lower top tax bracket. One of the greatest tax advantages during the early 1980s was to make long-term capital gains at the lower capital gains tax rates.

Overconcern about taxes can seriously confuse and cloud your normally sound investment judgment. Common sense should also tell you if you invest in tax shelters, there is a much greater chance the IRS may decide to audit your tax return.

The tax-shelter game is a fertile field for potential scams and fraudulent promotions. *Time* magazine on December 5, 1983, discussed the charge of a federal grand jury in New York City that Sentinel Government Securities and Sentinel Financial Instruments was the largest criminal tax fraud in U.S. history. Hollywood leftist Norman Lear was apparently taken for $1.8 million, according to the article.

This is America, where anyone who really works at it can be successful. Learn how to make a net profit, and when you do, be happy about it, rather than complaining about having to pay tax because you made a profit. Would you rather have a loss so you have no tax to pay?

Recognize at the start that Uncle Sam is always your partner and he will participate in his normal share of your wages and your investment gains.

I have never bought a tax-free security or a tax shelter. This has left me free to concentrate on finding the best investments possible. On occasion when these investments worked out, I paid my taxes on them just like everybody else. The United States' system of freedom and opportunity is the greatest in the world, so learn to use it.

Are Income Stocks Recommended?

I do not believe most people should buy common stocks for dividends or income. In theory, income stocks should be safer, but don't be lulled into believing they can't decline sharply.

People think utility and bank stocks are conservative and that you can just sit and hold them because you are getting your dividends. Ask any investor about owning Continental Illinois Bank in 1984 when the stock plunged from $25 to $2, or any of the electrical utilities caught up in nuclear power plant problems. Electric utilities nosedived in 1994.

If you do buy income stocks, don't strain to buy the highest dividend yield available. That will probably entail greater risk and lower quality. Trying to get an extra 2% or 3% yield can expose your capital to larger losses. **Dividends can also be cut if they are not being adequately covered by a company's earnings per share.**

If you need income, my advice is to buy the very best stocks you can find and simply withdraw 6% or 7% of your investment each year for living expenses. You could sell off a few shares and withdraw $1\frac{1}{2}$% per quarter. Higher rates of withdrawal are not generally advisable, since in time they could lead to possible depletion of your principal.

Are Warrants Safe Investments?

Most investors should shy away from low-priced warrants. It is another complex specialized field that sounds fine in concept but which few investors understand. Warrants give a person the right to buy so many shares of a company's common stock at a specific price, up to a certain date. Many warrants are cheap in price and, therefore, seem appealing. The real question comes down to whether the common stock is correct to buy. Most investors will be better off to forget the field of warrants.

Should You Buy New Stock Issues?

Should the average individual investor buy new issues on the initial offering? I don't generally recommend it. There are several reasons.

First, the few outstanding new issues are going to be in such hot demand by institutions that if you are able to buy them on the offering, you may only be able to buy a tiny allotment. If you can acquire all the stock you want, in many cases it may not be an outstanding issue.

Although most underwritings seem to be underpriced in the 1990s, new underwritings can occasionally be overpriced, and since they have no well-established market, you cannot be sure whether they are over-priced or not. This speculative area should, in most cases, be left to experienced institutional investors who can afford the necessary in-depth research and who are able to spread their new issue risks among many different equities.

Larger individual investors who can afford several expensive and var-ied services may want to consider Value Line's New Issue Service. However, many of the stock offerings being followed here that were ini-tially filed with the SEC may not actually come public. The *IPO Reporter,* a Florida-based service, also provides information on new issues.

Once an initial public offering has been trading in the marketplace for two or three months or more, you have additional valuable market price and volume action data on which to judge the situation. Stocks that have formed proper price bases should definitely be considered by experienced investors who understand correct selection and timing techniques. This can be a great source for new ideas.

There are always standout companies with superior new products and excellent current earnings to be considered from among the broad list of businesses that become publicly held in the previous three months to three years. *I.B.D.*'s New America page covers many of them.

Even so, new issues can be more volatile and occasionally suffer mas-sive corrections during difficult bear markets. This usually happens after a period of wild craze in the new-issue market, where any and every offering seems to be a "hot issue." For example, a new-issue boom developed in the early 1960s and in the beginning of 1983.

Merger Candidates Can Be Erratic

Should the individual investor speculate in merger candidates? No, not normally. It is usually safer to buy sound companies, based on your C-A-N S-L-I-M evaluation, than to try to guess whether or not a company will be sold.

Some merger candidates run up substantially in price on rumors of a possible sale only to suddenly drop sharply in price when a potential deal falls through or other unforeseen circumstances occur. In other words, it can be a risky, volatile business and in most instances should be left to experienced professionals.

Should You Buy Foreign Stocks?

How about foreign stocks? Don't they have terrific potential? Yes, a few foreign stocks have great potential at the right time and the right place, but I don't advise individual investors to waste much time investing in foreign stocks. The potential profit should be two or three times as large as that in a standout U.S. company to justify the additional risk of owning a foreign stock. For example, the player in foreign securities must understand and follow closely the general market of the particular country involved. Sudden changes in the country's interest rates, currency, or governmental policy could, in one sweeping action, make your investment considerably less attractive. There have also been such one-sided moves as nationalization of companies by countries.

It is not really necessary for individuals to find foreign stocks when there are over 8000 securities to select from in the United States. Foreign stocks should probably be left to professionals who specialize in this field. There are a few good mutual funds that excel in this specialty.

In 1982, some of our large banks learned the hard way the substantial added risk they assumed when making loans and investments in foreign countries.

Avoid Penny Stocks

The Canadian and Denver markets list many stocks you can buy for only a few cents a share. The reason I suggest you avoid gambling in such cheap merchandise is that everything sells for about what it's worth. You get what you pay for.

These seemingly cheap securities are unduly speculative and low in quality. The risk with them is higher than with better-quality, higher-priced investments. The opportunity for questionable or unscrupulous promotional practices is also greater. I do not like to buy any common stock that sells below $10 or $12 a share. If you want to fly, why not go first class?

Do You Belong in Futures?

Should you speculate in commodities or other futures? Probably not. Commodity futures are extremely volatile and much more speculative than most common stocks are. It is not an arena for the inexperienced or small investor unless you want to gamble or lose money quickly.

However, once an investor has four or five years' experience and has unquestionably proven his or her ability to make money in common stocks, the "strong of heart" might consider this medium.

In commodities it is even more important to be able to read and interpret charts. The chart price patterns in commodity prices are similar to those in individual stocks. Being aware of futures charts can also help stock investors evaluate changing basic economic conditions in the country.

There are a relatively small number of futures in which you can trade. Therefore, astute speculators can concentrate their analyses. The rules and terminology of commodity trading are different and the risk is far greater, so investors should definitely limit the proportion of investment funds which might be committed to futures. There are worrisome events, such as limit down days, where a trader is not even allowed to sell and cut a loss. Futures can be treacherous and devastating.

Most futures fall under the group categories of grains, precious metals, industrial metals, foods, meats, oils, woods and fibers, financial issues, and stock indexes. The financial group includes government securities such as T-bills and bonds, plus foreign currencies. One of the more active stock indexes traded is the S&P 100.

Large commercial concerns, such as Hershey, use the commodity market for "hedging." Hershey, for example, might lock in a current price by temporarily purchasing cocoa beans in May for December delivery, while arranging for a deal in the cash market.

Should You Buy Gold, Silver, or Diamonds?

Should you invest in gold, silver, diamonds, or other precious metals or stones? Some investors have lost a great deal of money investing in such commodities.

Many of these items were once promoted in a superaggressive fashion with little protection afforded the small investor. There was no SEC to protect against exaggerated, or possibly fraudulent, claims made by some dealers in precious metals. Many books were written boldly predicting gold would bolt to several thousand dollars and our country would go down the drain.

Gold, silver, diamonds, and other items of this nature are commodities. In recent years, they became highly speculative commodities. When the frenzy died down, many investors were left with investments they had bought at inflated price levels.

The dealer's profit markup in these investments was excessive in some cases. Furthermore, these investments did not pay interest or dividends during a period of very high interest rates.

Gold, silver, and diamonds all made very major long-term tops in 1980. At some point these commodities will rally back to a degree. However, due to the wild speculative furor that occurred, there is no way to know how much time must pass to completely clean out past excesses.

There will be periodic short, quick runups in gold, caused by fears or panics regarding potential problems in certain foreign countries. But, this type of commodity trading can be a pretty emotional and unstable game, so I suggest extreme care and caution.

The Soviet totalitarian economic system and that of most captive satellite Iron Curtain countries have been dismal failures. The Soviet Union's continued agricultural failures and vast spending for armaments create recurring pressures for them to sell gold, oil, and other assets to obtain badly needed currency and items their economy is unable to successfully and efficiently produce. This does not add to gold's appeal.

A certain amount of the past speculation in gold was fueled by the Arab world during the inflationary period when the price of oil was rapidly escalating. This situation has now changed somewhat. Because of excessive oil prices in the 1970s and early 1980s, the long-term world demand for oil slowed.

To prevent excessive dependence on imported oil from OPEC and future costly inflationary binges, the United States could and should press hard to open the deep interior of Alaska for oil drilling. I spent a few years stationed in Alaska while in the Air Force and can say that only a couple of thousand people a year visit this extremely remote area, where the temperature falls to 70 degrees below zero in the winter. It should be developed for the benefit of 250 million human beings.

Silver may find fewer uses as photography companies convert to discs and films that no longer use silver.

Diamonds were hawked to the public with almost fraudulent sales pitches, claiming diamonds are guaranteed to go up every year in price because they had always gone up. People were erroneously told that the diamond-market price is totally controlled and set by DeBeers.

Many investors were surprised to learn, as prices collapsed during 1980, that the law of supply and demand also works for diamonds. New sources of supply for diamonds also came into the world market.

As you can surmise, I do not normally recommend investing in metals or precious stones. It is possible at some point that small investments in such items will become timely and reasonable. However, even in this case, investors still may have to contend with large price markups and a lack of ready marketability. Marketability becomes a vital issue when you decide to sell and have trouble finding a willing buyer.

Should You Invest in Real Estate?

Should you invest in real estate? Yes, at the right time and in the right place. In the past, a greater percentage of individual investors in real estate have probably made money than have investors in stocks.

I am completely convinced that every able-bodied citizen should work toward either owning a home, a savings account, or common stock.

Two-thirds of American families report they own their own homes. The typical equity in a home in 1984 was $40,000. Even most insurance companies have made more from their big real estate equity investments than they have from bond and stock investing. That is in part because real estate has been easier for most people to understand.

Home ownership has always been a goal of Americans. Their ability to obtain long-term borrowed money through mortgages and the like, with only a small down payment as equity, has created the leverage necessary for Americans to make large real estate investments possible.

Time and leverage have usually paid off. However, this has not always been true. People can and do lose money in real estate if:

1. They buy in an area that is slowly deteriorating or is not growing.

2. They buy at inflated prices after several boom years and just before severe economic setbacks in the economy or in the particular geographic area where they own real estate. This might occur if there are major industry layoffs or the closing of an aircraft or steel plant that is an important mainstay to a local area.

3. They get themselves personally overextended with real estate payments that are too high, and their source of income is reduced by the loss of a job or an increase in rental vacancies, if they own rental property.

4. They make a poor initial selection, the area deteriorates, or they're hit by fires, floods, tornadoes, or earthquakes.

They say there are three golden rules to buying real estate—location, location, and location!

If you live in the Sunbelt area, you'll have an advantage because that's where much of the past and future growth in the United States has and will occur.

Southern California, Arizona, Texas, Nevada, and Florida are the fastest growing Sunbelt locations. California is already the largest state in the union, with 33 million in population and good year-round weather.

Texas will one day be the second-largest state in population. Houston, Dallas, Ft. Worth, San Antonio, and Austin are just a few of its dynamic areas. Lots of land is available in this giant state, and the state government doesn't overtax or overregulate. But be careful. Dallas is more of a distribution and evolving technology center, and Houston is more dependent on the oil industry. In early 1983, the unemployment rate in Houston was higher than in Dallas due to softness in the oil industry.

Florida has been known for past real estate booms followed by occasional busts when the speculative fever got too hot. Florida will continue to develop rapidly, and light industry should evolve.

Tourists and retired people alike will keep on finding their way to this fabulous land. Tampa-St. Petersburg and the surrounding area is one of the regions pensioners seem to prefer. Around the turn of the century, sunny Florida will become the third-largest state in terms of U.S. population, and New York will be the fourth largest.

Your own home is probably the first real estate investment you will make. Location is key here also. However, timing and financing are now becoming vital factors too.

If you have to pay an inflated price plus a 10% mortgage, you will be up to your ears in payments. Your risk-reward ratio has to increase. If you use creative financing that could force you to refinance in three to five years, your risks materially increase because you don't know what loan conditions may be like in the future.

There will be many other forms of imaginative financing. These absolutely must be investigated very carefully because most of them could force you, the buyer, to assume greater risks or payments down the road.

Remember, it is definitely possible to lose money in real estate or to lose your house if you can't under any and all future circumstances continually meet the payments. I would also shun the widely promoted, starry-eyed, nothing-down craze.

Real Estate Questions for You to Ask

Within or around a particular city, which locations are best? Ask yourself some questions. What are the better areas? Quality usually holds up best in the long run.

In which direction is the city most likely to grow? Are you close to good schools and shopping areas? How easy would this house be to resell later? Does it have all the features other families would want? How about the neighbors and the neighborhood? What do these people do? Is the home overbuilt for the area? What have other houses in the immediate vicinity sold for?

Where are the main traffic arteries or freeways, and do you have reasonable access to them? How long will it take you to get to and from work each day? Is a long trip worth the time, fatigue, and gas expense?

Then there are questions of a different type. Could there be any possible problems in the future, like a new freeway a half block away; new assessments for streets, sewers or lights; or a worn plumbing or heating system or roof that may have to be replaced? Is the foundation solid and is the land the house is built on sound? Has the house passed all required inspections? Are you in a high-risk area for fire, earthquakes, or floods? Can you get insurance?

Then you come to the financing. What will your total monthly payments be? Can they escalate and if so, how much? Will you be able to handle the increases? Are you sticking your neck out a little or a great deal? What are all the hidden costs, taxes and insurance, "points" charged to obtain a loan? How much total cash will you have to come up with in addition to the down payment? Can you positively get a clear title? Are there unreasonable prepayment penalties in the lender's agreement? Where will you get the money to make a balloon payment if one will be coming due?

Real estate can be an excellent investment if you take your time and make sure you know exactly what you are doing. Two twin opportunities that real estate offers are tax advantages (depreciation and tax deduction for interest on your home or on commercial or rental property and expenses), and leverage (using other peoples' money).

However, leverage has killed more than one amateur real estate operator who greedily overexpanded, so beware of trying to use leverage to acquire too many pieces of property. That's dangerous. You could be building a house of cards that will be blown down in the next healthy recession. Don't get carried away; use your head! Also, tax laws can change.

You should, furthermore, be careful of putting too large a down payment on property you buy because when you eventually sell, you may not be able to get all your cash out. You will probably have to take back a large amount of paper in the form of a second mortgage. And remember, second mortgages have no legal right to the property and are subject to substantial discounts when you try to sell and convert them to cash.

I would also be a little less interested in investing in condominiums because you will, in effect, own an apartment without much land. Frequently, land appreciates more over the years than does the structure.

A friend of mine who was in charge of real estate investments for the New York Life Insurance Company for 25 years had the following advice: "In office buildings or apartments, location and economic factors that will affect the area in the future are key. Is the area dependent on one industry? What is the unemployment rate? Is this the type of facility or unit that is going to be in demand? If the demand is for $20 per square foot units and you build for $25, you'll have trouble. Or if people are wanting three bedrooms and you build one-bedroom units, you will get hurt." These factors, he feels, are more important than the fact that a facility has a big-name tenant on the lease.

From a future supply-and-demand point of view, there is an interesting angle to land: they aren't making any more of it.

13

How You Could Make a Million Owning Mutual Funds

Mutual funds are outstanding investment vehicles after you learn how to utilize them correctly. Most people, however, do not have a solid understanding or conviction about mutual funds.

The first absolutely essential point to understand is that the **big money in mutual funds is always made by sitting through several business cycles.**

In other words, **to reap large returns from funds, you have to have the strong belief and patience to sit tight for 10 or 15 years or longer.** It's like real estate. You may not make anything if you buy and later become impatient or shortsighted and sell out after only three or four years. It simply takes time. Nervous Nellies are not good fund shareholders.

Investors in open-end investment companies, as mutual funds are sometimes called, tend to buy the best-performing fund after it has had a huge performance year. The next year or two will probably show slower or poorer results followed by an inevitable economic recession. This is usually enough to scare out those with less conviction or the "I want to get rich quick" fund holders.

Sometimes shareholders will switch to another fund that someone convinces them is much safer (usually at exactly the wrong time) or has a "hotter" recent performance record. Switching breaks up your long-range holding plan. I suppose you should switch if you have a really bad fund or the wrong type, like an income or industry fund when you should own a diversified growth fund, but too much switching quickly destroys what must be a long-term commitment.

Bear markets can last from nine months to two years or more and if you are going to be a successful long-pull investor in funds, you'll need to acquire the courage and perspective to live through numerous discouraging bear markets. Have the vision to build yourself a great long-term growth program, and stick to it.

I have sold mutual funds, known many top fund portfolio managers, provided research to hundreds of mutual funds, managed two mutual funds myself, and started the New USA Mutual Fund in 1992. In 1966, one of the funds was up over 10%, when the Dow was down 23% in a bear market. The other fund set a performance record for diversified growth funds of +116% in the following year. A huge number of stocks in its portfolio doubled. We had even planned that our goal at the beginning of the year was to be the number one fund for the year.

The fund did not do as well the next year. We had size problems, as assets under management in the fund and individual accounts increased dramatically. We also owned too many thin, volatile holdings, as we had just invented Datagraphs in January 1968 and, for the first time, had information on microfilm of several thousand smaller companies no one had ever seen before.

Some people thought we were a "flash in the pan" with one lucky year, but most were unaware that twice before, in 1963 and 1965, we had also made 100% or more in many individual accounts.

In 1963, the lowest-performing individual account I managed was up 115%. It was a cash account. From its inception, the fund ranked in the top 22% of all common stock funds until the day it was sold to another investment organization. This is an important fact most media people overlooked. An even more important point is that those original shareholders who held onto their shares as they were merged into the new company had a total increase of over 1,100%, which is the vital point I'm trying to make. The super big gains from mutual funds come from compounding over a span of years. Funds should be an investment for as long as you live. Diamonds are supposed to be forever—well, so are your mutual funds. So buy right and sit tight, period!

How to Become a
Millionaire the Easy Way

Here is what I regard as the ideal manner for a shrewd mutual fund investor to plan and invest. Pick a diversified domestic growth fund that performed in the top quartile of all mutual funds over the last three to five years. It will probably have *averaged* an annual rate of return of about 20%. The fund should also have a better-than-average record in the latest 12 months when compared to other domestic growth stock funds.

Steer away from funds that concentrate in only one industry or one area like energy, electronics, or gold. The investment company you pick does not have to be in the top three or four in performance each year to give you an excellent profit over 10 to 15 years.

The fund can be either a no-load, with no commission, or load, or one where a sales commission is charged. If you buy a fund with a sales charge, discounts are offered according to the amount you invest and some funds have back-end loads which you may want to check. The commission paid is substantially less than the mark-up you pay to buy insurance, a new car, a suit of clothes, or your groceries. You can also sign a letter of intent, which will allow a lower sales charge to apply to any quantity purchase made over the following 13 months.

When you purchase a mutual fund, you are hiring professional management to make decisions for you in the stock market.

Most diversified funds should be treated differently from individual stocks. A stock may decline and never come back in price. That's why the loss-cutting policy is necessary.

However, a well-selected fund run by an established management organization will, in time, almost always recover from the steep corrections that naturally occur during numerous bear markets. This is because mutual funds are broadly diversified and should participate in each recovery cycle in the American economy.

Therefore, I believe an extraordinarily different strategy should be employed with mutual funds. Each time you get into the thick of an economic recession and the newspapers and TV tell you how terrible things are, why not add to your fund when it is off 25% to 30% from its peak price. It might even be a possible time to borrow a little money and buy more shares. If you are patient, within two or three years the shares should be up sharply in price.

Remember, you're going to hold through many economic cycles, so why not be smart and add to your investment during each bear market? You can also reinvest your dividends and capital gains distributions and benefit from compounding over the years. When you buy your growth mutual fund, you should make up your mind at the outset that you are positively going to sit through the next three or four bear markets or economic recessions. This will give you the maximum opportunity to make really big money.

How about Income Funds?

If you need income, you may find it more advantageous not to buy an income fund. Instead, you could select the best possible fund available and set up a withdrawal plan equal to $1\frac{1}{2}\%$ per quarter or 6% or 7% per year. Part of the withdrawal would come from dividend income received and part from your capital, but the fund should generate enough growth over the years to more than offset the withdrawal of capital, if it is limited to 6% or 7% per year.

There are many organizations, such as Fidelity, Thomson, AIM, Scudder, Twentieth Century, Oppenheimer, Dreyfus, United Funds, Vanguard Group, and IDS Mutual that offer a family of funds with varied objectives and the right to switch to any other fund in the family at a nominal transfer fee. These families could offer you the added flexibility of making prudent changes many years later. The mid- to small-cap growth funds in a family are generally the better performing choices.

How Many Funds Should You Own?

As time passes, you may discover a second fund you would also like to begin accumulating in another long-term program. If so, do it. At the end of 10 or 15 years, you might own a worthwhile amount of two or even three funds, but there is no reason to diversify broadly, so don't overdo it. Those rare individuals with multimillion-dollar portfolios could spread out in more funds which would allow them to place almost unlimited sums into a more diverse group of funds. If this is done, some attempt should be made to own different-style managers. For example, money may be spread among one value-type growth fund, one aggressive growth fund, one small cap fund, one global fund, and so on.

If you own a growth fund which, by definition, invests in more aggressive growth stocks, it should go up more in bull-market years and fall off more in price than the general market in some bear market years. This is fairly common and in keeping with the nature of most growth portfolios, so don't get alarmed and panic out at the wrong time. During the poor periods, try to look ahead several years. Daylight follows darkness.

When Is the Best Time to Buy a Fund?

Any time is the best time. You'll never know when the perfect time is and waiting will usually result in your paying a higher price.

Should You Buy a Global or International Fund?

Yes, these could be a sound investment and provide further diversification, but I would definitely limit the percent of your total fund investment in this higher risk sector to 15% or 20% of your overall fund investments. International funds can, after a period of good performance, suffer several years of laggard poor performance.

The Size Problem of Large Funds

Asset size is a problem with most funds. If a specific fund has billions of dollars in assets, it will be less flexible in retreating from the market or in acquiring meaningful positions in smaller, better-performing stocks.

Therefore, I would generally avoid most of the very largest mutual funds. However, if you have a fund that has performed well for you over the years and it has now grown large but still performs reasonably well, maybe you should sit tight. Remember, the big money is always made over the long haul.

Checking Management Fees and Turnover Rates

Some investors try to evaluate the management fees and portfolio turnover rate of a fund. In most cases this nit-picking is not necessary.

In my experience, some of the best-performing growth funds have higher turnover rates. The Fidelity Magellan Fund, during its three biggest performance years, averaged an annual turnover rate of over 350%. CGM Capital Development Fund, managed by Ken Heebner, had a turnover rate of 272% and 226% in 1990 and 1991 respectively and was the top-performing fund from 1989 to 1994. You can't be active and on top of the market and do nothing. A good fund manager will sell stocks when he or she is worried about the overall market or a specific group, believes a stock is overvalued, or finds another, more attractive stock to purchase. That's what you hire a professional to do. Also, institutional commission rates that funds pay are extremely low, only a few cents per share of stocks bought or sold.

Are Monthly Investment Plans for You?

I do not generally favor monthly investment plans, where an investor adds $100 or so every month to a fund program. My reason is practical. Most people do not stick with them religiously. Therefore, they delude themselves by thinking they are going to achieve substantive long-term goals with such plans. If, on the other hand, you can have money automatically withheld and deducted every month for you, your program is sound.

If you can, it is best to evaluate your choices very carefully, then try to make a larger initial purchase and have the courage to stay with it. I also do not think people should make long-term investments in bond or preferred funds. Common stocks perform better.

If you want to check performance records, most magazines produce an annual survey that evaluates the performance of most of the funds. Your stockbroker or library should have special fund performance rating services such as Arthur Weisenberger or the Lipper service. *Investor's Business Daily* rates the prior 3-year record and shows the year to date and the prior year's percentage change in asset value for all mutual funds that are quoted daily in the newspaper. Additionally, several times a week it carries an article on a different fund and its investment activities.

An **open-end fund** continually issues new shares when people want to buy them. Shares are normally redeemable at net asset value whenever present holders wish to sell. This is the most prevalent form of mutual fund.

A **closed-end fund** issues a fixed number of shares. Generally, shares are not redeemable at the option of a shareholder. Redemption takes place through secondary market transactions. Most closed-end fund shares are listed for trading on exchanges. There are ordinarily better long-term opportunities found in open-end mutual fund investing than in owning closed-end funds that are subject to the whims and discounts below book value of the auction marketplace.

A *few* people successfully trade aggressive no-load growth funds on a timing basis, using moving average lines. There are several services that specialize in fund switching. This requires considerable experience, timing, skill, and emotional discipline. I do not advise the typical investor to attempt to trade no-load funds, because mistakes would probably be made in timing of buy and sell points. Get aboard for the long pull.

Finally, some individual or professional stock traders use growth stock funds for their IRA or Keogh retirement plans.

Why Many People Lose Money in Top-Performing Funds

Believe it or not, half of the people invested in some of the best-performing funds in the country may lose money. How can that happen? Very few people buy during a bear market. They're afraid. Far more people buy much later, during a bull market, when they feel much more assured. Some of these people then sell out over the next year or two when performance is slower or down. Why not buy and sit tight for the rest of your life and make a big fortune?

The Five Dumbest Mistakes Mutual Fund Investors Can Make

1. Failing to sit tight for an absolute minimum of 10 to 15 years.
2. Worrying about a fund's management fee, turnover rate, or dividends paid.
3. Being affected by news in the market when you're supposed to be investing for the long pull.
4. Selling out during bad markets.
5. Being impatient and losing confidence too soon.

Here are some strategies from a few of the smartest and best mutual fund portfolio managers in the business:

AIM Aggressive Growth Fund's Harry Hutzler and Jonathan Schoolar emphasize companies with a small market capitalization of $200 to $300 million. They evenly divide assets among 200 or so holdings to avoid having a bomb detonate in the portfolio if they had 4% or 5% in any one stock. They like stocks posting accelerating and better than expected earnings and also prefer to see both sales and earnings growing vigorously. Earnings reports are "where the rubber hits the road." Hutzler and Schoolar do not visit companies and will sell when earnings start decelerating or come in below expectations. They stay glued to the news wires for indications that earnings will be a lot higher or lower than expected.

Donald Chiboucas of Thomson Opportunity Fund states that their investment process is based on the theory of positive momentum-positive surprises, which asserts that a good company doing better than generally expected will experience a rise in its stock price. Conversely, a company falling short of expectations will experience a drop in its stock price. Thompson looks for signs both on a company level and an industry level including capacity utilization rate. They break down every industry and company to their bellwether indicators that will signal surprises. They closely watch about 12 areas of a company's business.

Twentieth Century Ultra's forte is picking the very best growth stocks and they too look for companies showing strong earnings and sales growth. Their policy of remaining heavily invested at all times does, however, create volatility.

Michael DiCarlo of John Hancock Special Equities says they start by ranking each industry sector based on expected earnings per share growth as well as current business conditions. Then, within roughly the top five groups, he picks the companies with the best potential for price appreciation using a bottom-up approach. Generally, DiCarlo looks for companies with growing revenue and earnings of at least 25% per year, preferring those that are able to do this consistently.

To summarize, the way to make a fortune in mutual funds is almost always by your long-term sitting, not your thinking. If you purchase $10,000 of a diversified domestic growth stock fund that is able to average about 15% a year over a period of many years, here is what could occur, compliments of the magic of compounding and time:

First five years	$ 10,000	goes to $ 20,000
Next five years	$ 20,000	goes to $ 40,000
Next five years	$ 40,000	goes to $ 80,000
Next five years	$ 80,000	goes to $160,000
Next five years	$160,000	goes to $320,000
Next five years	$320,000	goes to $640,000
Next five years	$640,000	goes to $1.28 million

Now suppose you also only added $2,000 each year to your program and let it compound over the years and you also bought a little extra during each bear market while the fund was temporarily down from its peak 25%. What do you think you'd be worth?

Although there are no absolute guarantees in this world, and yes, there are always taxes, the example above is somewhat close to what's been happening with the better growth mutual funds over the last 50 years and the American Stock Market has been growing since 1790. (See the chart on page xiv at the front of this book.) So, in my opinion, faith and confidence in America's long-term future is a very shrewd and intelligent position to take and stick with for as long as you live.

PART 3
Investing like a Professional

14

Models of the Greatest Stock Market Winners— 1953–1993

Now that you've previewed C-A-N S-L-I-M and know when to sell and cut a loss or nail down a profit, I should mention that a number of the models of *Greatest Stock Market Winners, 1953–1993* we actually recommended or bought. Have you ever heard the saying "those who can, do, and those who can't, either teach or write"? Well, we did the work, produced the results and now, afterwards, have put it down in writing to, we hope, help you.

Tracing the Growth of a Small Account

In 1961, all my classmates in the first PMD program chipped in $10 and started the first PMD Fund with the grandiose total of $850. It was partly for fun; each classmate had one beginning share worth $10 in the fund. Marshall Wolf, then with National Newark & Essex Bank in Newark, New Jersey, and later an executive vice president at Midlantic National Bank, had the thankless job of Secretary-Treasurer, keeping the records, informing the gang, and filing and paying taxes each year. I got the easy job of managing the money.

It is an interesting account to study because it proves you can start very small and still beat the game if you stick with sound methods and are allowed plenty of time. The account on September 16, 1986, **after prior taxes were paid,** was worth $51,653.34. The profit was over $50,000 and a share was worth $518. That is nearly a fiftyfold gain in about 25 years. Here are some of the actual buy-and-sell records to illustrate in vivid detail the execution of many of the basic concepts we have discussed up to this point.

SHARES	STOCK	DATE BOUGHT	PRICE PAID	DATE SOLD	PRICE SOLD	GAIN OR LOSS
5	Bristol Myers	1/1/61	$64\frac{7}{8}$	2/21/61	$78\frac{3}{4}$	
7	Bristol Myers	1/4/61	$67\frac{1}{4}$	2/21/61	$78\frac{3}{4}$	149.87
18	Brunswick	2/21/61	$53\frac{3}{4}$	3/10/61	68	223.35
29	Certain-teed	3/10/61	$42\frac{1}{8}$	4/13/61	$39\frac{3}{4}$	(104.30)
24	Stan. Kollsman	4/13/61	$45\frac{3}{4}$	6/27/61	45	
	Stan. Kollsman			6/27/61	$43\frac{3}{8}$	(82.66)
25	Endevco Corp.	4/26/61	13	5/25/61	$17\frac{1}{2}$	102.96
10	Lockheed	6/13/61	$44\frac{7}{8}$			
10	Lockheed	6/27/61	$46\frac{3}{8}$			
5	Lockheed	7/25/61	$48\frac{1}{2}$	8/29/61	$48\frac{1}{4}$	7.55
6	Crown Cork	9/1/61	$108\frac{1}{2}$			
5	Crown Cork	9/1/61	110	10/2/61	$103\frac{1}{4}$	(100.52)
20	Brunswick	10/11/61	$64\frac{1}{4}$	10/24/61	$58\frac{1}{8}$	
	Brunswick			11/1/61	54	(223.49)
3	Polaroid	10/31/61	$206\frac{3}{4}$			
3	Polaroid	11/1/61	209	2/21/61	180	(191.68)
30	Korvette	2/28/62	41	3/30/62	$47\frac{7}{8}$	
30	Korvette	4/5/62	$52\frac{1}{4}$	4/13/62	$54\frac{1}{4}$	183.96
10	Crown Cork	5/28/62	$99\frac{1}{4}$	5/22/62	$97\frac{1}{4}$	(50.48)
30	Lockheed	6/15/62	$41\frac{1}{4}$	6/2/62	$39\frac{3}{4}$	(81.02)
5	Xerox	6/20/62	$104\frac{3}{4}$			
5	Xerox	6/25/62	$105\frac{1}{4}$	7/12/62	$127\frac{1}{8}$	190.30
10	Homestake Mining	7/16/62	$59\frac{1}{2}$	7/24/62	$54\frac{1}{4}$	
10	Homestake Mining	7/16/62	$58\frac{3}{4}$	7/24/62	$54\frac{1}{4}$	(87.66)
10	Polaroid	7/31/62	105	7/19/62	$97\frac{7}{8}$	(101.86)
30	Korvette	10/24/62	$21\frac{7}{8}$	9/28/62	$35\frac{1}{8}$	385.94
10	Chrysler	10/30/62	59			
15	Chrysler	11/1/62	$60\frac{3}{4}$	1/15/63	$83\frac{3}{8}$	545.40
15	RCA	1/16/63	$62\frac{1}{2}$			
15	RCA	1/18/63	$65\frac{1}{4}$	2/28/63	62	(111.02)
25	Coastal States	2/28/63	$31\frac{3}{8}$	3/14/63	$32\frac{1}{8}$	(8.46)
14	Chrysler	2/27/63	$92\frac{1}{2}$			
8	Chrysler	3/14/63	93	4/16/63	$109\frac{1}{8}$	300.03
25	Control Data	4/23/63	$44\frac{1}{8}$	5/13/63	$49\frac{5}{8}$	102.55
25	Intl. Minerals	5/6/63	$52\frac{7}{8}$	5/15/63	$54\frac{7}{8}$	11.47
22	Chrysler	5/13/63	$54\frac{3}{8}$	6/10/63	$61\frac{3}{4}$	
25	Chrysler	5/17/63	$55\frac{5}{8}$	6/10/63	$61\frac{3}{4}$	211.30
15	Syntex	6/11/63	$89\frac{1}{4}$	9/23/63	$146\frac{1}{8}$	
10	Syntex	8/7/63	$114\frac{1}{2}$	9/23/63	$146\frac{1}{8}$	
15	Syntex	10/9/63	$149\frac{1}{8}$	10/22/63	225	2975.71
15	Control Data	7/9/63	$69\frac{1}{8}$	7/17/63	$67\frac{1}{4}$	(59.62)
15	RCA	1/8/64	102.02	2/11/64	$105\frac{5}{8}$	53.98
15	RCA	1/9/64	106.19	2/11/64	$105\frac{5}{8}$	(8.49)
15	RCA	1/10/64	107.33	2/11/64	$105\frac{5}{8}$	(25.54)
50	Pan Am	2/17/64	65.53	3/9/64	68	123.29

(Continued)

SHARES	STOCK	DATE BOUGHT	PRICE PAID	DATE SOLD	PRICE SOLD	GAIN OR LOSS
25	McDonnel Air	3/11/64	62.17	5/11/64	60	(54.26)
25	Chrysler	3/12/64	47.88	4/7/64	43.87	(100.35)
25	Chrysler	3/13/64	49.27	4/7/64	43.87	(135.06)
30	Chrysler	3/17/64	50.21	4/30/64	46.08	(123.83)
30	Consol. Cigar	3/19/64	49.35	4/20/64	47¼	(62.87)
25	Greyhound	4/7/64	55.47	5/1/64	57.63	53.88
20	Greyhound	4/8/64	58.55	5/1/64	57.63	(18.52)
15	Xerox	4/21/64	95.23	5/1/64	93	(33.41)
15	Xerox	4/29/64	98.53	5/5/64	95	(52.95)
30	Chrysler	5/13/64	52.14	7/8/64	48¾	(101.69)
50	Chrysler	5/13/64	52.32	6/11/64	46⅝	(290.79)
50	Chrysler	5/13/64	52.34	6/30/64	49	(166.82)
50	Cerro Corp	7/2/64	49	9/16/64	56	349.51
20	Cerro Corp	7/6/64	50.68	9/16/64	56	106.50
50	NY Central RR	7/8/64	41.65	11/16/64	49.05	369.89

Notice that while there were about 20 successful transactions through 1964, there were also 20 losing transactions. The average profit was around 20% and the average loss, about 7%. If losses had not been cut in Standard Kollsman, Brunswick, and a few others, later price drops would have caused much larger losses. This small cash account concentrated in only one or two stocks at a time. Follow-up buys were generally made if the security moved up in price.

The account made no progress in 1962, a bad market year, but was already up 139% by June 6, 1963, *before* the first Syntex buy occurred. By the end of 1963, the gain had swelled up to 474% on the original $850 investment.

The 1964 year was a struggling, lackluster year with no real gain. However, worthwhile profits were made in 1965, 1966, and 1967, although nothing like 1963, which was certainly an extremely unusual year. Since there simply is not room in this book to show 20 long, boring pages of stock transactions, let me mention the next 10 years showed further progress, but there were net losses in 1969 and 1974.

Another period of interesting progress started in 1978 with the purchase of Dome Petroleum. All decisions beginning with Dome are shown on the following page.

SHARES	STOCK	DATE BOUGHT	PRICE PAID	DATE SOLD	PRICE SOLD	GAIN OR LOSS
100	Dome Petroleum	12/28/78	77			
20	Dome Petroleum			2/26/79	97⅞	
320	4/1 split on 6/6/79			10/17/80	63	14,226.72
300	Fluor	10/17/80	56½	2/9/81	48¼	(3,165.82)
50	Fluor	10/17/80	56⅞			
100	Pic'N'Save	6/4/81	55			
300	3/1 split 6/29/81			7/6/82	15	(1,094.00)
100	Espey Mfg.	11/19/81	46¾	6/8/82	38	
50	Espey Mfg.	11/19/81	47	4/23/82	46	(1,313.16)
100	MCI Comm	4/23/82	37	8/20/82	36⅜	(123.50)
96	MCI Comm	7/6/82	45½			
	2/1 split on 9/20/82			1/3/83	38¼	2,881.92
200	Pic'N'Save	8/20/82	18½	7/16/84	19¼	3,892.00
45	Hewlett Packard	9/10/82	53	8/11/83	82⅞	1,307.35
100	Pic'N'Save	8/27/82	19½			
185	Pic'N'Save	1/3/83	38⅛			
	2/1 split on 12/1/83			2/1/85	23¼	4,115.02
200	Price Co.	7/6/84	39¼			
326	Price Co.	2/1/85	53¾			
8	Price Co.			3/25/85	57	
	2/1 split on 2/11/86			6/17/86	49⅞	26,489.87
15	Price Co.			3/20/86	43¼	

A valuable lesson can be learned about why most stocks sooner or later need to be sold. Dome Petroleum eventually declined below $2! Note also that the account was worn out of Pic'N'Save on July 6, 1982, at $15, but we bought it back at $18 and $19, even though it was at a higher price, and made a large gain by doing so.

Another engaging example of the C-A-N S-L-I-M principles being properly applied is the one of David Ryan, a research associate and winner of the 1985, 1986, and 1987 U.S. Investing Championships. David entered the stock division of the contest in January 1985 with his own account in the market and won the national derby with a 161% increase for the year. In 1986 he increased 160% and in 1987 was up another 118%.

Here are some of the characteristics of David Ryan's winning stocks at the time he bought them:

1. Average annual earnings growth rate, 24%.
2. Median EPS percentage increase, current quarter, 34%.

3. Average P/E, 15.

4. Average Relative Strength, 85.

5. Relative Strength line up an average of 6.5 months.

6. Median shares outstanding, 4.6 million.

7. Median average daily volume, 10,000 (not critical).

8. Median industry group strength, top 30%.

9. Average alpha, 1.78.

10. Average after-tax margin, 7.3% (not critical).

11. Median stock price, $24.

Another associate, Lee Freestone, participated in the U.S. Investing Championship in 1991 when he was just 24 years old. Using the C-A-N S-L-I-M techniques, he came in second for the year with a result of 279%. In 1992, he gained a 120% return and again came in second. The U.S. Investing Championship is not some paper transaction derby. Real money is used and actual transactions are made in the market.

Examples of Great Winners to Guide You

A selected group of the greatest stock market winners are presented here and on the following pages. They are models of the most successful investments in the United States between 1953 and 1993. Study them carefully, and refer to them often, because they are examples of what you must look for and learn to spot in the future. The thin line below prices is a relative strength line.

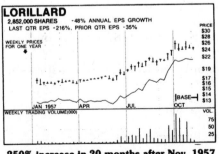

250% increase in 20 months after Nov. 1957

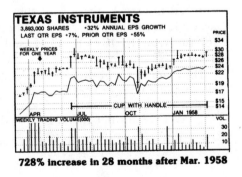

728% increase in 28 months after Mar. 1958

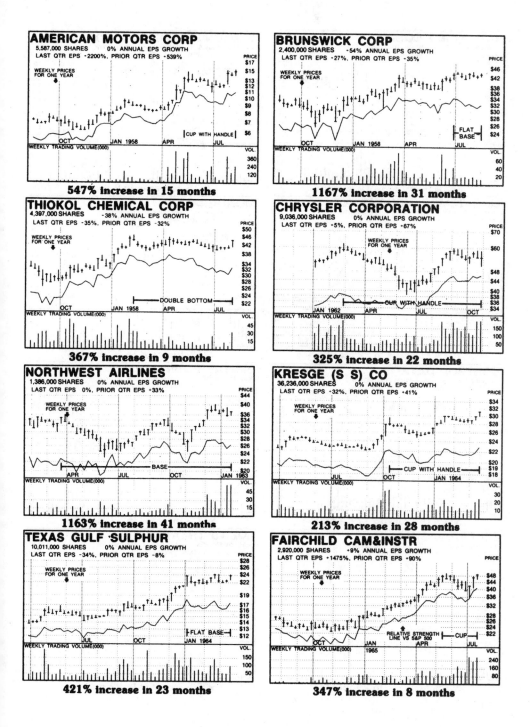

AMERICAN MOTORS CORP
5,587,000 SHARES   0% ANNUAL EPS GROWTH
LAST QTR EPS -2200%, PRIOR QTR EPS -539%

WEEKLY PRICES FOR ONE YEAR

CUP WITH HANDLE

WEEKLY TRADING VOLUME(000)

OCT   JAN 1958   APR   JUL

547% increase in 15 months

BRUNSWICK CORP
2,400,000 SHARES   -54% ANNUAL EPS GROWTH
LAST QTR EPS -27%, PRIOR QTR EPS -35%

WEEKLY PRICES FOR ONE YEAR

FLAT BASE

WEEKLY TRADING VOLUME(000)

OCT   JAN 1958   APR   JUL

1167% increase in 31 months

THIOKOL CHEMICAL CORP
4,397,000 SHARES   -38% ANNUAL EPS GROWTH
LAST QTR EPS -35%, PRIOR QTR EPS -32%

WEEKLY PRICES FOR ONE YEAR

DOUBLE BOTTOM

WEEKLY TRADING VOLUME(000)

OCT   JAN 1958   APR   JUL

367% increase in 9 months

CHRYSLER CORPORATION
9,036,000 SHARES   0% ANNUAL EPS GROWTH
LAST QTR EPS -5%, PRIOR QTR EPS -67%

WEEKLY PRICES FOR ONE YEAR

CUP WITH HANDLE

WEEKLY TRADING VOLUME(000)

JAN 1962   APR   JUL   OCT

325% increase in 22 months

NORTHWEST AIRLINES
1,386,000 SHARES   0% ANNUAL EPS GROWTH
LAST QTR EPS 0%, PRIOR QTR EPS +33%

WEEKLY PRICES FOR ONE YEAR

BASE

WEEKLY TRADING VOLUME(000)

APR   JUL   OCT   JAN 1963

1163% increase in 41 months

KRESGE (S S) CO
36,236,000 SHARES   0% ANNUAL EPS GROWTH
LAST QTR EPS +32%, PRIOR QTR EPS +41%

WEEKLY PRICES FOR ONE YEAR

CUP WITH HANDLE

WEEKLY TRADING VOLUME(000)

JUL   OCT   JAN 1964

213% increase in 28 months

TEXAS GULF SULPHUR
10,011,000 SHARES   0% ANNUAL EPS GROWTH
LAST QTR EPS -34%, PRIOR QTR EPS -8%

WEEKLY PRICES FOR ONE YEAR

FLAT BASE

WEEKLY TRADING VOLUME(000)

JUL   OCT   JAN 1964

421% increase in 23 months

FAIRCHILD CAM&INSTR
2,920,000 SHARES   +9% ANNUAL EPS GROWTH
LAST QTR EPS +1475%, PRIOR QTR EPS +90%

WEEKLY PRICES FOR ONE YEAR

RELATIVE STRENGTH LINE VS S&P 500   CUP

WEEKLY TRADING VOLUME(000)

1965   JAN   APR   JUL

347% increase in 8 months

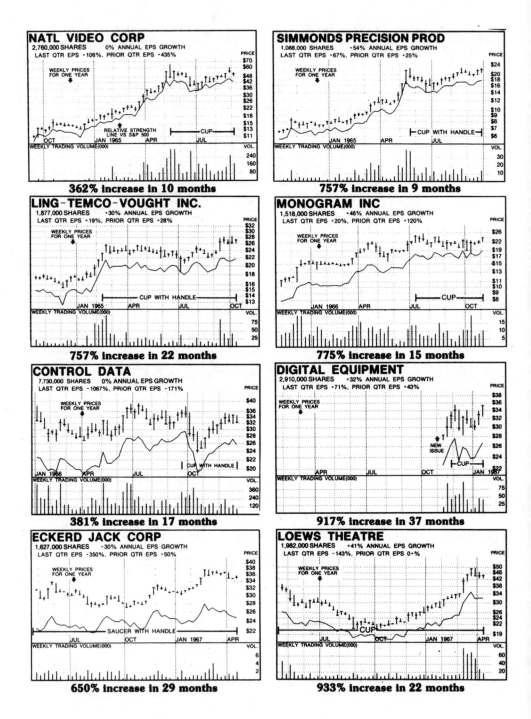

NATL VIDEO CORP
2,760,000 SHARES   0% ANNUAL EPS GROWTH
LAST QTR EPS +108%, PRIOR QTR EPS +435%

362% increase in 10 months

SIMMONDS PRECISION PROD
1,088.000 SHARES   +54% ANNUAL EPS GROWTH
LAST QTR EPS +67%, PRIOR QTR EPS +25%

757% increase in 9 months

LING-TEMCO-VOUGHT INC.
1,877,000 SHARES   +30% ANNUAL EPS GROWTH
LAST QTR EPS +19%, PRIOR QTR EPS +28%

757% increase in 22 months

MONOGRAM INC
1,518,000 SHARES   +46% ANNUAL EPS GROWTH
LAST QTR EPS +20%, PRIOR QTR EPS +120%

775% increase in 15 months

CONTROL DATA
7,730,000 SHARES   0% ANNUAL EPS GROWTH
LAST QTR EPS -1067%, PRIOR QTR EPS -171%

381% increase in 17 months

DIGITAL EQUIPMENT
2,910,000 SHARES   +32% ANNUAL EPS GROWTH
LAST QTR EPS +71%, PRIOR QTR EPS +43%

917% increase in 37 months

ECKERD JACK CORP
1,627,000 SHARES   -30% ANNUAL EPS GROWTH
LAST QTR EPS -350%, PRIOR QTR EPS +50%

650% increase in 29 months

LOEWS THEATRE
1,982,000 SHARES   +41% ANNUAL EPS GROWTH
LAST QTR EPS +143%, PRIOR QTR EPS 0+%

933% increase in 22 months

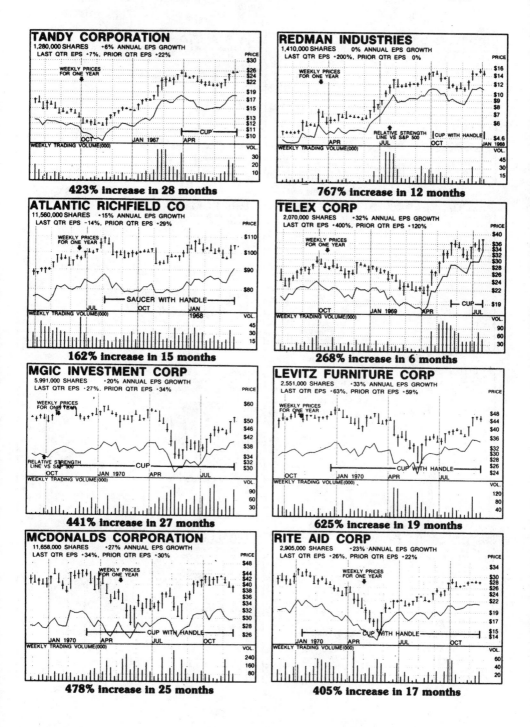

TANDY CORPORATION
1,280,000 SHARES +6% ANNUAL EPS GROWTH
LAST QTR EPS +7%, PRIOR QTR EPS +22%

423% increase in 28 months

REDMAN INDUSTRIES
1,410,000 SHARES 0% ANNUAL EPS GROWTH
LAST QTR EPS +200%, PRIOR QTR EPS 0%

767% increase in 12 months

ATLANTIC RICHFIELD CO
11,560,000 SHARES +15% ANNUAL EPS GROWTH
LAST QTR EPS -14%, PRIOR QTR EPS +29%

162% increase in 15 months

TELEX CORP
2,070,000 SHARES +32% ANNUAL EPS GROWTH
LAST QTR EPS +400%, PRIOR QTR EPS +120%

268% increase in 6 months

MGIC INVESTMENT CORP
5,991,000 SHARES +20% ANNUAL EPS GROWTH
LAST QTR EPS +27%, PRIOR QTR EPS +34%

441% increase in 27 months

LEVITZ FURNITURE CORP
2,551,000 SHARES +33% ANNUAL EPS GROWTH
LAST QTR EPS +63%, PRIOR QTR EPS +59%

625% increase in 19 months

MCDONALDS CORPORATION
11,658,000 SHARES +27% ANNUAL EPS GROWTH
LAST QTR EPS +34%, PRIOR QTR EPS +30%

478% increase in 25 months

RITE AID CORP
2,905,000 SHARES +23% ANNUAL EPS GROWTH
LAST QTR EPS +26%, PRIOR QTR EPS +22%

405% increase in 17 months

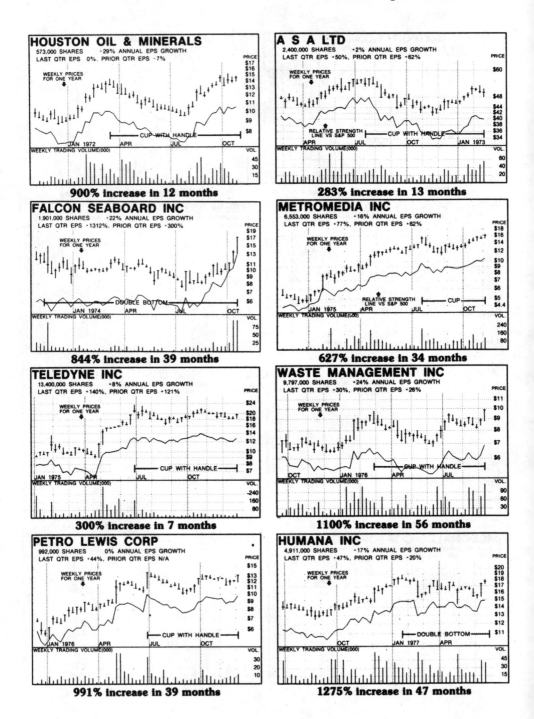

HOUSTON OIL & MINERALS
573,000 SHARES   -29% ANNUAL EPS GROWTH
LAST QTR EPS 0%. PRIOR QTR EPS -7%

900% increase in 12 months

A S A LTD
2,400,000 SHARES   -2% ANNUAL EPS GROWTH
LAST QTR EPS -50%, PRIOR QTR EPS -62%

283% increase in 13 months

FALCON SEABOARD INC
1,901,000 SHARES   -22% ANNUAL EPS GROWTH
LAST QTR EPS -1312%, PRIOR QTR EPS -300%

844% increase in 39 months

METROMEDIA INC
6,553,000 SHARES   -16% ANNUAL EPS GROWTH
LAST QTR EPS -77%, PRIOR QTR EPS -62%

627% increase in 34 months

TELEDYNE INC
13,400,000 SHARES   -8% ANNUAL EPS GROWTH
LAST QTR EPS -140%, PRIOR QTR EPS -121%

300% increase in 7 months

WASTE MANAGEMENT INC
9,797,000 SHARES   -24% ANNUAL EPS GROWTH
LAST QTR EPS -30%, PRIOR QTR EPS -26%

1100% increase in 56 months

PETRO LEWIS CORP
992,000 SHARES   0% ANNUAL EPS GROWTH
LAST QTR EPS -44%, PRIOR QTR EPS N/A

991% increase in 39 months

HUMANA INC
4,911,000 SHARES   -17% ANNUAL EPS GROWTH
LAST QTR EPS -47%, PRIOR QTR EPS -20%

1275% increase in 47 months

FLIGHTSAFETY INTL INC
3,027,000 SHARES   •33% ANNUAL EPS GROWTH
LAST QTR EPS •15%, PRIOR QTR EPS •12%
WEEKLY PRICES FOR ONE YEAR
DOUBLE BOTTOM
WEEKLY TRADING VOLUME(000)
943% increase in 46 months

STORAGE TECHNOLOGY CORP
4,630,000 SHARES   •46% ANNUAL EPS GROWTH
LAST QTR EPS •32%, PRIOR QTR EPS •29%
WEEKLY PRICES FOR ONE YEAR
CUP WITH HANDLE
WEEKLY TRADING VOLUME(000)
429% increase in 13 months

SMITHKLINE CORP
29,930,000 SHARES   •10% ANNUAL EPS GROWTH
LAST QTR EPS •22%, PRIOR QTR EPS •11%
WEEKLY PRICES FOR ONE YEAR
SAUCER WITH HANDLE
WEEKLY TRADING VOLUME(000)
138% increase in 8 months

BOEING CO
42,579,000 SHARES   •36% ANNUAL EPS GROWTH
LAST QTR EPS •77%, PRIOR QTR EPS •108%
WEEKLY PRICES FOR ONE YEAR
RELATIVE STRENGTH LINE VS S&P 500
CUP WITH HANDLE
WEEKLY TRADING VOLUME(000)
200% increase in 26 months

PRIME COMPUTER INC
2,610,000 SHARES   •68% ANNUAL EPS GROWTH
LAST QTR EPS •158%, PRIOR QTR EPS •153%
WEEKLY PRICES FOR ONE YEAR
CUP WITH HANDLE
WEEKLY TRADING VOLUME(000)
1500% increase in 40 months

WANG LABS INC CL B
11,195,000 SHARES   •19% ANNUAL EPS GROWTH
LAST QTR EPS •80%, PRIOR QTR EPS •46%
WEEKLY PRICES FOR ONE YEAR
CUP WITH HANDLE
WEEKLY TRADING VOLUME(000)
1543% increase in 34 months

RESORTS INTL CL A
3,285,000 SHARES   •56% ANNUAL EPS GROWTH
LAST QTR EPS N/A , PRIOR QTR EPS •933%
WEEKLY PRICES FOR ONE YEAR
CUP WITH HANDLE
WEEKLY TRADING VOLUME(000)
733% increase in 5 months

COMPUTERVISION CORP
2,404,000 SHARES   0% ANNUAL EPS GROWTH
LAST QTR EPS •110%, PRIOR QTR EPS •41%
WEEKLY PRICES FOR ONE YEAR
CUP WITH HANDLE
WEEKLY TRADING VOLUME(000)
1233% increase in 27 months

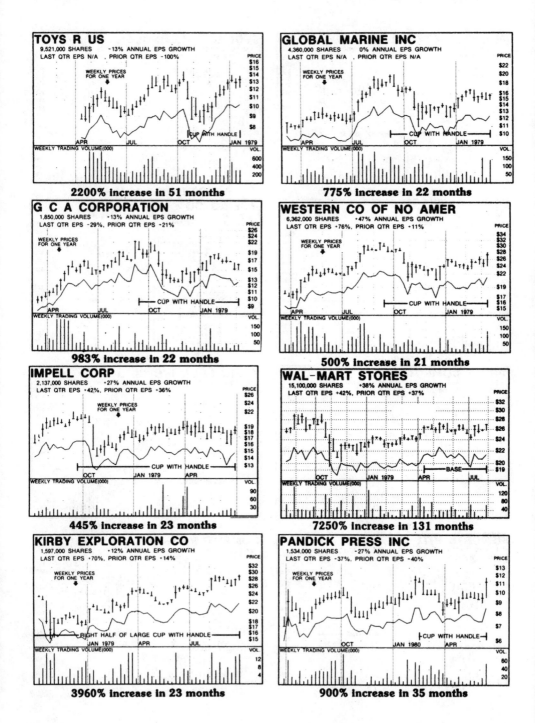

TOYS R US
9,521,000 SHARES   -13% ANNUAL EPS GROWTH
LAST QTR EPS N/A . PRIOR QTR EPS -100%

2200% increase in 51 months

GLOBAL MARINE INC
4,360,000 SHARES   0% ANNUAL EPS GROWTH
LAST QTR EPS N/A . PRIOR QTR EPS N/A

775% increase in 22 months

G C A CORPORATION
1,850,000 SHARES   -13% ANNUAL EPS GROWTH
LAST QTR EPS -29%, PRIOR QTR EPS -21%

983% increase in 22 months

WESTERN CO OF NO AMER
6,362,000 SHARES   +47% ANNUAL EPS GROWTH
LAST QTR EPS +76%, PRIOR QTR EPS +11%

500% increase in 21 months

IMPELL CORP
2,137,000 SHARES   +27% ANNUAL EPS GROWTH
LAST QTR EPS +42%, PRIOR QTR EPS +36%

445% increase in 23 months

WAL-MART STORES
15,100,000 SHARES   +38% ANNUAL EPS GROWTH
LAST QTR EPS +42%, PRIOR QTR EPS +37%

7250% increase in 131 months

KIRBY EXPLORATION CO
1,597,000 SHARES   +12% ANNUAL EPS GROWTH
LAST QTR EPS +70%, PRIOR QTR EPS +14%

3960% increase in 23 months

PANDICK PRESS INC
1,534,000 SHARES   +27% ANNUAL EPS GROWTH
LAST QTR EPS -37%, PRIOR QTR EPS -40%

900% increase in 35 months

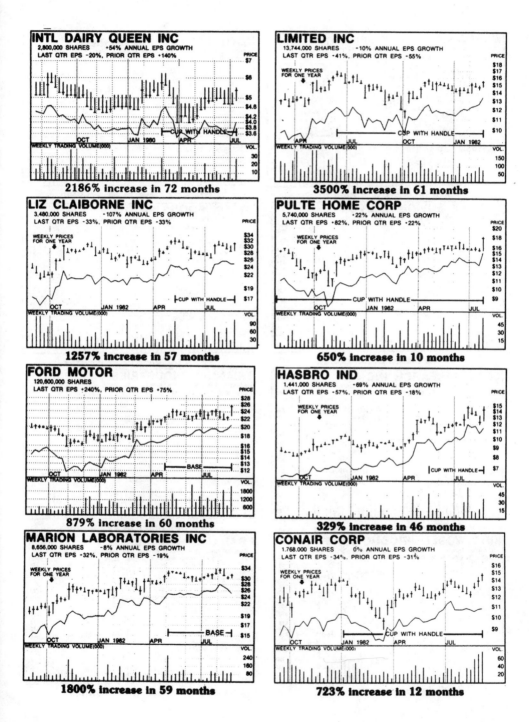

INTL DAIRY QUEEN INC
2,800,000 SHARES   +54% ANNUAL EPS GROWTH
LAST QTR EPS -20%, PRIOR QTR EPS +140%

2186% increase in 72 months

LIMITED INC
13,744,000 SHARES   -10% ANNUAL EPS GROWTH
LAST QTR EPS -41%, PRIOR QTR EPS -55%

3500% increase in 61 months

LIZ CLAIBORNE INC
3,480,000 SHARES   -107% ANNUAL EPS GROWTH
LAST QTR EPS -33%, PRIOR QTR EPS -33%

1257% increase in 57 months

PULTE HOME CORP
5,740,000 SHARES   +22% ANNUAL EPS GROWTH
LAST QTR EPS +82%, PRIOR QTR EPS +22%

650% increase in 10 months

FORD MOTOR
120,600,000 SHARES
LAST QTR EPS +240%, PRIOR QTR EPS +75%

879% increase in 60 months

HASBRO IND
1,441,000 SHARES   +69% ANNUAL EPS GROWTH
LAST QTR EPS +57%, PRIOR QTR EPS +18%

329% increase in 46 months

MARION LABORATORIES INC
8,656,000 SHARES   -8% ANNUAL EPS GROWTH
LAST QTR EPS +32%, PRIOR QTR EPS +19%

1800% increase in 59 months

CONAIR CORP
1,768,000 SHARES   0% ANNUAL EPS GROWTH
LAST QTR EPS -34%, PRIOR QTR EPS -31%

723% increase in 12 months

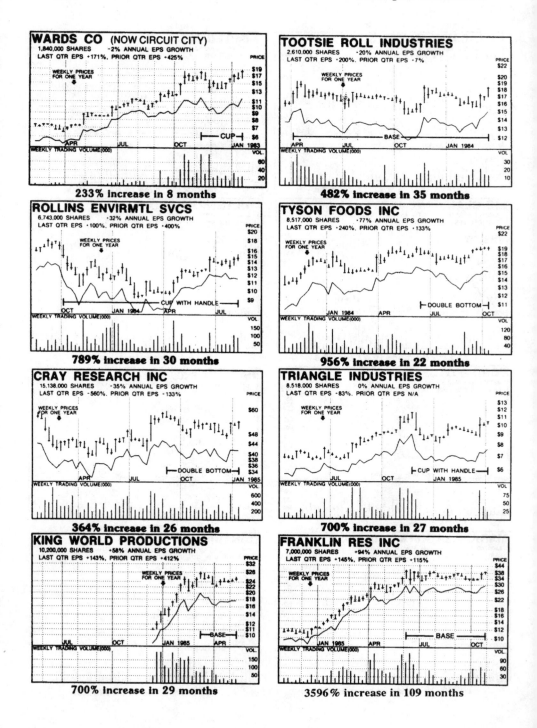

WARDS CO (NOW CIRCUIT CITY)
1,840,000 SHARES   -2% ANNUAL EPS GROWTH
LAST QTR EPS +171%, PRIOR QTR EPS +425%

233% increase in 8 months

TOOTSIE ROLL INDUSTRIES
2,610,000 SHARES   -20% ANNUAL EPS GROWTH
LAST QTR EPS +200%, PRIOR QTR EPS +7%

482% increase in 35 months

ROLLINS ENVIRMTL SVCS
6,743,000 SHARES   -32% ANNUAL EPS GROWTH
LAST QTR EPS +100%, PRIOR QTR EPS +400%

789% increase in 30 months

TYSON FOODS INC
8,517,000 SHARES   -77% ANNUAL EPS GROWTH
LAST QTR EPS +240%, PRIOR QTR EPS +133%

956% increase in 22 months

CRAY RESEARCH INC
15,138,000 SHARES   -35% ANNUAL EPS GROWTH
LAST QTR EPS -560%, PRIOR QTR EPS -133%

364% increase in 26 months

TRIANGLE INDUSTRIES
8,518,000 SHARES   0% ANNUAL EPS GROWTH
LAST QTR EPS -83%, PRIOR QTR EPS N/A

700% increase in 27 months

KING WORLD PRODUCTIONS
10,200,000 SHARES   +58% ANNUAL EPS GROWTH
LAST QTR EPS +143%, PRIOR QTR EPS +412%

700% increase in 29 months

FRANKLIN RES INC
7,000,000 SHARES   +94% ANNUAL EPS GROWTH
LAST QTR EPS +145%, PRIOR QTR EPS +115%

3596% increase in 109 months

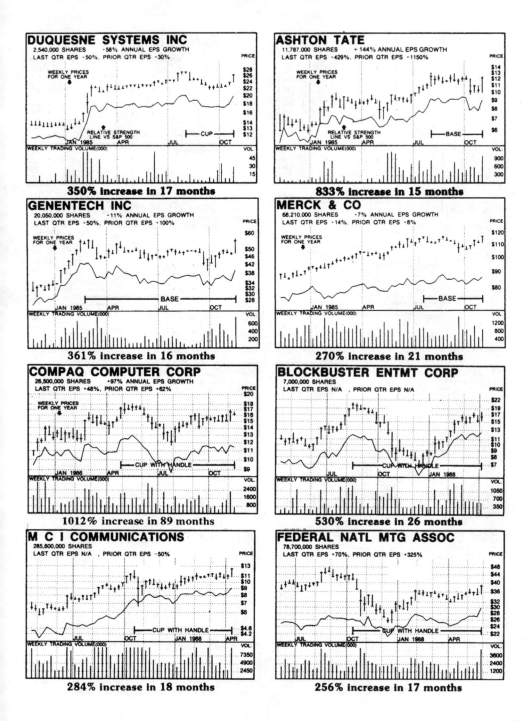

DUQUESNE SYSTEMS INC
350% increase in 17 months

ASHTON TATE
833% increase in 15 months

GENENTECH INC
361% increase in 16 months

MERCK & CO
270% increase in 21 months

COMPAQ COMPUTER CORP
1012% increase in 89 months

BLOCKBUSTER ENTMT CORP
530% increase in 26 months

M C I COMMUNICATIONS
284% increase in 18 months

FEDERAL NATL MTG ASSOC
256% increase in 17 months

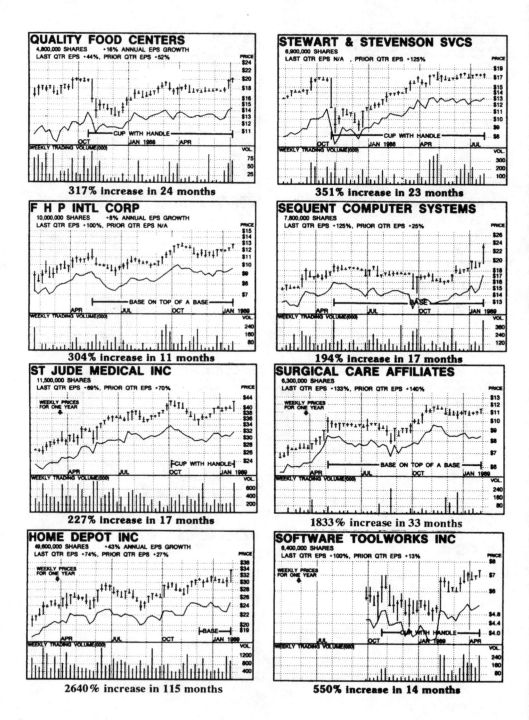

QUALITY FOOD CENTERS
4,800,000 SHARES   +16% ANNUAL EPS GROWTH
LAST QTR EPS +44%, PRIOR QTR EPS +52%

317% increase in 24 months

STEWART & STEVENSON SVCS
6,900,000 SHARES
LAST QTR EPS N/A , PRIOR QTR EPS +125%

351% increase in 23 months

F H P INTL CORP
10,000,000 SHARES   +8% ANNUAL EPS GROWTH
LAST QTR EPS +100%, PRIOR QTR EPS N/A

304% increase in 11 months

SEQUENT COMPUTER SYSTEMS
7,800,000 SHARES
LAST QTR EPS +125%, PRIOR QTR EPS +25%

194% increase in 17 months

ST JUDE MEDICAL INC
11,500,000 SHARES
LAST QTR EPS +69%, PRIOR QTR EPS +70%

227% increase in 17 months

SURGICAL CARE AFFILIATES
6,300,000 SHARES
LAST QTR EPS +133%, PRIOR QTR EPS +140%

1833% increase in 33 months

HOME DEPOT INC
49,600,000 SHARES   +43% ANNUAL EPS GROWTH
LAST QTR EPS +74%, PRIOR QTR EPS +27%

2640% increase in 115 months

SOFTWARE TOOLWORKS INC
6,400,000 SHARES
LAST QTR EPS +100%, PRIOR QTR EPS +13%

550% increase in 14 months

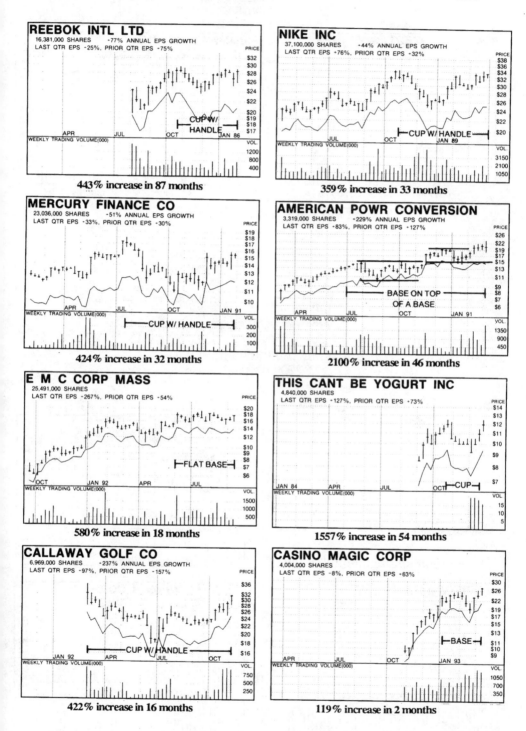

REEBOK INTL LTD
16,381,000 SHARES   -77% ANNUAL EPS GROWTH
LAST QTR EPS -25%, PRIOR QTR EPS -75%

CUP W/ HANDLE

443% increase in 87 months

NIKE INC
37,100,000 SHARES   -44% ANNUAL EPS GROWTH
LAST QTR EPS -76%, PRIOR QTR EPS -32%

CUP W/ HANDLE

359% increase in 33 months

MERCURY FINANCE CO
23,036,000 SHARES   -51% ANNUAL EPS GROWTH
LAST QTR EPS -33%, PRIOR QTR EPS -30%

CUP W/ HANDLE

424% increase in 32 months

AMERICAN POWR CONVERSION
3,319,000 SHARES   -229% ANNUAL EPS GROWTH
LAST QTR EPS -83%, PRIOR QTR EPS -127%

BASE ON TOP OF A BASE

2100% increase in 46 months

E M C CORP MASS
25,491,000 SHARES
LAST QTR EPS -267%, PRIOR QTR EPS -54%

FLAT BASE

580% increase in 18 months

THIS CANT BE YOGURT INC
4,840,000 SHARES
LAST QTR EPS -127%, PRIOR QTR EPS -73%

CUP

1557% increase in 54 months

CALLAWAY GOLF CO
6,969,000 SHARES   -237% ANNUAL EPS GROWTH
LAST QTR EPS -97%, PRIOR QTR EPS -157%

CUP W/ HANDLE

422% increase in 16 months

CASINO MAGIC CORP
4,004,000 SHARES
LAST QTR EPS -8%, PRIOR QTR EPS -63%

BASE

119% increase in 2 months

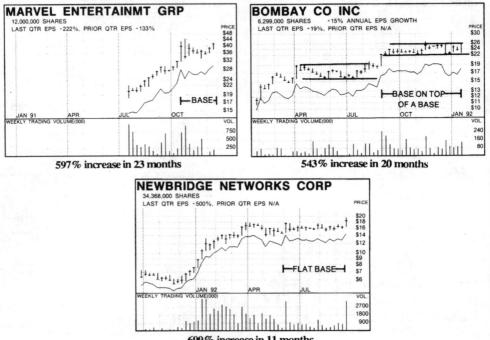

597% increase in 23 months

543% increase in 20 months

699% increase in 11 months

Sell or Short-selling Models

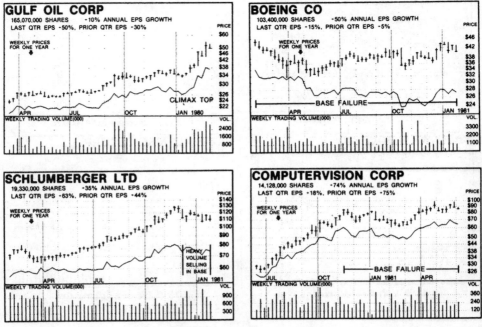

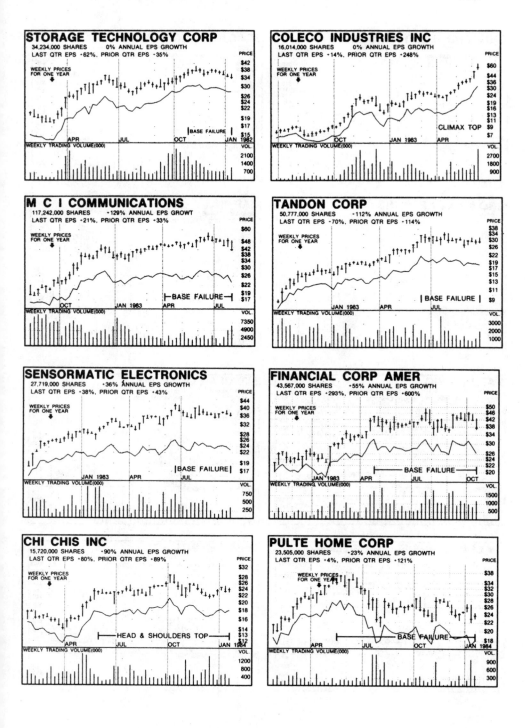

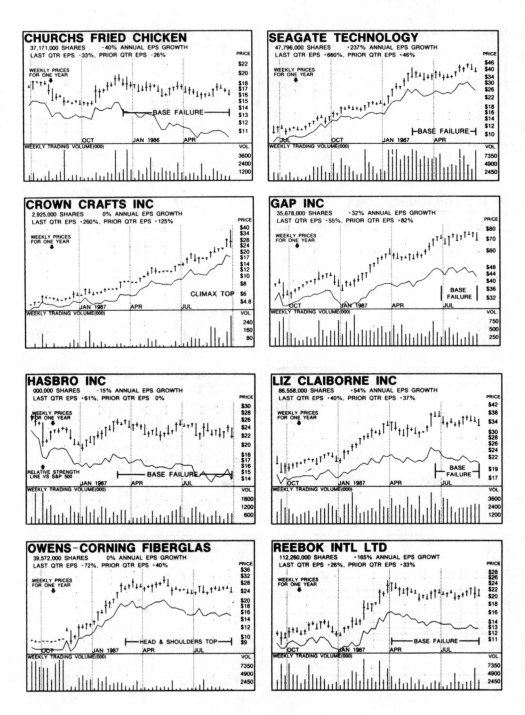

CHURCHS FRIED CHICKEN
37,171,000 SHARES   -40% ANNUAL EPS GROWTH
LAST QTR EPS -33%, PRIOR QTR EPS -26%
WEEKLY PRICES FOR ONE YEAR
BASE FAILURE
PRICE
$22
$20
$18
$17
$16
$15
$14
$13
$12
$11
OCT   JAN 1986   APR
WEEKLY TRADING VOLUME(000)
VOL.
3600
2400
1200

SEAGATE TECHNOLOGY
47,796,000 SHARES   +237% ANNUAL EPS GROWTH
LAST QTR EPS +660%, PRIOR QTR EPS +46%
WEEKLY PRICES FOR ONE YEAR
BASE FAILURE
PRICE
$46
$40
$34
$30
$26
$22
$18
$16
$14
$12
$10
JUL   OCT   JAN 1987   APR
WEEKLY TRADING VOLUME(000)
VOL.
7350
4900
2450

CROWN CRAFTS INC
2,925,000 SHARES   0% ANNUAL EPS GROWTH
LAST QTR EPS +260%, PRIOR QTR EPS +125%
WEEKLY PRICES FOR ONE YEAR
CLIMAX TOP
PRICE
$40
$34
$28
$24
$20
$17
$14
$12
$10
$8
$6
$4.8
JAN 1987   APR   JUL
WEEKLY TRADING VOLUME(000)
VOL.
240
160
80

GAP INC
35,678,000 SHARES   +32% ANNUAL EPS GROWTH
LAST QTR EPS +55%, PRIOR QTR EPS +82%
WEEKLY PRICES FOR ONE YEAR
BASE FAILURE
PRICE
$80
$70
$60
$48
$44
$40
$36
$32
OCT   JAN 1987   APR   JUL
WEEKLY TRADING VOLUME(000)
VOL.
750
500
250

HASBRO INC
000,000 SHARES   -15% ANNUAL EPS GROWTH
LAST QTR EPS +61%, PRIOR QTR EPS 0%
WEEKLY PRICES FOR ONE YEAR
RELATIVE STRENGTH LINE VS S&P 500
BASE FAILURE
PRICE
$30
$28
$26
$24
$22
$20
$18
$17
$16
$15
$14
JAN 1987   APR   JUL
WEEKLY TRADING VOLUME(000)
VOL.
1800
1200
600

LIZ CLAIBORNE INC
86,558,000 SHARES   +54% ANNUAL EPS GROWTH
LAST QTR EPS +40%, PRIOR QTR EPS +37%
WEEKLY PRICES FOR ONE YEAR
BASE FAILURE
PRICE
$42
$38
$34
$30
$28
$26
$24
$22
$19
$17
OCT   JAN 1987   APR   JUL
WEEKLY TRADING VOLUME(000)
VOL.
3600
2400
1200

OWENS-CORNING FIBERGLAS
39,572,000 SHARES   0% ANNUAL EPS GROWTH
LAST QTR EPS -72%, PRIOR QTR EPS -40%
WEEKLY PRICES FOR ONE YEAR
HEAD & SHOULDERS TOP
PRICE
$36
$32
$28
$24
$20
$18
$16
$14
$12
$10
$9
OCT   JAN 1987   APR   JUL
WEEKLY TRADING VOLUME(000)
VOL.
7350
4900
2450

REEBOK INTL LTD
112,260,000 SHARES   +165% ANNUAL EPS GROWT
LAST QTR EPS +26%, PRIOR QTR EPS +33%
WEEKLY PRICES FOR ONE YEAR
BASE FAILURE
PRICE
$28
$26
$24
$22
$20
$18
$16
$14
$13
$12
$11
OCT   JAN 1987   APR   JUL
WEEKLY TRADING VOLUME(000)
VOL.
7350
4900
2450

Study these patterns. History will repeat itself. All models show the stock's chart pattern just before the point where you want to take action. For example, the first model in this series of charts, Lorillard, broke out of its five-week sideways price base from $24 to $27 the very next week in November. If you bought as it traded at $27, Lorillard advanced to $98 or 250% in the following twenty months. You are seeing pictures of the most outstanding price accumulation patterns just before enormous price moves began.

15

How to Read Charts like an Expert And Improve Your Stock Selection and Timing

X-rays and brain scans are "pictures" doctors study to diagnose what is actually occurring in a human being. EKGs and ultrasound echo waves are recorded on graph paper or televisionlike terminals to show what is happening to the human heart. Maps are plotted and set to scale to help people tell exactly where they are and how to get where they want to go. Seismic data is traced on charts to help geologists study which structures or patterns seem most likely to contain oil. Economic indicators are plotted on graphs to assist in their interpretation. The price-and-volume history of a stock is recorded on graph paper to help determine if a stock is strong and healthy or if it is weak and behaving in an abnormal fashion.

A doctor would be irresponsible not to use X-rays and EKGs, and investors are foolish not to use and learn to interpret price patterns. Chart books allow you to follow a huge number of different stocks in a highly organized, time-saving way. You can subscribe to any one of the many chart services and receive complete updates weekly. In them there is just too much valuable information about what is realistically going on that you can't easily get any other way. That's why doctors study X-rays and EKGs and why knowledgeable professional investors study and try to understand and interpret charts.

Charts record and represent pure facts on thousands of stocks. Prices that actually occurred are a result of daily supply and demand in the

largest auction marketplace in the world. Facts on markets are much more reliable than 98% of the personal opinions and academic theories circulating about the stock market today.

Milton and Rose Friedman, distinguished economists, devoted the first 28 pages of their excellent best-selling book, *Free to Choose,* to the power of the marketplace and the unique ability of prices to transmit important and accurate information to decision makers.

Those investors who train themselves to properly decode price movements have an enormous advantage over those who are either too lazy or too ignorant to learn about such seemingly irrelevant hocus-pocus. Reading charts is easy to learn if you will take a little time.

I have seen many high-level investment professionals ultimately lose their jobs because they didn't know very much about market action.

Learn to Use Historical Precedents

History repeats itself in the stock market. Many price patterns and price consolidation structures that stocks form are repeated over and over again, just as geological formations recur.

Therefore, **price patterns taken from successful stocks in the past few years should definitely be used as models or precedents for future selection of successful stocks.** Attorneys and geologists rely heavily on precedents; why shouldn't you do the same?

Our record book of *Greatest Stock Market Winners* was compiled to provide historical patterns and important precedent data which could be used by institutional investment professionals as models when searching for successful stocks.

Chart patterns are simply areas of price correction and consolidation, usually after an earlier price advance. The primary challenge in analyzing price consolidation structures is to diagnose if the price and volume movements are normal or, instead, signal significant weakness or distribution.

Major advances occur off sound price patterns and bases. Faulty base structures and completely obvious patterns that everyone sees bring failure.

Price patterns are certainly not Ouija-board magic fakery. Fortunes are made by those who take the time to learn how to properly interpret a graph's market action. Professionals that scoff at, or do not believe in, such important tools are openly confessing their total ignorance of the use of modern highly sophisticated measurement and timing mechanisms.

Search for Cup-with-a-Handle Price Patterns

One of the most fundamental chart-base price patterns looks like a cup with a handle when the outline of a cup is viewed from the side. Cup patterns last, in time duration, from 7 to as many as 65 weeks (most are usually three to six months). The *usual* percentage correction from the absolute peak to the low point of the price pattern varies from 12% or 15% to 33%.

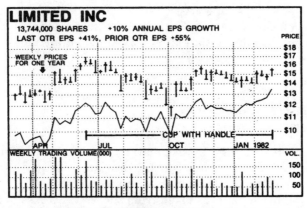

Cup with handle: 3500% increase in 61 months

It is normal for growth stocks to create a cup pattern during intermediate general market declines and correct $1\frac{1}{2}$ to 2 times the market averages, sometimes up to $2\frac{1}{2}$ times. However, stock downturns exceeding $2\frac{1}{2}$ times the decline of the general market averages during bull markets are usually too wide and loose and should be regarded with suspicion. As discussed earlier, your best choices generally are stocks with base patterns that deteriorate the least during an intermediate market decline.

A very few volatile leaders can plunge as much as 40% or 50% in a bull market. Base patterns correcting over this amount while in bull markets have a higher failure rate if they attempt to make new price highs and resume their advance. The reason is that a downswing over 50% from a peak to a low means the stock must increase 100% from its low to get back to its old high. Many stocks making new price highs after such a huge move may fail 5% to 15% beyond their breakout price.

Here is one glowing exception. Sea Containers descended about 50% during a sharp intermediate decline in the 1975 bull market. It then formed a perfectly shaped cup-with-handle price structure and proceeded to increase 554% in the next 101 weeks. I presented this stock, with its 54% annual-earnings growth rate and its latest quarterly earnings up 192%, along with several other equities to Fidelity Research & Management in Boston during a monthly consulting meeting in early June 1975. One of the portfolio managers became instantly interested in the stock upon seeing such big numbers.

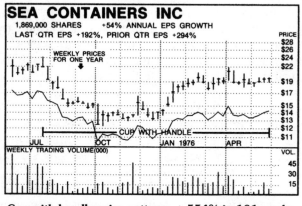

Cup-with-handle price pattern: + 554% in 101 weeks

Coming out of a major bear market, some patterns that have decreased 50% to 60% or more can succeed. The percent decline is, in these cases, a function of the severity of the bear market and the extent of the stock's prior price runup.

The bottom part of a cup pattern should be rounded and give the appearance of a "U" rather than a very narrow "V." This characteristic allows the stock time to proceed through a needed natural correction with two or three final little weak spells around the lows of the cup.

This scares out or wears out the remaining weak holders and takes other speculators' attention away from the stock. A sounder foundation of strong owners who are much less apt to sell during the next advance is thereby forged.

Basic Characteristics of Handle Areas

The forming of the handle area is usually more than one or two weeks in duration and has a downward price drift or price shakeout (where the price drops below a prior low point made a few weeks earlier) near the end of its down-drifting movement. Extreme trading volume dry ups will normally occur near the lows in the price pullback phase of the handle.

Cups without handles have a somewhat higher failure rate, although some stocks with smaller capitalizations do successfully advance without forming a handle.

When handles do occur, they should form in the upper half of the overall base structure, as measured from absolute peak to the low of the cup. This should be above the stock's 200-day moving average price line. Handles forming in the lower half of a base or completely below the stock's 200-day line are weak, failure-prone price structures. Demand up to that point has not been strong enough to enable the stock to recover more than half of its prior decline.

Additionally, handles that consistently drift upwards along their price lows have a higher probability of failing when they break out into new highs. This wedging-upward characteristic along low points in the handle does not allow the stock to undergo the needed correction or shake-out after having advanced from the low of the base into the upper half of the pattern. This high-risk characteristic tends to occur in either third- or fourth-stage bases, laggard stock bases, or very active market leaders that become too widely followed and obvious.

A price drop in a proper handle should be contained within 10% to 15% of its peak unless the stock forms a very large cup, as in the unusual case of Sea Containers. Downturns in handles exceeding this percentage during bull markets look wide and erratic and are, in most cases, improper, excessive, and risky.

Constructive Patterns Have Tight Price Areas

There should also be some tight areas in price patterns of stocks under accumulation. Tightness in this sense means small price variations from high to low for the week, with several weeks' prices closing unchanged or remarkably near to the previous week's close in price.

Find Pivot Points and Watch "Volume % Change"

When a stock charges through an upside buy point, which Livermore referred to as "the pivot point or line of least resistance," the day's volume should increase at least 50% above normal. It is not uncommon for a new market leader to increase its daily volume 500% to 1000% during a major breakout.

The winning individual investor can afford to wait and begin buying at these precise pivot points. This is where the real move starts and all the exciting action originates. If you try to buy before this point, you will be premature and in many cases the stock will never get to its buy point. If you buy more than 5% to 10% past the point, you are late.

Your object is never to buy at the cheapest price or near the low but to begin buying at exactly the right time. This means you have to learn to wait for a stock to move up and trade at your buy point before making an initial commitment.

Pivot buy points are not necessarily at a stock's old high; many occur 5% to 10% below a stock's former high point. Sometimes you can get a slight head start by drawing a down trendline across certain peak points in the stock's price pattern and begin your purchase as the trendline is broken. However, you have to be right in your chart and stock analysis to get away with this.

How to Spot a Saucer-with-Handle Price Pattern

A saucer with a handle is a price pattern similar to the cup with a handle except the "saucer" part tends to be longer and more shallow. If using the name "cup with a handle" or "saucer" sounds unusual, consider that for years you have recognized and called certain constellations "the big and little dipper."

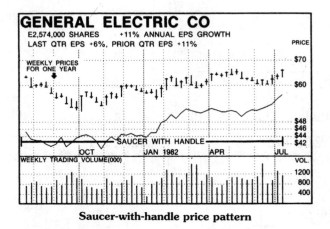

Saucer-with-handle price pattern

A strong price pattern of any type should always have a definite price uptrend prior to the beginning of its base pattern. You should look for a minimum of a 30% increase in price in the prior uptrend, together with improving relative strength and a very substantial increase in volume at some point during the prior uptrend.

The General Electric chart on the previous page shows an example of a saucer-with-handle price structure.

Recognizing a Double-Bottom Price Pattern

A double-bottom price pattern looks like the letter "W." This pattern does not occur as often as does the cup price structure. It is usually important that the second bottom of the "W" touch the price level of the first bottom or, as in most cases, undercut it by one or two points, thereby creating a shakeout.

Double bottoms may also have handles, although it is not always essential. Depth and horizontal length are similar to that of the cup formation. In theory, a double bottom may not be quite as powerful as a proper cup with a handle, since to make the double bottom, the stock had to twice fall back to its low point. See Texas Oil & Gas and Dome Petroleum below for outstanding examples of double-bottom price patterns found during 1977 and 1978. The buy points are 32 and 42.

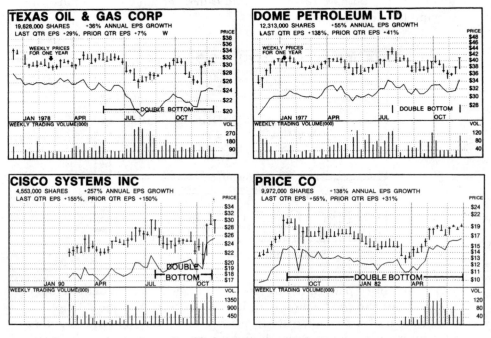

Double-bottom price pattern

Definition of a Flat-Base Price Structure

A flat base is another rewarding price structure. It is usually a second-stage base that occurs after a stock has advanced off of a cup-with-handle, saucer, or double-bottom pattern. The flat base moves straight sideways in a fairly tight price range for at least six or seven weeks and does not correct more than 10% to 15%. Standard Oil of Ohio in May 1979 and SmithKline in March 1978 are good examples of a flat base. Pep Boys in March of 1981 formed a longer flat base.

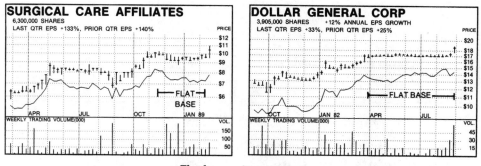

Flat base price patterns

High, Tight Flags Are Rare

A high, tight flag price pattern is rare and occurs no more than once or twice a year. It begins by moving approximately 100% to 120% in a very short period of time (four to eight weeks) and then corrects sideways, usually in three, four, or five weeks, no more than 10% to 20%. It is the strongest pattern but is certainly risky and very difficult to correctly recognize or interpret. Many stocks can skyrocket 200% or more off this formation. (See E. L. Bruce, June 1958; Certain-teed, January 1961; Syntex, July 1963; Rollins, July 1964.)

The E. L. Bruce pattern in the second quarter of 1958, at around $50, provided a perfect precedent or model for the Certain-teed advance which occurred in 1961, and Certain-teed in turn became a model for Syntex in 1963. Just about everyone can be helped by studying models. Even our pilots in wartime were trained by using silhouette models of planes as a guide to recognizing various types of enemy aircraft.

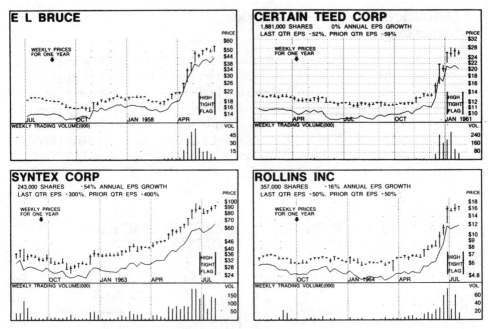

High, tight flag price pattern

Deciphering a Shakeout-Plus-Three-Points Situation

If a stock drops below its low price while it is in a base-building period, the stock can usually be bought when it recovers by three points back through the broken low point. The three-point rule can be tricky to interpret and is used only on stocks in approximately the $30 to $60 dollar price range.

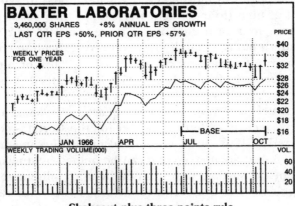

Shakeout-plus-three-points rule

What Is a Base on Top of a Base?

During the latter stages of a *bear market,* in a few stocks a contrary condition occurs that can result in aggressive new leaders in the market. I call this slightly bewildering case a base on top of a base.

What happens is that a powerful stock breaks out of its base on the upside but is unable to increase 20% to 25% because the general market begins another leg down. The stock, therefore, builds a second price-consolidation area just on top of its previous base while the general market keeps making new lows.

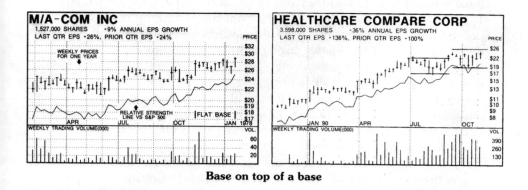

Base on top of a base

When the bearish phase in the overall market eventually ends, the security will probably be one of the first to race into new high ground and launch a tremendous advance. The stock is like a spring being depressed and held down by the pressure of a heavy object. Once the heavy object (a bear market decline) is removed, the spring is free to do what it wanted to do all the time.

M/A-Com and Boeing were two of our best institutional buy recommendations made just before we placed a full-page "bullish ad" in *The Wall Street Journal* on March 29, 1978. Both had a base-on-top-of-a-former-base price structure. One advanced 180%, the other 950%. Healthcare Compare is an example that occurred coming out of the 1990 bear market in November 1990. It bolted from 24 to 175.

Wide-and-Loose Price Structures are "Failure Prone"

Another interesting price phenomenon is the one we label wide-and-loose price structures. Patterns with this characteristic almost always fail, although some of them may later tighten up their price structure and finally make a large-scale advance.

New England Nuclear and Houston Oil & Minerals are two cases of price structures eventually tightening up from previously wide, loose, and erratic price movements. I use these two examples because I missed both of them at the time. It is always wise to review big winners you missed to try to find out why you didn't recognize them when they were exactly right and ready to soar into outer space.

New England Nuclear formed a wide, loose, faulty price structure that looked like a double bottom from points A, B, C, D, and E. (See page 171.) It declined approximately 40% from the beginning at point A to point D. That was excessive. Note the additional clue provided by the declining trend of its relative strength line throughout the false structure. Buying at point E was wrong. The handle was also short and not drifting down or having a shakeout.

New England Nuclear formed a second base from point E to F to G. However, if you tried to buy at point G, you were wrong again. It was premature because the price structure was still wide and loose. From point E to F was a prolonged period down with relative strength in a steep decline. The rise straight up from the bottom at point F to its bogus breakout point G was too fast and erratic, covering only three months. Three months of improving relative strength versus the prior seventeen months of decline in relative strength was not sufficient to turn the previous poor trend into a positive one.

The stock then declined from G to H to form what appeared to be a handle area for the possible cup formation from E to F to G. However, if you bought at point I on the breakout attempt, the stock failed again. The reason: the handle was too loose—it degenerated 20%. But after failing this time, the stock at last tightened up its price structure from I to J to K and 15 weeks later, at K, broke out of a very tight sound base and advanced almost 200%. Note the stock's relative strength line from point K back to point F. So you see, there really is such a thing as the right and wrong time to buy a stock. But it's demanding.

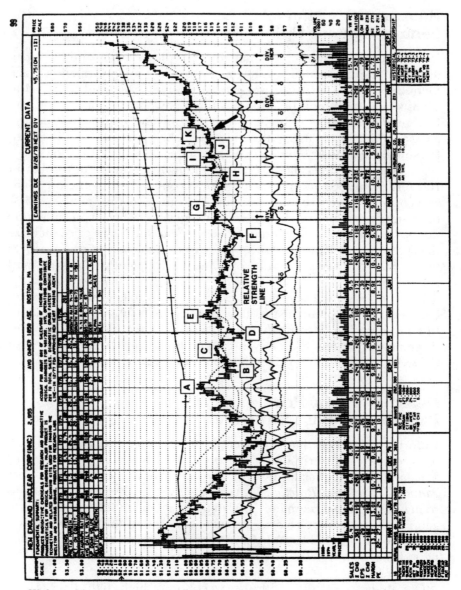

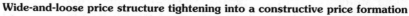

Wide-and-loose price structure tightening into a constructive price formation

Houston Oil & Minerals
Pattern Tightens Up

Houston Oil is an even more dramatic example of a wide-and-loose pattern that later tightened up into a constructive price formation. (See following page.) A to B to C was extremely wide, loose, and erratic. B to C was straight up from the bottom without any pullback in price. C and D were false attempts to break out of a faulty and improper structure, and so was H. Afterwards, a tight nine-week base formed from H to I to J. (Note the extreme volume dry up along the December 1975 lows.)

This structure was called to my attention by an alert stockbroker in Hartford, Connecticut, but I had been so conditioned by the two prior years of poor price structures and toppy earnings that my mind was slow to change when the stock suddenly changed its behavior in only nine weeks. I was also probably intimidated by the tremendous price increase that occurred in Houston Oil in the earlier bull market during 1973. Once again, this just proves that opinions are frequently wrong but markets seldom are.

It also points out a very important principle. It takes time for human beings to change opinions that have built up for a substantial period. In this instance the current quarterly earnings turning up 357% after three down quarters didn't even change my incorrect bearish view of the stock to a bullish one. The right buy point was in January 1976.

Detecting Faulty Price
Patterns and Base Structures

Unfortunately, there has not been any original or thorough research done on price-pattern analysis in the last 50 years. In 1930 Richard Schabacker, a financial editor of *Forbes,* wrote a book entitled *Stock Market Theory and Practice.* In it, he discussed many patterns, such as triangles, coils, and pennants. Our detailed model building and investigations of price structure over the years have shown the patterns he discussed to be unreliable and risky. They probably worked in the latter part of the "roaring 20s" when any and every old thing ran up in a wild, climactic frenzy.

Our studies show that, with the exception of high, tight flags, which are relatively rare, reliable base structures must have a minimum of six to eight weeks of price consolidation. Most coils, triangles, and pennants are simply weak foundations without sufficient time or price correction to become proper and safe bases.

John McGee and Robert D. Edwards wrote a book in 1948 called *Technical Analysis of Stock Trends.* The book is fairly expensive and

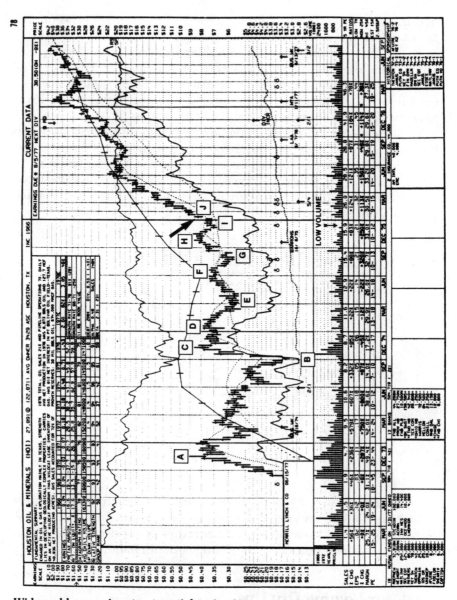

Wide-and-loose price structure tightening into a constructive price formation

appears to have copied many of the same faulty patterns presented in Schabacker's earlier book.

In 1962 William Jiler wrote an easy-to-read book, *How Charts Can Help You in the Stock Market,* which explains many of the correct principles behind technical analysis. However it, too, seems to have continued the display and discussion of certain of these predepression era, failure-prone price patterns.

Triple bottoms and head-and-shoulder bottoms are also structures widely mentioned in several books on technical analysis. These we have found to be weaker structures. A head-and-shoulders bottom may succeed in a few instances, but it has no strong prior uptrend, which is a necessary element for most powerful market leaders.

While head-and-shoulder bottoms are not as sound as previous writers have claimed, head-and-shoulder top price structures are one of the more reliable price patterns signifying a top in a stock. But be careful—with just a little knowledge of charts, you can misinterpret what is a correct head-and-shoulders top. Many professionals do not properly interpret the price structure.

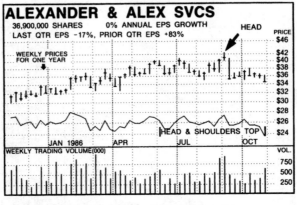

Head-and-shoulders top price pattern

A triple bottom is a looser, weaker, and less-attractive base pattern than a double bottom because the stock corrects and falls back sharply to its absolute low three different times rather than twice, as with a double bottom, or one time, as in the strong cup with handle.

Look for Volume Dry Ups
Near Lows of a Price Pattern

Nearly all proper bases will show a dramatic volume dry up for one or two weeks along the very low of the base pattern and in the low area of the handle. This means that all of the selling has dried up and there is no more stock coming into the marketplace. Healthy stocks under accumulation almost always show this symptom. The combination of tightness in prices (daily or weekly price closes being very near each other) and dried-up volume is generally quite constructive.

How to Use Relative Strength Correctly

Many fundamental security analysts think technical analysis means buying stocks with the strongest relative strength.

You do not buy stocks that show the highest relative price strength on some list of best performers. You buy stocks that are performing relatively stronger than the general market just as they are beginning to emerge from a sound base-building period. The time to begin selling is when the stock advances in price rapidly, is extended materially from its base, and is showing extremely high relative strength.

Analysts have a great deal to learn if they believe all that technical research amounts to is the buying of high relative strength momentum stocks.

What Is Overhead Supply?

A critically important concept to learn in analyzing price movements is the principle of overhead supply. It is really quite simple. If a stock advances from $25 to $40, then declines back to $30, most of the people who bought late in the upper $30s and at $40 will have a loss in the stock unless they were quick to sell and cut their loss (which most people don't do). Therefore, if the stock later increases in price back to the high $30s or $40 area, all the investors that had losses can now get out even.

Human nature is pretty much the same most of the time. So it is normal that a number of these people will sell when they see a chance to get their money back after having been down a significant amount.

Good chartists (a typically tiny group of investors) know how to recognize the price areas that represent heavy overhead supply. They will never make the fatal mistake of buying a stock that has a large recent amount of overhead supply. This is one type of serious mistake many inexperienced fundamental analysts tend to make.

On the other hand, if a stock is able to fight its way through all its overhead supply, it may be safer to buy even though the price is a little higher because the stock proved itself to have sufficient demand to absorb the concentrated supply zone. Of course, a stock that has just broken out into new high ground for the first time has no overhead supply to contend with, which adds to its appeal.

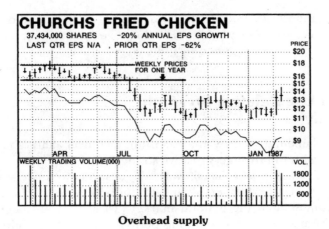

Overhead supply

Excellent Opportunities in Unfamiliar Newer Stocks

Alert winning investors should have a way to track every week all of the new stock listings and new issues that have emerged on the scene during the previous two or three years. This is important because some of these newer and younger companies will be among the stupendous performers of the next year or two. A newspaper's OTC section can possibly help you stay on top of the myriad of new companies.

Commonly, some new issues move up a small amount and then retreat to new price lows during a bear market. This creates a rather unimpressive record. When the next bull market begins, some of these forgotten newcomers will, unnoticed, sneak back up, form a base pattern, and suddenly take off and double or triple in price.

Most investors miss these outstanding price moves because they occur in new names that are largely unknown to the average market watcher. Following chart books each week can help you spot these unfamiliar, newer companies. It also is essential for a chart service to follow a large number of stocks so you don't miss a big new leader simply because the stock didn't appear in the service.

Levitz Furniture, Rite Aid, and National Chemsearch in 1970, and Toys R Us in 1978 are a few examples of the situation mentioned above.

Successful, young hi-tech growth stocks tend to enjoy their fastest earnings growth between their fifth and tenth years in business.

Big Volume Clues Are Valuable

Big daily and weekly volume provides another extraordinarily valuable tip-off to a trained chart reader looking for potentially large winners. Fannie Mae in May 1988, Software Toolworks in September 1989, and Nordstrom are examples of outstanding stocks that flashed such a key indication immediately before tremendous price increases.

Huge volume weeks with price advancing, followed by extreme volume dry ups in other weeks, illustrates a picture of maximum contrast in volume levels. This is very constructive. Using a daily chart service in conjunction with weekly basis graphs can frequently let you see unusual volume activity that happened on only one particular day.

Analysis of volume, or the number of shares of stock being traded, is a subject worth careful study. It can certainly help you recognize if a stock is under accumulation or distribution. Once you acquire this skill, you won't have to rely as much on the personal opinions of analysts and experts. Big volume at major points is indispensable.

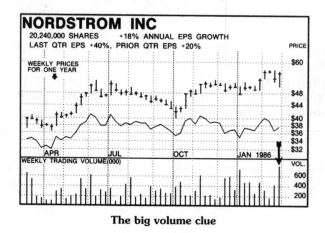

The big volume clue

Volume is your best measure of supply and demand and institutional sponsorship, two vital ingredients in successful stock analysis. Perhaps you may want to consider getting a chart book and starting to learn how to time your purchases correctly. It's simply too costly to continue making buys at the wrong time, or worse, buying stocks that are not under accumulation or have unsound price structures.

A Loud Warning to the Wise!

Let me offer one last bit of judicious guidance. If you are new to the stock market or the strategies outlined in this book, or more importantly, you are reading this book for the first time near the beginning or middle of a bear market, do not expect the presumed buy patterns to work. Most will be defective.

The patterns can be too wide and loose, with third- and fourth-stage bases; wedging or loose, sloppy handles; handles in the lower half of the base structure; narrow "Vs" moving straight up from the bottom of a base into new highs, without any handle area forming. The patterns can show laggard stocks with puny relative strength lines and price structures with too much adverse volume activity.

It isn't that bases, breakouts, or the method isn't working any more, it's that the time and the stocks are simply wrong. The price and volume patterns are phony, faulty, and unsound. The general market isn't right. It is selling time. Even a skunk isn't going to make a cent.

Be patient, keep doing your studying, and be 100% prepared. At the least expected time when all the news seems terrible, winter will ultimately pass and a great new, super bull market will suddenly spring to life. The practical techniques and disciplines discussed here should work for you for many, many future economic cycles.

The following graph from Daily Graphs by Daily Graphs Inc. illustrates what a cup-with-handle-pattern looks like on a daily chart.

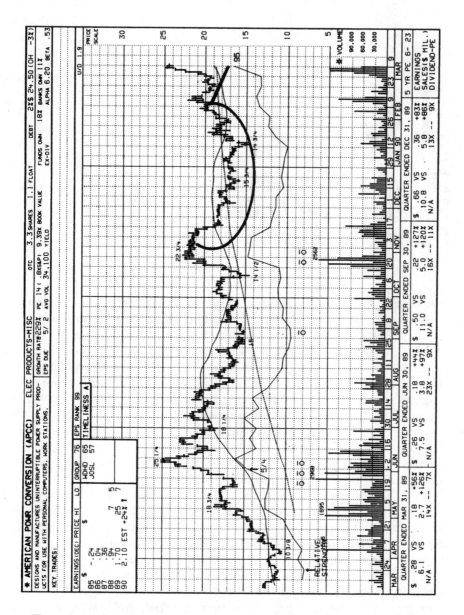

To summarize: **Learn to read and use charts if you want to improve your stock selection and timing.** It's easier than you think to scan a daily chart book once a week, so don't pass up this gold mine of opportunities.

16

How to Make Money Reading the Daily Financial News Pages

For years, institutional investors garnered all the valuable investment information. However, today you can obtain an amazing amount of professional financial data and background from a daily newspaper.

City newspapers generally show at least a minimum of stock price tables in their business sections. National daily business newspapers do not give advice or recommendations; however, they do provide general economic news and an understanding of financial alternatives for serious investors and people desiring successful business careers.

Anyone who wants to achieve financial independence and a secure retirement income should consider reading the financial news pages. It is a good way to regularly keep up with the action of your investments and "red flag" those you are thinking about buying.

But do you know how to use all this special news data? You might think so; however, there may be essential measurements you have skipped over. The tables and graphs that follow are from *Investor's Business Daily,* a national business newspaper I started in April 1984; they will help explain how to read financial features data.

Business newspapers should be organized to save time for busy executives and investors. Most people first read the "News Digest" on the front page. You can scan brief headlines in a flash and stay up to date on the prime economic, business, and world news. Articles are digested in short, two- or three-paragraph stories. Sometimes a graph of a "just released" economic indicator, such as housing starts, Gross National Product, retail sales, auto sales, or unemployment, is also shown.

Busy readers usually next glance at the feature stories appearing on the right-hand side of the front page to see if one of the four top-level national issue, Leaders and Success, News For You, or Investor's Corner articles strikes their fancy. To further save you time, all front page feature stories are limited in length and completed on the very next page.

Page 4 is usually the Executive Update section. Frequently you'll find articles here on the latest high-tech and computer systems. The New America page that follows is an absolute must-read for all investors. Every day there are 3 to 4 stories on fast-growing, entrepreneurial companies. If you read this each day, in 3 months' time, you will know about most of the exciting new companies in America. Many may be tomorrow's big winners.

Next, many investors read the daily stock market column. It tells the important "goings on" in the market the day before highlighting stocks that displayed unusual action.

You can proceed from page 1 to 2 to 3 (front to back), rather than jumping all around or starting toward the rear of the paper, to check the stock tables. New York Stock Exchange prices are printed up front in Section I because this is a focal point people want to check quickly.

Virtually all U.S. newspapers use the Associated Press price tables in their papers. There has been little change in this basic information provided to the public for 50 years or more. For example, they show the yield, P/E, high, low, closing price, net price change for the day, and volume of trading for several thousand stocks. This is the standard data most investors see, but it does not give you the complete picture.

Specifically, four critical additional news items are provided every day in the *Investor's Business Daily* New York Stock Exchange, AMEX, and NASDAQ tables, items that cannot be found in your local paper or in *The Wall Street Journal*.

Earning per Share Rank Indicates a Company's Relative Earnings Growth

The first "additional" news item in *Investor's Business Daily* is the earnings per share (EPS) rank, which calculates every company's growth in earnings per share over the last five years and the stability of that growth. A company's percentage change in earnings per share for the two most recent quarters, versus the same quarters a year ago, is combined and then averaged with its five years' earnings growth record. The result is compared with all other common stocks in the price tables and ranked on a scale from 1 to 99, with 99 being the highest. An 80 EPS rank means that particular company's bottom-line earnings results are in the top 20% of the more than 7000 corporations being measured.

NYSE

EPS Rank	RelSt	Acc. Dis.	52-Week High	52-Week Low	Stock	Symbol	Closing Price	Chg.	Vol.% Change	Vol. 100s	PE	Day's Price High	Day's Price Low	
48	20	C	3 7/8	2	KimmnEnvrn	KVN	2 3/8	- 1/8	+35	138	13	2 1/2	2 3/8	
70	**78**	**A**	**NH**	**24 5/8**	**KingWorld**	**KWP**	**41 7/8**	**+1 1/8**	**+67**	**1527**	**16**	**42 1/8**	**40 3/4**	o
	32	C	11 1/4	9	Kleinwrt Ben	KBA	9 5/8	- 1/8	-48	55	..	9 3/4	9 5/8	
43	23	B	65	50 5/8	KnightRidder	KRI	52 7/8	+ 1/2	+23	1100	21	53 1/8	52 1/2	o
38	26	C	13 5/8	6 1/2	Knogo Corp	KNO	9	- 1/8	+36	135	20	9 1/4	9	k
30	5	D	7/8	**NL**	KogerPrprtes	KOG	3/32	....	-4	499	..	3/32	3/32	b
82	**79**	**B**	**43 3/8**	**20 3/4**	**Kohls**	**KSS**	**43 1/4**	**+1 1/8**	**-80**	**205**	**33**	**43 1/4**	**42 1/8**	o
75	66	A	7 5/8	2	Kollmorgen	KOL	6 5/8	....	+25	135	..	6 3/4	6 5/8	
	32	B	16 1/4	11 3/4	Korea Fund	KF	13 7/8	....	-14	582	..	13 7/8	13 3/4	
	28	C	13 1/4	10	KoreanInvst	KIF	11 1/8	+ 3/8	+11	185	..	11 1/8	10 3/4	
46	55	B	**27**	19 3/4	Kranzco	KRT	24 5/8	- 3/4	-42	103	..	25 1/2	24 5/8	
98	81	A	**21 3/4**	11 3/8	Kroger	KR	20 7/8	....	-69	1205	15	21	20 1/2	k o
28	36	B	16 1/2	11 1/2	Kuhlman Cp	KUH	14 1/4	- 1/8	-28	69	..	14 3/8	14 1/4	k
53	87	B	**122 7/8**	55 3/4	KyoceraCorp	KYO	116	- 1/2	-88	5	..	116 1/4	116	
68	32	D	21 3/4	11 3/8	Kysor Indstrl	KZ	16 3/8	+ 1/4	-73	39	9	16 1/2	16 1/4	k
					— L —									
28	19	C	13 3/8	8 1/8	LA Gear	LA	9 1/4	- 1/8	+99	2689	..	9 3/8	9	k o
19	36	B	10 5/8	4 1/4	LacMinerals	LAC	7 1/2	+ 1/8	-55	1650	..	7 1/2	7 3/8	o
67	63	B	**43 3/8**	32 1/4	LGEEnergy	LGE	43	- 1/4	**+212**	512	17	43 3/8	43	
66	45	B	5 5/8	3 3/8	LL&E RyltTr	LRT	4 5/8	....	-64	80	17	4 5/8	4 1/2	
[illegible]	[illegible]	[illegible]	**19 7/8**	13 1/4	MooreCorp	MCL	18 7/8	- 1/4	-[illegible]	443	99	19 1/8	18 3/4	o
	34	[illegible]	13 1/4	10 1/4	Morgn Gren	MGC	11	- 1/4	-61	52	..	11 1/4	11	
61	79	A	**14 1/4**	7 3/4	MorgnKeegn	MOR	13 7/8	- 1/8	+66	257	6	14 1/8	13 3/4	
17	34	C	8 3/8	5 3/8	MorganPrds	MGN	6 3/8	- 3/8	-76	46	..	6 3/4	6 3/8	
	76	A	**24 1/2**	15 3/4	MrgnStEmrg	MSF	23	- 1/4	+17	531	..	23 1/8	22 7/8	
7	41	.	**15 7/8**	15	MrgSEmMkD	MSD	15 1/4	- 1/8	-23	466	..	15 1/4	15 1/8	
95	86	A	**86 3/8**	46	Morgan Stan	MS	84 7/8	- 3/4	-44	1274	10	85 3/4	84 3/4	o
97	60	B	**79 3/8**	59 3/8	Morgan J P	JPM	75	....	-24	3567	12	76 1/8	75	k o
44	66	B	**27 1/8**	17 7/8	MorrisnKnud	MRN	25 1/4	- 7/8	-3	757	49	26 1/8	25 1/4	o
11	1	E	2 1/2	7/16	Mtg&RealtyTr	MRT	15/32	- 1/32	+16	227	..	9/16	15/32	
47	77	B	**89 3/8**	53 3/4	Morton Intl	MII	87 1/4	+ 3/8	-54	616	34	87 3/8	86 3/4	k o
7	51	.	**13 5/8**	11 1/4	Motorcoach	MCO	13 1/4	- 1/8	-55	697	..	13 3/8	13 1/8	
94	**88**	**B**	**99 1/8**	**41 3/8**	**Motorola Inc**	**MOT**	**93 3/4**	**+2**	**-7**	**9896**	**35**	**94 3/4**	**92 5/8**	k o
66	84	A	**34 3/4**	13 1/2	Mueller Inds	MLI	31 7/8	....	-46	380	18	32 1/4	31 7/8	
7	28	.	**15**	14 1/8	MuniassetFd	MUA	14 1/4	- 1/8	-97	3	..	14 1/4	14 1/4	
7	27	.	**15 1/8**	14 1/4	MentorInFd	MAF	14 3/8	+ 1/8	-71	35	..	14 3/8	14 1/4	
	36	C	**10 1/8**	8 5/8	MuniHiIncm	MHF	9 7/8	+ 1/8	-60	70	..	9 7/8	9 3/4	
	40	B	**8 7/8**	7 1/2	MuniIncOpp	OIA	8 3/8	- 1/8	+132	783	..	8 1/2	8 3/8	
	43	D	**8 7/8**	7 5/8	MuniOppTr2	OIB	8 1/2	- 1/8	+114	787	..	8 5/8	8 1/2	
	49	B	**9 7/8**	8 1/8	MunIncOpyIII	OIC	9 3/4	....	+15	135	..	9 7/8	9 3/4	
	43	B	**11 1/2**	10	MuniInTrst1	TFA	11 1/4	+ 1/8	+22	308	..	11 3/8	11 1/8	

Four relevant and vital news items: EPS rank, relative strength, accumulation/distribution, and volume % change
(Note: Closing price appears after stock symbol to save time.)

This, of course, could be crucial intelligence because it gives an objective, relative measurement of the actual earnings results produced by all of the leading corporations in American industry.

You can now compare the audited earnings record of one company to that of companies in other industries or you can compare IBM's past record to Digital Equipment, Hewlett Packard, Unisys, and all the computer and computer-related companies that make up the industry.

Since earning power and earnings growth are the most basic measures of a firm's success, EPS rank should be invaluable for screening the true leaders from the poorly managed, deficient, and lackluster laggards in today's emerging age of tougher worldwide competition.

EPS rank may be more meaningful than the widely followed Fortune 500 ratings that primarily list which corporations are the largest in size.

Corporate size rarely guarantees growth, innovation, profitability, or an increasing number of jobs for workers.

Earnings estimates are not used in the calculation because they are opinions and are sometimes inaccurate, whereas reported earnings are actual reported facts.

Relative Strength Rank
Shows How a Stock's Price
Has Performed

The second pertinent "extra" measurement is a stock's relative price performance during the latest 12 months. Relative strength measures the cold, realistic auction marketplace's appraisal of a stock, in spite of the theoretical value of the company or its past popularity, name, and image.

How did the stock's price behave in the market in the last year? Its running 12 months' performance is updated daily, compared to all other stocks, and then placed on the same easy-to-use 1 to 99 scale.

An 80 relative strength rank means the stock, pricewise, outperformed 80% of all other common stocks in the last year. During good markets, the potential implication of these two basic news measurements, EPS rank and relative strength rank, is considerable. During poor markets, relative strength measures that break below 70 might forewarn you of possible problem situations. Every stock's group strength is shown each Monday. *Investor's Business Daily* shows a list at the end of the NYSE tables of stocks that just fell below 70, 50, or 30 in relative price strength. These are generally companies to avoid.

Most of the superior stocks available for investment will usually rank 80 or higher on *both* EPS and Relative Strength. Since one is a fundamental measurement and the other is a marketplace valuation, insisting on both numbers being strong should, in positive markets, improve your selection process compared to the old, unscientific methods of faulty opinions, academic theories, stories, promotions, tips, and touts.

Of course, there is no guarantee that a company's terrific past or current record can't suddenly start to turn sour. That's why you should always have and use some type of loss-cutting strategy. Additionally, you'll need to do a little more research, such as checking the stock's daily or weekly chart to see if it is currently in a base (sideways area of price consolidation) or is extended in price above its base. Then study an S&P stock report tear sheet or a Value Line report to learn more about the company's basic business and new products.

As discussed earlier, **models of more than 500 of the best-performing companies, over a 40-year period, showed that the previous five years' earnings growth rate and percent increase of the latest two quarters' earnings was the most important fundamental common characteristic in the majority of excellent-performing companies. These successful models racked up an average relative strength number of 87 at the starting point, when they broke out of their first price-consolidation basing area, prior to their substantial price advance.**

Why should you invest your hard-earned dollars in a sluggish stock that trumpets a 30 EPS rank and 40 relative price-strength rank when there are dozens of first-rate choices with higher rankings? Companies with poor ratings can perform, but there are more disappointments in these lower categories. Also, even when a low-ranked company has a decent price move, one of the better-ranked stocks in the same industry probably advanced percentagewise much more. These combined measurements, in a way, are similar to the A.C. Neilson's TV viewer ratings of programs. Who wants to continue sponsoring a TV show that has especially poor ratings?

For a minute pretend you are the New York Mets' manager. Visualize it is "off season" and you are going to pick new players for next year's baseball team. Would you trade for, recruit, or sign only .200 hitters, or would you select as many .300 hitters as possible? The .200 hitters are available at a cheaper price, but how many ball games would you win with nine players in your lineup averaging .200?

When the bases are loaded in the ninth inning and the score is tied, who would you rather march to the plate: a .200 hitter or a .300 hitter? How often does an established .200 hitter blossom into a batting champion? Not often.

It's no different selecting and managing your portfolio of stocks. **To be a more consistent winner and finish in the first division ahead of the others, you need a roster of the very best players available—the ones sporting a *proven record* of excellence.**

With all the past talk about America's lack of competitiveness in many areas of our older basic industries, these practical, no-nonsense measurements have helped wake up corporate boards of directors. They have created pressure for changes in top managements that are continually producing pathetic second division results. Alert, responsible directors need to be aware of these longer-term company relative performance rankings.

Accumulation/Distribution

This proprietary measurement is based on price and volume change and tells you if your stock is under accumulation (professional buying) or distribution (professional selling). You'll probably want to pick "A" or "B" ranked companies and temporarily avoid the "D" and "E" ranked ones. They are under liquidation in the last 3 months.

Volume % Change Tracks Big Money Flow

The fourth valuable news measurement is volume % change. Most newspapers only publish a stock's trading volume for the day, but volume % change goes one giant revealing step further by keeping track of what the normal trading level for *every company* is during the prior three months. Stocks, like people, are different. One stock may average trading 10,000 shares a day, another 100,000 shares a day, and still another 1 million shares a day.

If a 10,000-share trader suddenly transacts 70,000 today, and its price jumps one point, the stock has popped up on a 600% increase in volume. The volume % change column will show a + 600. It's like having a "computer in your pocket to carefully monitor changing supply and demand for every stock."

Is this essential data for you to know? Imagine if your largest stock holding was down two points yesterday and the volume % change column showed your stock traded 500% greater volume than normal. Wouldn't you want to be aware of that fact?

The columns displaying the volume % change for thousands of stocks every day are one of the top reasons many specialists on the floor of the New York Stock Exchange and most professional portfolio managers, as well as many savvy public investors, read the *Investor's Business Daily* stock tables.

This data allows them to scrutinize the flow of money into and out of stocks. Many sophisticated investors and experienced or larger-producing stockbrokers also widely utilize this more advanced news dissemination.

Money managers usually save time reading the tables because all stocks up one point or more or those hitting new price highs are printed in large boldface type. Stocks down one point or more or making new price lows are underlined. You can scan the tables rapidly and be aware of all of the key market action for the day.

To further save readers time in today's fast-paced business world, the remaining print is easy to read, companies are spelled out more completely, and preferred stocks are displayed in a separate area.

Have you ever tried to find a common stock in the price tables and found there were six or seven issues all with the same or similar name, and you weren't sure which one was your stock? Old tables that show a company with seven preferred stock issues alongside the common stock can add to the delay and confusion in locating your common stocks.

Additionally, each Tuesday the stock tables show every company's P.E. ratio and Wednesday's tables give you the sponsorship rank. Thursday's tables contain the % of stock outstanding that is owned by management, and Friday's edition tells you the % dividend yield. Rather than showing only the P.E. and yield every day, since they seldom change that much and are not really the most vital data, IBD shows today's more knowledgeable investor seven other key items as well that, when taken together, are far more important for getting better investment results.

Be Alert to Stocks with the Greatest % Change in Volume

All newspapers show the 15 most active stocks, usually consisting of securities like IBM, AT&T, or General Motors, which each normally trade more than a million shares a day. *Investor's Business Daily,* on the other hand, shows a table of the "Common Stocks with the Greatest % Rise in Volume." This spotlights companies that have the largest increase above their own last 50 days of average daily trading volume.

The list is valuable because the computer surveillance picks up the small- and medium-sized, innovative, entrepreneurial organizations that may have a 500% increase in trading volume but never reach a total volume figure large enough to make the more commonly followed "Most Active" lists. These sophisticated screens may not appear in other publications. Pay close attention to the boldfaced stocks on the list.

Some newspapers list the stocks that are up most, percentagewise, in price. This list is almost universally worthless because it will show a $2 stock up $\frac{3}{8}$ of a point as stock up in price the greatest percent. They also show preferred stocks in the list. Low-priced stocks and preferred issues are of little use to most informed investors. You can't get rich prospecting in the junk pile.

Eliminating the cheaper, less relevant, low-quality stocks, plus the preferred issues, and concentrating on a meaningful list of 25 of the more significant securities $12 or higher is more useful. Stocks in this list that have options listed show a small "o" after the company's name to assist option traders.

Most newspapers typically provide a small block, "How to Read the Daily Stock Tables." Be absolutely sure to read these instructions as you would directions to any new product you buy. You'll learn many helpful facts that will save you money.

Option Tables Should Show Trading Volume

Stock option tables should give volume of trading for each option and combine all exchanges together in an alphabetical list. Many daily publications omit volume data. Volume helps measure liquidity and the amount of demand for an option. A long-term options table is also shown.

Call (C) Put (P)	E X C	Strike Price	Jun Vol.	Jun Last Price	Jul Vol.	Jul Last Price	Vol.	Last Price
A M P Inc						Stk Close	53⅜	**Aug**
C	C	55		no trade		no trade	5	2⅜
C	C	60	10	1/16		no trade		no trade
P	C	50		no trade	3	½	53	¾
A S T Research						Stk Close	25⅛	**Aug**
C	A	25	140	1	149	1⅞	62	2¼
C	A	30		no trade		no trade	15	¾
P	A	22½		no trade	5	⅝		no trade
P	A	25	3	1		no trade		no trade
Abbott Labs						Stk Close	74⅛	**Aug**
C	X	70	65	4⅞	9	5	20	6
C	X	75	193	1	61	2⅛	42	3
Amoco Corp						Stk Close	53	**Aug**
C	C	45	30	7¾		no option	20	8⅝
C	C	50	23	3⅛	272	3½	45	4⅛
C	C	55	242	¼	81	11/16	20	1⅛
C	C	60		no trade		no option	103	3/16
P	C	50	5	⅛	25	5/16	10	½
Amr President Co						Stk Close	25¼	**Oct**
C	P	30		no trade		no trade	5	⅝
P	P	22½		no trade	10	¼		no trade
P	P	30		no trade		no trade	2	4½
Anadarko Petrol						Stk Close	33¾	**Aug**
C	C	30		no trade		no trade	9	4¾
C	X	65	7	3⅛	3	3¾	39	4⅞
C	X	70	4	⅝	2	1¼		no trade
P	X	65	1	⅜		no trade		no trade
Bell Atlantic Corp						Stk Close	52	**Oct**
C	C	47½	380	5	426	4⅝		no trade
C	C	50	20	2⅜	8	3¼		no trade
C	C	52½		no option	6	1¼		no option
C	C	55		no option	5	9/16	2	1⅜
C	C	55	2	3/16		no option		no option
P	C	45		no trade		no trade	50	¼
P	C	47½		no trade		no trade	50	⅝
P	C	50	5	⅜		no trade		no trade

Useful volume data measures liquidity and demand for options

Always Check Stocks Making New Highs Daily (Graphically Displayed)

Another helpful feature is 30 graphic displays shown every day of stocks in the news on each of the New York and NASDAQ markets. If a stock makes a new price high for the year, a weekly graph of its high, low, closing price, and volume is shown covering the past 12 months. If more than 30 stocks make new highs, the ones with the highest EPS rank are pictured. If there are less than 30, the remainder of the list is completed with equities that had the greatest % change in their own trading volume.

This display is like a computerized tool for bringing to the surface all unusual day-by-day action so you will have a better chance to see all potentially emerging leaders. It does not miss many leaders; however, not all stocks shown will be successful and work out.

You would probably overlook most of these fascinating companies, particularly in the over-the-counter market, because the stocks are not widely known. These unrecognized, unfamiliar companies frequently blast off and become the new outstanding big winners of the year.

NASDAQ Stocks In The News

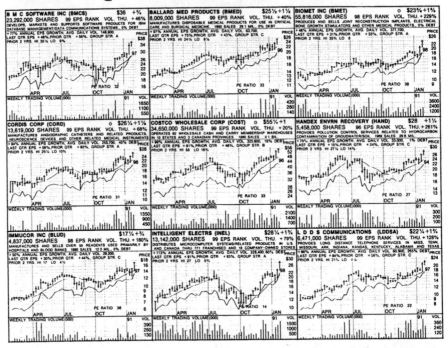

Each of these minigraphs of "Stocks in the News" are fact-packed with fundamental decision-making data such as: number of shares outstanding, EPS rank, company description, stock symbol, annual earnings growth rate, accumulation/distribution, % owned by management, percent company debt, group relative strength, stock relative strength line and number, average daily trading volume, price-earnings ratio, current quarterly earnings, high and low prices for the prior two years and if the stock has options.

In June of 1986, I picked a June 1985 paper at random and checked all 30 graphic displays shown in the June 1985 "OTC Stocks in the News" section. In the one year up to June 1986, 27 of the 30 had advanced in price and three had declined. In this instance the overall increase of all 30 stocks averaged 75%, while the general market averages for the same time period increased 25%. That certainly doesn't mean it will happen in the future, but at least in that strong bull market year, the method seemed to work better than did throwing darts at the stock tables. These graphs also picked up all of the real leaders.

Lists are provided for all NYSE, AMEX, and OTC stocks hitting new price highs or new lows. Initial new highs could be worth checking up on, especially in the OTC market, since few publications provide new high lists for over-the-counter securities. New high lists are uniquely shown by industry groups and they show the stock symbol and closing price for each stock. The symbol lets you quickly check on new ideas.

If You Want Success, Study
The General Market
Indicators Page

If you sincerely want to do well investing in the stock market or be more accurate in predicting what the American economy is likely to do, then you must be able to correctly interpret the direction of the daily general market averages.

To do this properly, you can't just look at one market average. *Investor's Business Daily* provides you with the Dow Jones 30 Industrials, two broader indexes, the S&P 500 index and *Investor's Business Daily* stock index, which covers 6000 New York Stock Exchange, American, and over-the-counter common stocks, and is the broadest possible market-value-weighted index of the equities market.

The NYSE daily advance-decline line, which measures cumulatively the number of stocks on the New York Stock Exchange advancing in price versus the number declining, plus a 200-day moving average price line for each market index, rounds out the measurements that you will need.

On the next page is a striking case in point of the importance of displaying several large, easy-to-read graphs of different market indexes together and paralleling exactly the same current nine-month period. At most major market tops and bottoms, subtle divergences occur between the various market averages.

As mentioned in Chapter 7 on general market direction, in December 1984 and early January 1985, the Dow Jones 30 Industrials made new lows, while the NYSE advance-decline line actually moved up and penetrated into higher ground three times. This was a clear "blinking light" alert that the broad market was getting stronger, while the weakness in the Dow Jones 30 Industrials was providing a totally false indication of the market's condition.

This divergence occurred right after discount-rate cuts on November 21 and December 21 of 1984. These interest-rate changes were shown on the same stock index chart that displays the advance-decline line. A stunning rally quickly ensued.

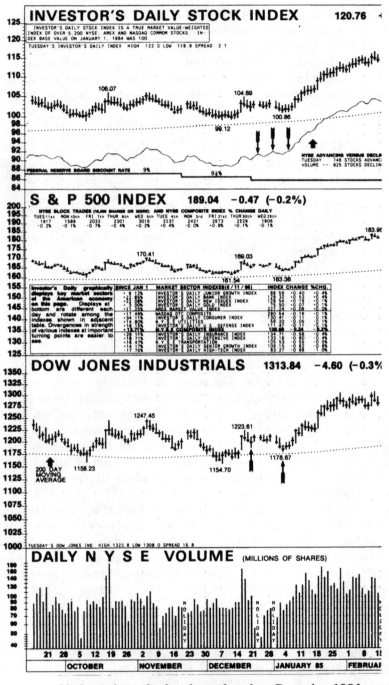

**Market indexes displayed together show December 1984
bullish divergence**

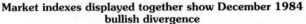

At other strategic turning points, the Dow Industrials may break below one of its important earlier price support zones and the *Investor's Business Daily* stock index, which represents the entire market, may hold above its previous lows established during the same period—thereby flashing a positive sign. These are refinements you need to recognize on a day-to-day basis.

Scanning this data once a week is not enough, because these signals occur on one specific day, and it's important to spot them when they happen. Do you think good piano players get that way by practicing only once a week?

Psychological Market Indicators Are Important

Items such as the percentage of investment advisory services that are bearish or bullish, odd-lot short sales as a percentage of total odd-lot sales (the higher the percentage of short selling by small investors, the more positive it should be for the stock market), and cash positions of mutual funds are some of the more important psychological measurement tools that can be viewed along with the several market averages.

Key Market Sector Graphs Let You Hone In

Nine different major market sector graphs appear daily at the bottom of the general market indicators' page. The economy is divided into broad economic sectors. You can rapidly monitor every significant sector such as high-tech, junior growth stocks, consumer companies, health care securities, and even a new issue index.

The percentage change in each index is quoted every day in a small market sector box so you can separate the best-performing sectors of the market from the below-par areas. The New York Stock Exchange composite, the Dow Jones Transportation, and the utilities index are also shown in this box each day.

Over-the-counter and American Stock Exchange indexes are graphically provided on the OTC and AMEX price table pages, along with a special OTC/AMEX market column devoted to reporting on this enticing world of emerging growth opportunities.

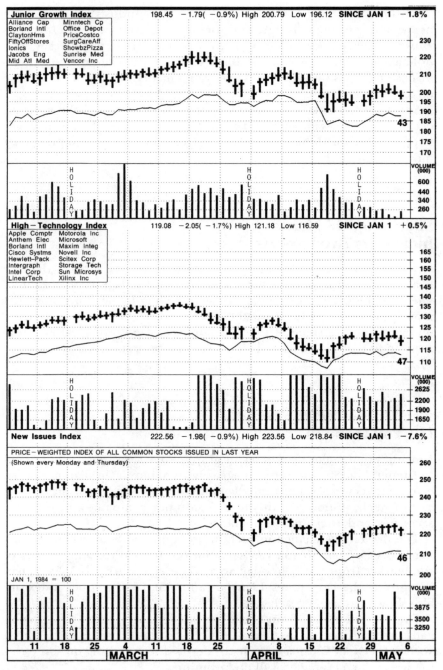

Key market sector graphs

During early 1994, using data in the market sector box, you could easily see that the high-tech sector was the leading market segment performancewise, with junior growth stocks next in strength, and the utility index seriously underperforming the market averages.

MARKET SECTOR INDEXES FOR 2/18/94

Sorted Monday, Wednesday & Friday by best % performance in last 3 months. List is sorted Tuesday & Thursday by best % gain year to date. Boldface sectors performed better than NYSE composite yesterday.

SINCE JAN 1	3 MONTH %CHANGE	(★ On Left, Top 4 Indexes Since Jan. 1) (★ On Right, Top 4 Indexes Yesterday)	INDEX	YESTERDAY'S CHANGE	%CHANGE
+ 8.27%★	+ 13.54%	**HIGH – TECH INDEX**	128.23	– 0.00	– 0.00%★
+ 4.12%★	+ 10.00%	**JUNIOR GROWTH INDEX**	210.52	– 0.85	– 0.40%
– 0.19%	+ 6.78%	**BANK INDEX**	251.09	– 0.69	– 0.27%
+ 2.69%★	+ 5.84%	**NEW ISSUES INDEX**	247.47	– 1.17	– 0.47%
+ 2.18%★	+ 5.40%	**VALUE LINE INDEX**	465.82	– 1.58	– 0.34%
+ 1.55%	+ 4.57%	**NASDAQ OTC COMPOSITE**	788.85	– 1.39	– 0.18%★
+ 1.30%	+ 4.55%	**U.S. DEFENSE INDEX**	126.96	– 1.17	– 0.91%
+ 1.88%	+ 3.60%	**DOW JONES TRANSPORTATION**	1795.42	– 3.09	– 0.17%★
+ 0.95%	+ 2.90%	**MEDICAL/HEALTHCARE**	742.16	– 5.85	– 0.78%
+ 0.30%	+ 1.43%	**N.Y.S.E COMPOSITE INDEX**	259.87	– 1.51	– 0.58%
– 0.96%	+ 1.28%	**N.Y.S.E FINANCE**	214.73	– 1.20	– 0.56%
+ 0.16%	+ 0.31%	**INSURANCE INDEX**	237.14	– 0.93	– 0.39%
– 3.97%	– 2.69%	**DEFENSIVE INDEX**	563.80	– 2.51	– 0.44%
– 7.21%	– 3.85%	GOLD INDEX	78.94	– 2.77	– 3.39%
– 2.92%	– 5.14%	SENIOR GROWTH INDEX	256.41	– 2.31	– 0.89%
– 2.95%	– 7.33%	**CONSUMER INDEX**	319.28	– 0.32	– 0.10%★
– 9.05%	– 7.38%	DOW JONES UTILITY	208.54	– 3.56	– 1.68%

Observe Prices of 197 Industry Groups Daily

Newspapers generally show stock tables containing the prices of individual stocks. But it is also possible to see the price changes every market day for 197 industries.

On Monday, an alphabetical listing of groups highlights the prior week's price performance of each industry. The top 10 industries are shown in boldface print.

Every Tuesday the industry indexes are listed in order of those that produced the best price performance since the beginning of the year. This unique table varies its format to give you several points of view on each industry's performance and ranking.

Investor's Business Daily Industry Prices

Lists changes in 197 price-based indices(Jan. 1, 1984 = 100) every day.   **Top 10 in performance yesterday are boldfaced.**
† indicates best performing industries year to date.   Worst 10 industries in performance are underlined.

% Chg. Since Jan. 1	Industry Name	No. of Stocks In Grp	EPS Rnk	Rel Str Rnk	Sales % Gro Rate	Group Index Close	% Chg.
	— A – B —						
+0.0	Advertising	16	33	43	-13	280.61	-0.2
+5.2	Aerospace/Defense	10	43	80	-1	200.79	+0.2
-1.8	Aerospace/Defense Eqp	46	27	66	0	139.05	-0.2
+0.2	Agricultural Operations	24	23	68	8	268.23	-0.3
+11.6†	Auto Mfrs-Foreign	9	2	92	1	333.58	+0.2
-0.6	Auto/Truck-Original Eqp	43	88	88	3	296.69	+0.7
-2.6	Auto/Truck-Replace Prts	18	85	73	6	184.06	-0.5
-4.3	**Automobile-Mfg.**	6	91	50	0	318.41	+1.2
-10.1	Banks-Foreign	30	62	20	-5	270.24	-0.5
+0.3	Banks-Midwest	105	81	34	4	518.49	+0.3
+0.3	Banks-Money Center	8	98	14	0	217.11	+0.8
+4.2	Banks-Northeast	185	78	71	-2	281.31	+0.4
+2.4	Banks-Southeast	107	88	68	-1	339.69	+0.3
+5.8	Banks-Southwest	14	75	19	-9	85.33	+0.1
+8.7†	Banks-Super Regional	20	97	37	5	283.47	+0.7
-0.2	Banks-West	73	51	44	2	303.30	+0.4
-0.6	Beverages-Alcoholic	11	78	42	-2	202.42	+0.6
-8.2	Beverages-Soft Drinks	15	31	15	-3	513.55	-0.5
+1.8	Bldg Prod-Wood	15	71	86	-6	297.27	+0.4
+8.2†	Bldg-A/C & Heating Prds	12	46	69	14	210.43	-0.8
+0.3	Bldg-Cement/Concrt/Ag	15	43	62	2	285.18	-0.5
-0.8	Bldg-Constr Prods/Misc	49	56	94	-2	294.20	-0.9
-0.4	Bldg-Hand Tools	10	71	54	4	278.25	-0.7
+5.8	Bldg-Heavy Const	20	27	75	8	157.96	+0.4
-0.6	Bldg-Maintenance & Svc	16	81	59	4	266.05	-0.1
-0.3	Bldg-Mobile/Mfg & Rv	29	91	97	7	151.03	-0.3
-1.6	Bldg-Paint & Allied Prds	15	92	38	5	334.72	-0.3
-17.3	Bldg-Resident/Commrcl	38	75	10	-2	131.11	-1.2
-0.1	Business Services-Misc	113	51	84	6	186.34	-0.3
	— C – D – E —						
+4.5	Chemicals-Basic	15	17	49	0	296.92	-0.2
+3.4	Chemicals-Plastics	24	41	69	20	277.40	-0.3
-0.8	Chemicals-Specialty	56	46	58	1	370.74	-0.3
+0.1	Computer-Graphics	20	41	71	16	87.71	-0.3
-6.2	Computer-Integrated Syst	37	37	31	25	80.70	-0.2
-7.4	Computer-Local Networks	43	66	88	32	2570.02	-0.5
-5.6	Computer-Mainframes	10	23	76	-6	75.82	+1.0
-3.0	Computer-Memory Devices	36	14	97	17	137.81	+0.5
-10.6	<u>Food-Dairy Products</u>	13	31	8	-4	349.60	+1.8
+5.8	Food-Flour & Grain	7	5	55	4	346.57	+0.3
-0.7	Food-Meat Products	18	62	61	5	400.42	-0.5
-2.7	Food-Misc Preparation	45	62	45	4	445.24	0.0
-11.8	Food-Sugar & Refining	2	1	2	4	186.79	+0.6
-8.5	Funeral Svcs & Rel	3	96	22	17	437.80	-0.2
-8.6	Furniture	26	75	57	3	237.33	+0.1
+4.7	Household-Appliances	15	62	99	-10	344.39	-0.5
+2.5	Household-Audio/Video	18	20	85	5	152.07	-0.9
-3.0	Household-Textiles Furns	12	96	86	2	656.83	-1.9
-8.2	Housewares	11	88	54	6	210.57	-1.2
+4.2	Instruments-Scientific	40	43	85	7	214.16	+0.8
-5.8	Insurance-Acc & Health	22	94	35	10	284.60	-0.5
-5.6	Insurance-Brokers	11	83	18	6	262.90	-0.3
-1.4	Insurance-Diversified	8	96	8	2	189.64	-0.1
-4.6	Insurance-Life	57	71	32	6	304.45	-0.2
-4.0	Insurance-Mult Line	13	81	16	13	176.69	+0.5
-8.6	Insurance-Prop/Cas/Titl	118	92	99	4	341.01	+0.1
-0.9	Lasers-Sys/Components	31	11	25	8	85.83	+0.8
-14.4	Leisure-Gaming	64	37	3	-2	431.01	+0.9
+3.0	Leisure-Hotels & Motels	20	33	81	0	226.46	0.0
-7.6	Leisure-Movies	52	41	76	3	187.43	-0.4
-7.6	Leisure-Photo Equip/Rel	15	12	17	-4	164.42	-0.8
+4.4	Leisure-Products	54	51	48	-1	364.90	-0.1
-2.9	Leisure-Services	26	31	61	11	290.13	+0.1
-13.8	Leisure-Toys/Games/Hobby	34	14	20	10	358.22	-0.1
-6.7	Linen Supply & Related	7	81	29	8	428.51	-0.2
+5.2	Machine-Tools & Rel Prod	16	9	79	8	128.06	0.0
+19.4†	Machinery-Const/Mining	11	56	95	1	179.65	-0.7
+9.3†	Machinery-Farm	9	78	55	3	243.97	-1.2
+2.9	Machinery-Gen Industrial	58	56	79	2	268.27	-0.2
-1.3	Machinery-Mtl Hdlg/Autmn	18	37	52	0	138.41	+0.5
+1.3	Machinery-Printing Trade	9	14	52	-2	144.64	+0.8
-7.8	Machinery-Thermal Proc	6	37	46	13	342.51	-0.3
+0.0	Media-Books	16	75	70	7	376.60	0.0
-22.4	Media-Cable Tv	31	5	5	9	773.24	-0.1
-16.6	Media-Newspapers	19	66	49	3	222.85	-0.4
-16.6	Media-Periodicals	13	27	9	7	286.25	-0.7
-2.0	Media-Radio/Tv	45	62	60	2	411.20	-0.2
-18.6	Medical-Biomed/Genetics	141	4	41	18	200.61	-0.4
-8.5	Medical-Drug/Diversified	9	51	13	7	303.88	-0.8
-2.8	OilKGas-U S Exploi&Prod	161	8	12	9	77.16	+1.3
-2.6	**OilKGas-U S Integrated**	12	11	4	-1	159.32	+2.8
-6.0	Paper & Paper Products	36	16	77	-8	286.93	-0.6
-3.1	Pollution Control-Equip	58	31	89	3	288.23	-0.5
-6.0	Pollution Control-Svcs	104	20	78	11	233.27	+0.4
+3.0	Precious-Gems & Stones	12	3	78	-49	106.81	+0.7
+0.6	Printing-Commercial	17	88	64	10	316.98	+0.5
-4.0	Protection-Sfty Eq & Svc	46	27	56	3	197.07	+0.5
	— R – S —						
-2.4	Real Estate Development	22	11	23	-3	88.31	-0.4
-4.3	Real Estate Operations	34	23	27	-6	95.87	+0.2
+2.8	Retail-Apparel/Shoe	59	27	84	8	323.19	0.0
-6.5	Retail-Consumer Elect	19	85	74	17	261.52	-0.5
-1.3	**Retail-Convenience Strs**	8	81	90	-3	99.35	+1.8
+1.4	Retail-Department Stores	19	56	50	8	417.72	-0.4
-4.7	Retail-Discount&Variety	34	20	33	8	216.20	+0.1
+4.3	Retail-Drug Stores	13	83	45	8	194.32	-0.2
-15.4	Retail-Home Furnishings	22	83	26	5	208.92	-1.2
+4.6	Retail-Mail Order&Direct	27	71	83	15	329.69	-0.9
+0.2	Retail-Major Chains	4	83	18	9	345.09	-1.0
-6.6	Retail-Misc/Diversified	77	23	53	3	236.59	0.0
-6.4	Retail-Restaurants	117	66	65	4	256.06	-0.6
-2.5	Retail-Supermarkets	35	31	39	4	485.00	+0.3
-1.7	Retail/Whlse Office Supl	4	99	30	35	472.73	-0.4
-7.2	Retail/Whlse Computers	30	75	53	18	146.05	-0.6
-6.2	Retail/Whlse-Auto Parts	25	66	46	3	234.56	-0.2
+7.7†	Retail/Whlse-Bldg Prods	31	62	98	12	358.40	+0.1
-3.4	Retail/Wholesale-Food	20	81	29	0	235.42	-0.6
-9.7	Retail/Wholesale-Jewelry	20	51	36	4	261.70	+0.1
-2.7	Rubber-Tires/Misc	10	51	21	-4	440.79	-0.8
-8.4	Schools	15	62	51	3	125.48	-0.6
-0.8	Shoes & Rel Apparel	31	27	73	10	323.94	+0.1
-6.5	Soap & Clng Preparatns	11	56	24	5	384.27	+0.6
+2.1	Steel-Producers	23	71	81	-12	143.28	+0.4
-5.6	Steel-Specialty Alloys	9	16	37	2	241.29	0.0
	— T – U – W —						
-8.3	Telecommunctns-Cellulr	37	17	10	30	1071.63	-0.2
-10.1	**Telecommunications-Equip**	117	46	36	3	119.25	+1.7
-7.9	Telecommunications-Svcs	59	33	22	6	477.94	-0.5

Review Companies in a Leading Industry

Each day beneath the industry price table, a price-and-volume graph is presented of a top industry in the market. Under that is a list of the companies within that particular industry group. Many people find this screen worthwhile, so they cut it out to save for future research reference. The typical *Investor's Business Daily* is kept 13 days.

The number of companies in a leading industry can be extensive since the newspaper has exclusive contractual access to a proprietary historical database covering more than 8000 securities. Each industry list is arranged in order of companies with the highest EPS rank and relative-strength rank. Generally the top 20% of this list represent the stocks with a superior past record within their particular industry.

Companies In A Leading Industry

The Medical-Hlth Maint Org group ranked in top 30 prior six months
15 stocks are shown by total of EPS Rank and Relative Price Strength
o after symbol means OTC; a means Amex; * Calculated annually

Rank	Stock	Trade Symbol	EPS Rnk	REL STR	Acc Dis	Recnt Price	% off High Price	PE Ratio	5yr PE Hi	lo	Shrs Outstd (mil)	Avg. DlyVol (100s)	Last Qtr EPS	Last Qtr. Sales	Net % Profit Margin*	Return on Equity*	% Debt*	Beta
1	Mid Atlantic Med Svc Inc	MAMS o	99	96	A	30.63	..	35	35	7	14.5	3796	+ 59	+ 6	3.7	41.3	16	+1.68
2	Oxford Health Plans Corp	OXHP o	99	96	A	66.00	..	84	84	23	15.1	3091	+ 79	+106	4.4	27.3	0	+0.34
3	Intergroup Healthcare	IGHC o	95	94	A	48.75	8	25	26	10	9.8	443	+ 30	+ 36	9.5	31.0	14	+0.29
4	First Amer Health Concpt	FAHC o	92	97	A	9.50	5	32	40	3	2.4	79	+125	+ 22	31.2	25.9	0	+0.98
5	Physician Corp Of Amer	PCAM o	91	98	A	29.50	..	28	28	8	37.5	3328	+ 86	+ 48	6.7	59.5	32	....
6	Wellcare Mgt Group Inc	WELL o	91	95		26.13	..	41	41	18	5.9	562	+150	+ 96	4.0	588.0	178	....
7	Takecare Inc	TKCR o	92	89	A	64.75	..	22	22	7	12.5	1289	+ 24	+ 23	7.0	23.0	19	+2.11
8	Foundation Health Corp	FH	98	82	A	37.13	17	14	25	6	28.5	1936	+166	+ 47	6.8	24.1	46	+2.46
9	Healthsource Inc	HS	94	85	B	60.13	..	34	34	6	14.8	365	+ 32	+ 53	13.3	15.4	0	+2.49
10	U S Healthcare Inc	USHC o	98	80	B	66.50	..	27	38	9	107.8	9935	+ 64	+ 20	15.1	47.0	0	+1.63
11	United Healthcare Corp	UNH	98	78	A	85.50	..	39	39	10	76.4	2845	+ 52	+ 45	12.3	23.5	0	+1.99
12	United Amer Healthcare	UAH	95	80	A	13.88	20	18	27	6	6.6	228	+ 29	+ 38	23.9	19.8	9	+1.34
13	Pacificare Health Sys B	PHSYB o	94	81	B	44.75	10	20	25	10	27.3	920	+ 30	+ 33	3.4	42.0	9	−1.19
14	Sierra Health Svcs Inc	SIE a	80	93	A	26.75	4	20	21	4	12.4	603	+ 19	+ 10	8.3	42.7	18	+1.77
15	Ramsay Hmo Inc	RMO	92	80	A	42.13	1	24	27	4	7.4	284	+ 30	+ 33	7.1	15.4	4	+1.64

The Economy Page
Heads Up Second Section

The entire front page of the second section is devoted to coverage of the U.S. and the world economy. Breaking news, as well as a regular economics column entitled "Perspective," is provided daily.

Key Futures Graphs for
Traders and for Economic
Perspective

Twenty-four important futures are selected to present each day in graphic form. This is helpful not only to commodity traders but to corporate officials and students of the economy, because, for instance, the price of crude oil may influence inflation rates, as well as the price of airline stocks; lumber prices give a hint of the building industry's health. Today's savvy business people are interested in currency futures as well as in corn, cattle, and coffee prices. Spot (cash) and future price tables are also furnished for a wide variety of commodities. A special daily futures column is provided and all charts show stochastic price momentum lines.

Futures charts with stochastic lines

Check Up Versus Down
Corporate
Earnings Reports Daily

When corporations announce their quarterly earnings results, the reports are separated into those which increased earnings and those where earnings decreased. Additionally, the quarter's percentage change in earnings is shown. You may be interested in the company's stock, so the stock symbol, closing price, EPS and Relative Strength rank, plus industry group is provided. A list of Best Ups and Worst Downs is also provided.

Company Earnings News

Investor's Daily earnings reports are separated into those that are up and those that are down. This lets you see who's producing results and who isn't. The % change for the latest quarter is boldfaced and the stock symbol is shown. The ★ symbol signifies the change for the latest quarter is greater than or equal to 20%. The individual stock price, relative strength, and EPS rank reflect the closing values from yesterday's paper.

18 Ups
Median Change +61%

AGENCY RENT A CAR — AGNC 13%
Leasing Companies — Eps 52 Rel 50
Quar Apr 30: 1990 — 1989
Sales $66,486,000 — $61,331,000
Net Income 3,301,000 — 2,676,000
Share earns: — (OTC)
  Net Income 0.13 — 0.10
  % Change +30% ★

AMERICAN CLAIMS EVALUATN AMCE 9%
Financial/Business Svcs — Eps 93 Rel 96
Quar Mar 31: 1990 — 1989
Sales $1,345,014 — $786,982
Net Income 159,699 — 69,103
Share earns: — (OTC)
  Net Income 0.17 — 0.08
  % Change +113% ★
12 months:
Sales 4,363,835 — 2,687,118
Net Income 520,517 — 156,330
Share earns:
  Net Income 0.55 — 0.17
  % Change +224%

BRITISH GAS PLC ADR — BRG 36%
Oil&Gas-Intl Specialty — Eps 74 Rel 78
12 mo Mar 31:
  e1990 — e1989
Sales 7,983,000,000 — 7,526,000,000
Net Income 926,000,000 — 899,000,000

SOFTWARE TOOLWORKS INC TWRX 22%
Computer-Software — Eps 99 Rel 99
Quar Mar 31:
  es1990 — es1989
Sales $21,946,000 — $12,322,000
Income k1,670,000 — 740,000
Extrd gain b677,000 — ....
Net Income 2,347,000 — 740,000
Avg shares 20,274,000 — 16,014,000
Share earns: — (OTC)
  Income 0.08 — 0.05
  % Change +60% ★
  Net Income 0.12 — 0.05
12 months:
Sales 68,689,000 — 34,978,000
Income k1,914,000 — d–4,269,000
Extrd gain b677,000 — ....
Net Income 2,591,000 • d–4,269,000
Avg shares 18,293,000 — 14,822,000
Share earns:
  Income 0.10 — d–0.29
  Net Income 0.14 — d–0.29
b–Tax loss carryforward. d–Loss. e–Restated to include the effects of merger with Mindscape Inc accounted for as a pooling of interests. s–Share data adjusted to reflect a 100% stock dividend in April 1990. k–Includes $1.2 mil charges in connection with the merger.

MERRY GO ROUND ENT INC — MGR 26½
Retail-Apparel/Shoe — Eps 96 Rel 98
Quar May 05: s1990 — s1989
Sales $120,967,000 — $73,919,000
Net Income 6,615,000 — 1,666,000
Avg shares 22,310,700 — 20,918,400
Share earns: — (NYSE)

16 Downs
Median Change −25%

ACXIOM CORP — ACXM 21½
Computer-Services — Eps 98 Rel 77
Quar Mar 31: 1990 — 1989
Sales $25,175,000 — $20,303,000
Net Income 960,000 — 991,000
Share earns: — (OTC)
  Net Income 0.20 — 0.21
  % Change −5%
12 months:
Sales 89,734,000 — 74,278,000
Net Income 5,664,000 — 4,241,000
Share earns:
  Net Income 1.16 — 0.90
  % Change +29%

FLEETWOOD ENTERPRISES — FLE 28½
Bldg-Mobile/Mfg & Rv — Eps 40 Rel 76
Quar Apr 29: 1990 — e1989
Sales $431,586,000 — $425,490,000
Net Income 17,129,000 — 17,697,000
Avg shares 22,455,000 — 23,192,000
Share earns: — (NYSE)
  Net Income 0.76 — 0.77
  % Change −1%
12 months:
Sales 1,549,424,000 — 1,618,523,000
Net Income 55,039,000 — 70,468,000
Avg shares 22,755,000 — 23,050,000

Latest up-and-down corporate earnings reports

Smart Mutual Fund Price Tables that Tell Past Performance

Many prudent investors buy mutual funds. These unique tables may help you make sounder evaluations, because they show each fund's year-to-date total return plus the prior three years ranking of total results. *Investor's Business Daily* was the first newspaper to show performance data in its mutual fund tables. Six different graphs are also shown each day of outstanding funds and their most recent publicly available stock buys. The 10% which gained the most for the day are boldfaced in the tables.

Mutual Fund	'87-'90 Performance Rank	'90 % Wooks Chg	Last 4 Asset %Chg	Net Asset Value	Offer Price	NAV Chg

Mutual Funds
Wednesday, May 16, 1990
Investor's Daily tables show each fund's year-to-date and last 4 weeks % change in net asset value.

Top 2% in % performance yesterday in boldface

— A —

AAL Mutual: Assets 232 million
CapitalGrwth p	+ 1 + 3	11.35	11.92 –	.02
Income p	– 3 + 1	9.40	9.87 –	.01
MuniBond p	– 1 0	9.84	10.33 –	.01

AARP Investment: Assets 3.7 billion
CapitalGrwth	94 – 7 + 1	28.60	NL –	.02
GNMATreas	7 – 2 + 1	14.88	NL –	.01
GrwthIncome	43 – 5 + 1	24.09	NL –	.01
HighQuality	64 – 3 + 1	14.72	NL –	.01
TxFrGenlBnd	54 – 2 + 1	16.44	NL +	.01
TxFrShtTerm	25 – 1 0	15.13	NL +	.01

ABT Funds: Assets 270 million
EmergGrwth p	15 + 2 + 8	9.10	9.55 +	.02
GrwthIncome p	45 0 + 1	9.62	10.10 +	.01
SecIncome p	33 – 9 + 1	9.80	10.29 –	.01
UtilIncome p	86 – 5 + 3	12.85	13.49 –	.01

AHABalanced .... + 2 10.73 NL .....
| AddisonCap p | – 1 + 4 | 17.96 | 18.52 + | .01 |
Adtek 4 – 1 + 3 9.54 9.54 + .01
| AFA AvTech | 89 + 2 + 4 | 11.91 | 12.50 | ..... |
| AFATeleTech | 89 + 3 + 7 | 17.52 | 18.39 + | .12 |

AIM Funds: Assets 1.0 billion
Charter p	84 + 3 + 4	6.70	7.09	.....
Constellation p	89 + 10 + 5	8.88	9.40 +	.01
ConvertYld p	20 + 2 + 3	10.41	10.93 +	.03
HighYield p	11 – 9 + 1	6.28	6.59 +	.02
LimitedMat p	– 1 0	9.74	9.91	.....
Summit	55 + 3 + 5	7.99	–	.02
Weingarten p	86 + 5 + 5	12.38	13.10	.....

A M A Family: Assets 242 million
| ClassicGrwth p | 22 – 3 + 1 | 8.85 | NL – | .02 |

— F —

| FBLGrwthStk t | + 2 + 1 | 10.93 | 10.93 + | .01 |
FPA Funds: Assets 370 million
Capital	88 + 5 + 2	13.61	14.56 +	.02
NewIncome	78 – 4 + 1	9.47	9.92 –	.01
Paramount	96 – 3 + 1	12.57	13.44 +	.04
Perennial	60 – 2 + 3	20.39	21.81 +	.01
Fairmont – 9 0 14.63 NL – .10
Federated Funds: Assets 6.8 billion
CorpCash	4 – 7 – 1	7.76	NL +	.03
Exchange	32 + 3 + 3	56.05	NL –	.06
Bond	8 – 3 + 1	8.95	NL –	.01
InterGovt	63 – 2 + 1	9.52	NL	.....
FloatRate	50 – 2 0	9.18	NL	.....
GNMA	75 – 3 + 1	10.85	NL –	.01
Growth	84 + 1 + 4	20.15	NL +	.01
HighYield	31 – 9 – 1	7.84	NL	.....
Income	74 – 1 0	10.13	NL	.....
InterMuni	27 – 2 0	9.83	NL –	.01
Shortinter	11 0 0	10.12	NL	.....
ShrtIntGovt	46 – 1 0	9.91	NL –	.01
StockBond	57 0 + 2	15.13	NL –	.02

Equity	48 + 3 + 3	7.22	7.52	.....
FederalTxFr	49 – 2 + 1	11.26	11.73	.....
FLTaxFree	– 2 0	10.64	11.08	.....
GlobalOppInc	– 5 – 1	9.25	9.64 +	.01
Gold	97 – 9 – 1	13.52	14.08 +	.06
Growth	86 + 5 + 4	24.00	25.00 –	.02
HighYldTxFr	78 – 2 0	10.44	10.88	.....
Income	68 – 6 – 2	1.93	2.01	.....
InsuredTxFr	50 – 2 + 1	11.18	11.65	.....
MAInsrdTxFr	42 – 2 0	10.63	11.07 +	.01
MIInsrdTxFr	48 – 1 + 1	11.01	11.47 +	.01
MNInsrdTxFr	48 – 1 + 1	11.36	11.83	.....
MOTaxFree	.... + 1	10.60	11.04	.....
NJTaxFree	– 2 0	10.59	11.03	.....
NYTaxFree	52 – 2 0	10.81	11.26	.....
OHInsrdTxFr	49 – 1 + 1	11.13	11.59	.....
ORTaxFree	– 2 0	10.50	10.94	.....
PATaxFree	– 2 0	9.56	9.96	.....
Option	75 0 + 3	5.05	5.27	.....
PRTaxFree	52 – 1 0	10.70	11.15 +	.01
ShtIntGvtSec	– 1 0	10.08	10.23	.....
SpecialEqty	.... + 2	11.76	12.25 –	.01
TaxAdvGovt	– 2 + 1	9.97	10.39 –	.01

Smart mutual fund price tables

Last, a growth-fund index is graphically presented together with 50- and 200-day moving average price lines. The index can be used as another general market indicator, since it is made up of the combined performance of twenty growth funds, or a tool for those who use moving average lines to trade no-load funds on a timing basis.

Performance of World Stock Markets Are Charted

Of course for some people, investing is a global affair, so daily world-markets graphs portray how stock markets in 12 other countries are doing. Prices of selected foreign stocks are also listed.

New Issues, Corporate Offerings, and New Listings

Pending new corporate underwriting and other financing are listed showing you the dollar amount, indicated price, type of security offered, business description of each company, and the underwriting firm's name.

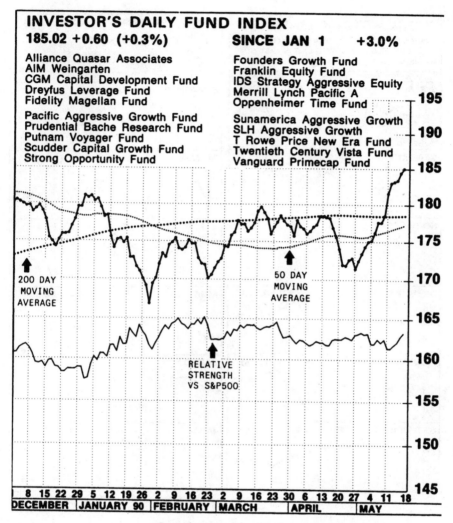

INVESTOR'S DAILY FUND INDEX

185.02 +0.60 (+0.3%)   SINCE JAN 1   +3.0%

Alliance Quasar Associates
AIM Weingarten
CGM Capital Development Fund
Dreyfus Leverage Fund
Fidelity Magellan Fund

Pacific Aggressive Growth Fund
Prudential Bache Research Fund
Putnam Voyager Fund
Scudder Capital Growth Fund
Strong Opportunity Fund

Founders Growth Fund
Franklin Equity Fund
IDS Strategy Aggressive Equity
Merrill Lynch Pacific A
Oppenheimer Time Fund

Sunamerica Aggressive Growth
SLH Aggressive Growth
T Rowe Price New Era Fund
Twentieth Century Vista Fund
Vanguard Primecap Fund

200 DAY MOVING AVERAGE

50 DAY MOVING AVERAGE

RELATIVE STRENGTH VS S&P500

8 15 22 29 5 12 19 26 2 9 16 23 2 9 16 23 30 6 13 20 27 4 11 18
DECEMBER | JANUARY 90 | FEBRUARY | MARCH | APRIL | MAY

Growth mutual fund index

Yield-Curve Graphic Display
Plus Selected Interest Rates

Interest rates are important to everyone. The Fed Funds rate, FRB Discount rate, rate of three-month Treasury Bills, the prime rate, rates of 30-year Treasury Bonds and tax-exempt bonds, rate of Moody's AA utilities, and 90 CDs' interest rates are graphed every day. A yield curve

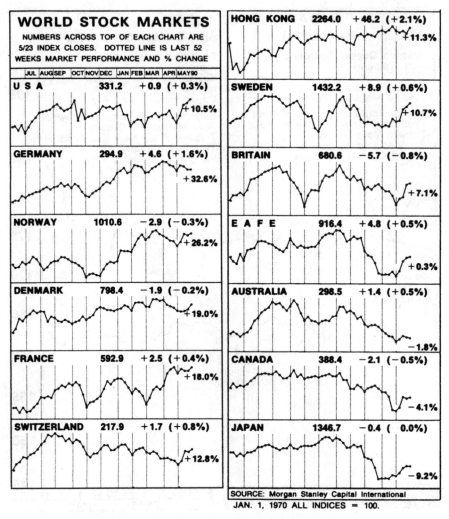

World stock market charts

of U.S. Treasury issues is also available daily. These important rates should help you better plan your business financing, personal financing, and investing.

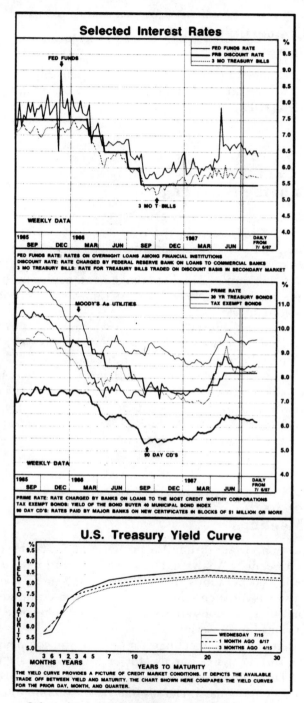

**Selected interest rates charts and U.S. Treasury
yield curve**

Separate Convertible Bond
Tables with Key Data

Convertibles are shown in their own table with valuable data such as
S&P ratings, yield to maturity, volume, conversion price, and premium
or discount calculated and provided in order to save you time.

New Ideas from the
Companies in the News Page

Some of America's most dynamic, growing companies are spotlighted
every day on the "Companies in the News" section near the back of
Section II. (See page 203.) The companies surveyed on this page come
from an industry which has outperformed at least 75% of all others during the previous six months. The high-ranked companies in that industry are profiled, by an experienced business reporter who reviews each
firm in an 800-word article.

Along with in-depth editorial coverage, there are also three graphs
probing the stock-price movements of the company for one, five, and
fifteen years. These daily, weekly, and monthly basis graphs are packed
with so much significant fundamental data that with them you hopefully
have a way to make better-informed financial decisions. Incidentally,
Investor's Business Daily featured Cisco Systems 12 times from
December, 1990 to August, 1992 while it was a young, new company,
before it was covered in another national newspaper.

Be a Visitor to the New York
Analysts' Meetings

One of the most important forums for professional investors is the New
York Society of Security Analysts. The presidents and chief executive
officers of leading corporations appear before the New York analysts to
discuss the prospects for their companies and to answer questions from
analysts. In fact, these sessions are so well regarded that some investors
pay important sums for transcripts of what transpires.

Reporters attend analysts' meetings not only for the company appearing at the New York analysts', but also for important analysts' meetings
in other cities. Those on-the-spot stories, along with graphs of the companies, are presented regularly. Here is one great example you missed if

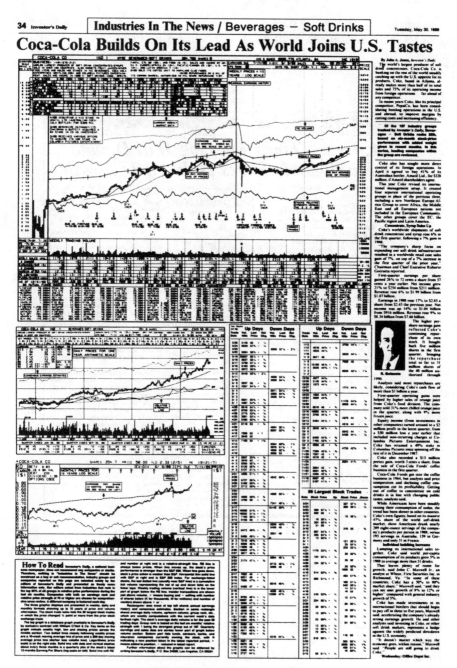

Industries in the News section

you weren't reading the paper on February 11, 1988. L. A. Gear jumped from $14 to an equivalent of $175 before it topped out.

L.A. Gear Thinks Backlog Will Double As Fashionable Shoes Help Fuel Growth

By Pamela Russell, *Investor's Daily*

NEW YORK — Poised with a hot style, show-biz advertising, and solid grounding in the import-clothing business, L.A. Gear Inc. chairman and president Robert Y. Greenberg said yesterday he expects order-backlog for his company's fashion-focused athletic footwear to double to $100 million by the end of June, from $50 million as of Nov. 30.

Greenberg said he based his forecast on the success of the company's booth at a New York tradeshow last weekend. The display featured a model of the city of Los Angeles, outfitted with 18 order stations.

Commenting that all 18 stations buzzed continually, Greenberg admitted, "I have no idea how much business we did at the show. I know we turned away at least 100 customers, said we see them at stores."

Noting one analyst's wide-ranging earnings estimate for fiscal 1988 of $1.85 to $2.35 a share, chief financial officer Elliot J. Horowitz said, "we think those numbers are very achievable." It earned $1.08 a share in the fiscal 12 months ended Nov. 30.

Sales to support those earnings will range from two to three times the $70 million volume of fiscal 1988, Greenberg said.

Earnings for the fiscal fourth quarter ended Nov. 30, 1987, soared 400% to $1.22 million, or 30 cents a share, from $244,000, or 6 cents, a year earlier. Sales climbed 175% to $22.55 million.

The full-year increase to $1.08 a share represented a 93% increase from

56 cents a year earlier. Net income advanced 150% to $4.37 million from $1.75 million, while sales rose 94% to $70.58 million from $36.3 million.

Supporting this growth are more than 100 shoe designs.

Sixty percent of sales are in women's shoes, with teenage women the focus. But, Greenberg observed, in shoe fashion, people of many ages think of themselves as teenagers. Thus, while the bulk of television and billboard promotions are leveled at young women, L.A. Gear devises a family of products, with men, boys, girls and infants together producing 40% of sales.

L.A. Gear gets all its product from factories in Korea and Taiwan. Greenberg estimated the Taiwan dollar and Korean won will continue to rise against the U.S. dollar. But he insisted his company will pass on necessary price increases, rather than cut margins to get market share.

One price-increase took effect in October; a second is scheduled for March. By this September, identical shoe models will sell for 20% more wholesale than they did in September 1987, he projected.

Sales and administrative expenses, including commissions of about 7% of gross sales, and advertising budgeted at 6% of sales, will remain level as a percent of sales as the company grows, according to Horowitz. The after-tax profit margin should approximate 6.5% to 7% for 1988, but "we'd like to get it to 8.5%," Horowitz added.

Foreign distributors are expected to double in number from 15 to 30 during fiscal 1988, Greenberg said. Distributors sign a contract committing themselves to an increasing level of orders for each year of the three years, and receive from L.A. Gear what is essentially a "turnkey business," Greenberg said, including company-produced advertising.

Distributors who fail to reach minimum order commitments may not have their contracts renewed, Greenberg added.

After shoes come jeans, Greenberg said. For the back-to-school season of 1988, or at the latest, the 1988 holiday season, L.A. Gear will ready a small women's jeans line. Greenberg hopes to generate $10 million in sales in the first twelve months. Though jeans advertising at first will be minimal, he said, "we'll just add jeans above the shoes in the ads."

L.A. Gear stock, which has been strong in recent sessions, added another ⅓ to 14½ yesterday on the Over-The-Counter market.

Friday: Cray Research Inc.

Coverage of a 1988 New York analysts' meetings

National Economic Analysis

Regular editorials may also have some impact, and with the one on the following page, we received a short, to-the-point letter from Don Regan, then Chief of Staff to the President. The letter said, "...rest assured this will get to all the right places and something will be done about it." The next month Paul Volker, then Federal Reserve Board Chairman, in a speech in Canada, mentioned that money supply was only one of a number of causes of inflation, and the following February the Fed began the first of four consecutive discount rate cuts during the subsequent six months.

Editorial

The Fed Fiddles As Rome Burns

By William O'Neil
Chairman of Investor's Daily

Should the Federal Reserve Board determine America's future economic growth? No! Their job should be to manage the nation's finances. One of the reasons we elect a president is to create a sound growth rate. If he fails, he is replaced.

How is the Fed doing? Not very well in the last 18 months. The Fed says the economy will be much better in 1985's second half. But they have been blinded by a narrow cure-all called M1. The Fed bought lock, stock and barrel Milton Friedman's overboard and unproven claim that money supply is the *one and only* important cause of inflation (a 1,000% increase in the price of oil from 1973 to 1981 was dismissed as just an irrelevant, temporary abberation.) So every time money supply lurches up, most Fed members, the Wall Street Journal and well-intentioned economists from academia shout: "We can't ease up now because M1 is up."

Martin Feldstein was replaced by Beryl Sprinkel and we've gone from the frying pan into the fire. Mr. Sprinkel warns money must be reined in or we're in for trouble.

Suppose M1 keeps moving up and the economy weakens. Would Mr. Sprinkel advise tighter money as our economy struggles for life? Why don't we abandon the council of economic ill-advisers and replace the Fed's out-of-tune (or touch) fiddling so we can go back to using common sense. Let's pay attention to the American economy and the level of interest rates.

Why And Where The Fed Is Off

The Fed should listen to what the market-

place is saying. The discount rate was raised *only once* this cycle, in April 1984, and it killed the growth of our auto, steel and computer industries. Later, the Fed cut the discount rate three times and the economy responded weakly. What does this tell us? Interest rates have been and are still too high! The discount rate needs to be lowered further.

Today's predicament is not like past cycles. It is harder to resurrect an economy in a late phase (34th month of recovery), when momentum has been slashed, than one in the trough of a recession. We have been in a deflationary period, interest rates are in an overall downtrend and real rates are substantially out of line with the current inflation rate of barely 3%.

The Fed seems bewildered. First they broadened M1 targets and now they are trying to figure out why money supply is up so much. The Fed theoretically controls money supply, yet they don't totally understand it; they can't reliably measure it and don't know for sure why it goes up and down. That's dangerous.

The Fed and Mr. Sprinkel should recognize that when investors get concerned they sell stocks and some of the money winds up in interest-bearing NOW accounts. Also, investors and business people reduce spending when they become uncertain or apprehensive and this could cause some checking accounts to increase.

Money Is Only One Inflation Cause

Our government rigidly believes money supply is the sole cause of inflation. Let me cite six additional inflation causes:

1. Wars and their aftermath (which create

serious shortages.)

2. Shortages of important commodities, products and services.

3. Shortages of labor (low unemployment). Labor is the largest cost item for many corporations.

4. Factories operating at a high percentage of capacity (shortage of productive capacity.)

5. Lack of competition (means higher prices.)

6. Tax and government policies (unrelated to money supply) that create unusual demand, i.e. full deductibility of interest expense on real estate and other key items; and Medicare, which initially gave the medical profession a blank check for the nation's health care and sharply increased demand for medical services.

Friedman states that, to his knowledge, "there is no example in history of a rapid increase in the quantity of money that was not accompanied by a roughly correspondingly substantial inflation." There is now: the rapid explosion of money supply in 1982 and 1983 resulted in a *decrease* in inflation for 1984 and 1985. The deflation was primarily caused by a positive contribution from most of the six items on the above list. It's time for the Fed to end its love affair with faulty money supply theories and consider lowering the discount rate to more normal levels that will encourage sound growth.

Reprinted by permission of Investor's Daily, September 25, 1985. Copyright Investor's Daily Inc., 1985

September 1985 editorial on Fed policy

Investor's Business Daily penned more than sixty editorials on the serious defects and errors in our government's 1993 proposed total reform of the American Healthcare system. These editorials were bound into a booklet that was purchased by hundreds of business, political, and media leaders. One daily reader, Jack Kemp, said *Investor's Business Daily* carried the most informative coverage on this critical national issue. Editorials appear daily on page 2.

How to Utilize the News
Pages in a Bear Market

Below is a list of ideas that should be helpful in a declining market:

1. Are more corporate earnings reports coming in below estimates?

2. Use the new low list in conjunction with the stock tables to show a stock's % change in volume when it makes a new price low.

3. Check the 90 minigraphs of "Stocks in the News" on the NYSE, AMEX, and OTC market. There will be fewer stocks making new highs and more showing huge increases in volume. Those closing down in price might be selling situations in a bear market, especially if they are not extended too far below price-basing patterns.

4. Notice if there is a shift to defensive securities such as Foods, Supermarkets, Gold, Tobacco, or Utilities. See if many defensive group graphs show up in Friday's newspaper at the bottom of the general market indicators page.

5. What are the weakest industry groups and the former leading groups?

6. Are more stocks consistently underlined in the price tables than are boldfaced?

7. Monitor quarterly earnings reports daily to spot poor reports in stock positions that may need to be sold.

8. Check price tables for companies with relative strength breaking below 70 and Volume % Change up when price is down.

9. Study the daily market averages on the general market indicators page to determine bad market conditions as well as the eventual beginning of the next bull market. Observe the Mutual Fund Index and performance of foreign market averages for further clues. Is the Fund Index persistently below its 200-day moving average line?

10. Watch for special news items daily on companies, industries, or the economy. And be sure to check the NASDAQ chart.

11. Track weakening stocks that perhaps should be sold.

12. Which sector indexes are the weakest?

13. Save and study the New America page to get ready for the next bull market.

17

The Art of Tape Reading:
Analyzing and Reacting to News

Tape reading is like seeing the Super Bowl football game live from the 50-yard line rather than reading about it in the paper the next day. You see all the grand action, you feel the electricity in the air, and you experience the overpowering emotion and excitement.

A tape reader is an investor or speculator who spends time watching both individual stock transactions as they are reported on the stock exchange ticker tapes and absorbing news as it flows over the news wires.

A good tape examiner acquires a feel for the market and can tell you whether stocks are behaving normally or not. Naturally, the number of good tape readers is like the number of football players who are good enough to play in a Super Bowl game.

Tape readers come in all sizes and shapes; many are "board room sitters" gazing at the electronic tape in their local broker's office. Very few of them do well, but you often hear them brag about their favorite stocks or opinions. In time you'll hear one say, "There goes Motors," as they see a stream of trading volume in General Motors stock.

Most stockbrokers peek at the tape, but once again only the minority really have a knack for it. In some cities, the tape is broadcast on daytime TV with a 15-minute delay for home viewers. I think the stock exchange may be wrong in placing the 15-minute-delay restriction upon public home-TV viewing. It could contribute to more nationwide public interest in the stock market and more reliable information if the exchange would reconsider and change its position. How would you like to see the scintillating Super Bowl on TV with a 15-minute delay? TV *real time,* over-the-counter trading should also be reported by ticker tape.

Institutional traders and some professional money managers also study the tape. Jack Dreyfus was such an avid tape reader that he had tapes put in every office in his accounting department. If he happened to leave his desk to go into the accounting area, he didn't want to risk missing any important trades.

Jesse Livermore and Gerald Loeb of E. F. Hutton always watched the tape. And of course, specialists on the floor of the New York Stock Exchange have tapes all throughout the Main Room, the Blue Room, and the Garage, as the different trading areas are called.

All transactions are supposed to be flashed on the ticker tape about three minutes after the trade actually occurs on the floor of the stock exchange. Sometimes, however, the volume of trading is so heavy even the high-speed tickers can't keep up with the activity, and the tape falls behind. This is called a late tape and it might be a more questionable time to buy or sell because it is sometimes harder to know what the actual prices are on the floor at the time you enter your orders.

Separating Leaders from Laggards, via the Tape

Competent, experienced tape readers can weed out the stock leaders from the feeble, laggard stocks in the market. How is this done?

After declining for several weeks, a market will finally turn and start to rebound. The observant tape reader will notice which stocks are the first ones to begin the rally.

The good tape student will also see which stock is drawing the largest quantity of buying, in terms of the size and volume of transactions. He or she will notice which equities move up with the greatest ease. If very good, the tape reader will probably be able to spot the true leader in the market.

Other stocks that are the last to respond in a rally, or stocks that only trade light volume, are more sluggish and are the laggard movers to avoid.

During short-term declines in a bull market, the tape reader may watch for stocks that for some reason persistently resist selling off along with the rest of the market.

The tape analyst looks for a sudden pickup in volume and activity in a stock previously quiet and inactive. They always look for the unusual activity.

The best tape readers are concerned more with volume in a stock than with just watching the price. Several 20,000-share trades in a company's stock are much more significant than a hodgepodge of 200- and 300-share trades.

It Isn't Your Aunt Sue Buying

For one thing, a 20,000-share trade in a $50 stock on a ⅜-point uptick from the prior trade represents a transaction involving $1 million (20,000 × $50). The assumption is that some buyer is willing to pay up three-eighths of a point to buy the stock. Because of the size you can also be pretty certain it isn't your Aunt Sue down the street buying, but probably a more informed buyer.

Before you decide you've discovered an easy way to make money solely by shadowing the ticker tape, let me assure you again the obvious hardly ever works in the stock market. Experienced professionals know investors are influenced by big trades appearing on upticks, so don't get too carried away with what could be a well-advertised tape trap.

The real problem with tape analysis is the tape reflects all trading, good and bad. Not all of the action you see on the tape is good, sound, correct buying. Professionals who deal in big blocks buy a large number of mediocre or poor stocks, or good stocks at the wrong time. So, it becomes a question of sifting the white elephants from the smart buying. Market manipulation by program traders also distorts prices.

Tape Reading Is Too Exciting and Emotional

Another problem with tape watching is it is positively too exciting and emotional. It requires constant discipline to avoid being swept along with the rampant fever when a stock keeps advancing until you're convinced it's going to go "straight through the roof."

When you get this feeling in the pit of your stomach, the stock is probably topping, since it will also look fantastic to everyone else. When it is that obvious, almost everyone has bought that can buy. Remember, the majority, or crowd, opinion is rarely right in the stock market.

If you sit by the ticker tape too much, you just get too close to the forest to see the trees. And above all, the most important things a winner must have in the stock market are perspective, discipline, and self-control.

Is the Stock in a Base or Is It Extended?

There is an easy, effective way to periodically read the tape and exercise strong discipline. Whenever you see tape activity that impresses you, refer to the stock's chart to see if the stock is in a base-building period or if it is extended from a base. If it is extended in price, leave it alone; it's too late. Chasing stocks, like crime, doesn't pay.

If the stock is in a base (sideways price-consolidation area), then check and apply the C-A-N S-L-I-M formula. Are current earnings up a meaningful amount? Is the five-year earnings record good?

More than half the stocks that look inviting on the tape will fail to pass the C-A-N S-L-I-M test and will prove to be deficient, mediocre investments. However, sooner or later convincing tape action will point you to a golden opportunity that passes all your criteria and could become a star performer.

Scan Chart Books Weekly and List Buy Prices

Another way to use the tape productively is to review a comprehensive graph book every week and make a list of stocks that meet your technical plus fundamental selection criteria.

Then jot down the pivot price where you would consider buying. Also write down the average daily volume for each stock on your prospect list.

Keep this shopping list with you every day for the next couple of weeks when you are watching the ticker tape or the market. In time, one or two of the stocks on your prospect list will begin prancing all over the tape and will approach your buy point. This is the time to get ready to make a possible buy decision—if the stock trades at your buy price and you conclude the day's volume will be up at least 50% above average. Generally, the more demand for a stock at the buy point, the better.

Look for a Shift in Quality Around the Top

After a short-term rally, or near a market top, a tape reader can frequently discern a shift in the quality of the tape. The top-notch leading stocks no longer lead the market up. Lower quality laggards and cheaper stocks now move to the front line of battle. This is a warning sign that all is not right in the market, and a sharp correction might be just around the next corner.

Watch Out When Defensive Stocks Begin to Appear

After an extended rally in the market, a tape reader may notice more defensive stocks (food and utility stocks) cropping up on the tape. This is an indication professional money is becoming apprehensive. In this case, you should be cautious in continuing to buy.

There are other little symptoms and market habits the tape observer will recognize. Some stocks have delayed openings and other stocks will stop trading during the day. At certain times activity will become so heavy that, to save time, digits are deleted from the ticker tape, with numbers left off certain prices and volumes.

At other periods stocks may rally in rapid fashion, which creates the impression of greater short coverings than normal. Periodically, the pace of the market may become very slow. In these lulls, the ticker is known as a "quiet or dull tape." Some traders say "don't sell a dull market."

Previously, the sound of the mechanical tape or the old paper tape moving alerted the tape reader to a pickup or slowdown in the pace of overall market activity. Now we have modern electronic tapes, which move without a whisper.

Still other markets may, to the trained tape reviewer's eye and ear, reflect a slow, steady pace of quiet, subtle accumulation. Sometimes on the day before a long holiday weekend, those on the job are quietly and steadily buying up stocks, while other less active souls are gone for the weekend and miss what's transpiring.

Tape readers expect the pace of activity to slow down around lunch time in New York (12:00 p.m. to 1:00 p.m., New York time, or 9:00 a.m. to 10:00 a.m., Los Angeles time). They also know the market frequently shows its true colors in the last hour of the day, either coming on and closing strong, or suddenly weakening and failing to hold gains established early in the day.

The careful eye can also spot a stock "churning" on the ticker tape. This happens when a great deal of trading volume occurs but poor price progress results.

In 1961, years before Bunker Hunt got involved in his silver fiasco, he phoned me one day and said he had just come from lunch at a downtown Dallas hotel. The rumor, he said, was that Clint Murchison was going to buy control of a particular company that sold at about $16 on the New York Stock Exchange.

He suggested buying the stock, and as he was talking, I watched the stock trade in unbelievable reams on the ticker tape. However, most of the prices were unchanged and the price was not making any real progress overall. I told Bunker to wait a few days. Something didn't make sense to me, because if these rumors were true, why was the stock churning on such immense activity and not making much headway?

Two days later, the news filtered out that Murchison had acquired control of a block of stock outside the marketplace and had been selling short in the market the day Bunker Hunt telephoned. The stock sold off on this surprising news. Now you have a firsthand example of why tips and rumors are dangerous and can get you into trouble.

Don't Buy on Tips and Rumors

I never buy stocks on tips, rumors, or inside information. It simply is an extremely unsound investment practice. Of course, tips, rumors, or inside information seem to be what most people are looking for. But, again, what most people believe and do in the market doesn't work; so beware!

Certain advisory services and some daily business newspapers carry regular columns fed by Street gossip, rumors, tips, and planted personal opinions or inside information. This, in my opinion, is not the most professional approach, nor is it too sophisticated. There are far sounder and safer methods of investing in the stock market.

Bernard Baruch emphasized the importance of separating the facts of a situation from tips, inside "dope," or wishful thinking. One of his rules was to beware of barbers, beauticians, waiters—of anyone bringing gifts of "inside" information or "tips."

Big Block Trades Represent Institutions

In today's institutionally dominated markets, large numbers of big blocks of stock trade every day. Many of these blocks of 10,000 to 500,000 shares or more are crossed by block houses (institutional brokerage firms specializing in large transactions). Sometimes they represent both sides of the order, acting as broker for both the buyer and seller. In certain of these cases it may be of value to know if a stock exchange specialist has taken any stock in position on the block trade.

Block houses positioning (buying for their own trading account) a block that trades on a big down tick from the prior trade will try to dispose of their stock as soon as possible over the next few trading days.

Block trades unchanged or only $\frac{1}{8}$ of a point above or below the prior trade are confusing and misleading to the public and are sucker bait for the uninitiated. Arbitrage and deliberate painting of the tape by crossing blocks that are being sold on $\frac{1}{8}$ of a point upticks complicate the analysis of large transactions.

Goldman, Sachs is perhaps the leading block house, with Salomon Brothers also being a giant factor in this specialty. Block firms take large risks and at times may run their block operations as a loss leader to attract greater syndicate, bond, or other commission business.

Learning Ticker Tape Stock Symbols

A good tape reader should learn the stock symbols of most of the leading stocks. All stocks have an abbreviated ticker symbol, such as GM for General Motors, T for American Telephone, and XON for Exxon.

Symbols are easy to learn. However, there are many newly listed stocks each year, so you have to keep abreast of new symbols. Some new listings, particularly on the American Stock Exchange or NASDAQ market, can become exciting growth leaders in certain types of market cycles where the AMEX or NASDAQ is in favor.

Below is an example of the New York Stock Exchange ticker tape. This sample shows a 10,000-share block of IBM which traded at $154\frac{5}{8}$ (the first two digits, *1* and *5*, are deleted) as well as 100-share trades in General Electric, J.P. Morgan, Hewlett Packard, American Express, and Merrill Lynch. A big block of 1,500 American Telephone and Telegraph traded at $34\frac{1}{2}$.

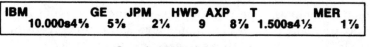

Sample NYSE ticker tape

Since many equities tend to move in industry groups, a seasoned tape reader will usually look for confirmation of strength in at least one other important stock in the same group. For example, if Aluminum Co. of America shows unusual strength in the market, you would expect either Alcan Aluminum, Reynolds Metals, or Kaiser Aluminum to also show strong price and volume action.

Don't Buy into Overhead Supply

Last, a professional tape reader always avoids buying securities as they approach former overhead supply price areas and will wait to see if a stock is able to break through its recent overhead supply zone before considering purchase.

Many amateur and even professional investors do not understand the fundamental but critical principle of overhead supply, so out of ignorance they make poor stock selections. Ignorance in the stock market always costs money.

Watch for Tape Distortion Around Year's End

A certain amount of distortion can occur in the activity in optionable stocks around option expiration dates. There is also a significant amount of year-end distortion in stocks during December and sometimes through January and early February.

The year's end is a topsy-turvy, tricky time for anyone to buy stock since numerous trades are made for tax considerations. Many low-grade losers will suddenly seem strong, while former leaders lie idle or correct. In time, this misleading activity dissipates and the true leaders reemerge.

General market sell-offs also occasionally start after the beginning of a new year, which further adds to the difficulty. Fake-out action can occur with one big "up" day followed by a big "down" day, only to be followed by another big "up" day. For these reasons, I would periodically just as soon take a vacation in January.

In addition to watching the New York Stock Exchange tape, which is now called a consolidated tape because it also shows transactions from regional exchanges, tape readers can view the Dow Jones News Tape, which continually provides company news and comments from around the world. Reuters also supplies an excellent news service.

Analyze Upticks and Down Ticks

One helpful tool in judging overall performance is to analyze a stock's upticks and down ticks. The total blocks over a period of time that occurred on plus ticks of $\frac{1}{4}$ point or more from the previous trade can be compared to the total volume on $\frac{1}{4}$-point or more down ticks in a stock.

The *Daily Graphs* service has a computerized screen that tabulates the top 50 stocks in the overall market for the past week in terms of net plus ticks shown on the stock exchange ticker tape. A separate list of the top 50 on-balance minus tick stocks is also given. These lists might be significant in picking up net accumulation or distribution in stocks. But be careful. Not every stock under accumulation by an institution is a correct investment decision. They, too, make many lackluster choices.

An active do-it-yourself investor with enough study might, in time, even be able to recognize when specific large institutions are buying. This could be done by analyzing and becoming very familiar with quarterly portfolios of several of the most active and aggressive large institutional portfolios.

When a stock trades at its buy price, the individual investor can usually afford to wait for the first block or two to show on the tape. The small investor, if skillful, has the advantage of waiting until the force behind the move is so powerful that the stock has to thrust out of its base pattern. The institutional buyer usually feels a need to start a little earlier, due to its size disadvantage.

Investors should be careful not to assume that a big block on the down side from the previous trade is always a dark sign. Once a block overhanging the market is out of the way, a stock customarily will finally rally. Specialists that take blocks on big down ticks will usually try to dump their position on upticks afterwards.

View Key Stocks as General Market Indicators

Some tape detectives feel specific stocks are predictive of the entire market. The saying used to be, "As General Motors goes, so goes the market." This is not necessarily always true. However, at times certain key industry leaders in the stock market, such as IBM, may be viewed in this fashion. Many professional traders feel if Merrill Lynch stock gets in trouble, the general market may be headed down. This may be true in some, but not all, cases.

Another telling tape reading indication is when a powerhouse that had led its industry into new highs in the last year or two fails to lead its group anymore when others in the industry make new highs.

Thus, for the winning amateur investor **who has the time and self-control,** learning to read the ticker tape properly could be a useful tool to add to other investment skills.

Interpret and React to Major News

When news of consequence hits the street about the U.S. economy, our government, foreign countries, or international events, the capable tape sleuths are sometimes less concerned with whether the news is good or bad than they are in analyzing the news effect on the market.

For example, if the market yawns at national news that appears to be bad, the investor will feel positive since this is an indication the underlying market may be stronger than originally believed.

On the other hand, if highly positive news strikes the market and stocks give ground slightly, the tape analyst might conclude the underpinnings of the market are weaker than previously believed. The essential point is not always whether the news is good or bad but how the market handles itself in face of seemingly positive or negative news.

Sometimes the market overreacts or even counteracts favorable items or disappointing news. On Wednesday, November 9, 1983, someone ran a full page ad in *The Wall Street Journal* predicting rampant inflation and another 1929 depression. The ad appeared during the middle of an intermediate correction in the market. Its warnings were so overboard and exaggerated that the market immediately responded with a rapid 17-point advance and the beginning of a rally that lasted for several days.

There is also a marked difference between a market that tumbles for a couple of days on definite scare news, which is easy to understand and explain, and one which slumps noticeably on no apparent news at all.

The experienced tape investigator will have a good memory or keep records of all past major news events and how they affected the market. These would include important items, such as President Eisenhower's heart attack, the Cuban missile crisis, the Kennedy assassination, an outbreak of war, the Arab oil embargo, and rumors of various government actions such as wage and price controls, U.S. flagging of Kuwait oil tankers in the Persian Gulf, or unsound legislation pending in Congress.

Old News versus New News

Both good and bad news becomes old news after being repeated several times, and it will frequently have the opposite effect on the stock market than it had when the item initially appeared. This is, of course, the opposite of how propaganda and disinformation work in totalitarian countries—the more a lie or distortion is repeated to the masses, the more it comes to be accepted as a truth. When a news item has become widely known or anticipated, it is usually discounted by experienced individuals in the marketplace, blunting the effect of its release.

News can also be very paradoxical and confusing to the market neo-phyte. For example, a company can have a bad quarterly earnings report released and the stock may go up in price when the news is reported. When this occurs, it is often because the news was known or anticipated ahead of time and a few professionals may decide to buy or cover short sales once all of the bad news is finally out. Some institutions may feel they are wily to follow the old saw, "Buy on bad news." Others believe they should provide support for one of their large positions at a difficult time.

Analyzing the News Media

There are several excellent books written on the subject of analyzing national news. Humphrey Neill, author of the 1931 classic *Tape Reading and Market Tactics,* also wrote *The Art of Contrary Opinion,* which carefully examines the way identical news stories are reported quite differently in the various cities' newspaper headlines, and how that can be misleading to stock owners.

His contrary opinion investment theory is developed by illustrating how frequently conventional wisdom or accepted consensus opinion expressed in the national news media turns out to be ill-conceived or wrong.

Media expert Bruce Herschensohn wrote a short, easy-to-read book entitled *The Gods of Antenna.* It specifically tells how our national TV news can manipulate and bias the news to influence and help form public opinion. It was published in 1976 by Arlington House in New Rochelle, New York. Another book on the subject is *The Coming Battle for the Media,* published in 1988 by William Rusher.

The most outstanding study on the subject was published in 1986 by Adler & Adler, 4550 Montgomery Avenue, Bethesda, Maryland, entitled, *The Media Elite,* by authors Rothman and Lichter. In it, they interview 240 journalists and top staffers at *The New York Times, The Wall Street Journal, The Washington Post,* and *Time, Newsweek,* and *U.S. News & World Report* magazines, and the news departments of ABC, CBS, NBC, and PBS. When asked to rate their fellow workers' leanings, they said by a margin of seven to one their co-workers were mostly on the liberal left versus the conservative right. Eighty-five percent of the top national journalists were found to be liberal and voted the Democratic ticket in recent elections.

How the national news is edited and presented does dramatically affect every investor, our economy, public opinion, and public confidence in the economy, our government, our President, and the stock market.

To succeed financially as individual investors or as a nation, we need to learn to separate with better insight and perspective the relevant accurate facts from the national media's own political agenda, personal opinions, feelings, beliefs, or desires.

18

How to Pick the Best
Industry Groups, Subgroups,
and Market Sectors

Common stocks, like people, tend to move in groups. Each market cycle is led by specific industries. One time, computer and electronic stocks may be the leading groups, and in another period, retail or defense stocks will. According to computer analysis, 37% of a stock's price movement is due to subgroup influence and 12% to major group influence.

Normally the leading industry throughout one bull market will not come back and lead in the next cycle, although there are some irregular exceptions to this rule. Groups that emerge later in a bull market now and again are early enough in their own stage of improvement to weather a bear market and resume advancing to set the pace in the next bull market.

In our institutional service every week the computer arranges each of the 200 groups in order of their group relative-price strength for the last six months. The strongest categories are shown in Volume I of the Database books and the weaker groups are contained in Volume II each week. Buyers operating on the undervalued philosophy love to do their prospecting in Volume II.

Analysis has shown that stocks in the top 50 or 100 groups, on average, perform better than those in the bottom 100. We are, therefore, more interested in companies in Volume I of the institutional service.

As a typical rule, the top quartile of groups perform substantially better pricewise than do the bottom quartile of groups. **In the period from 1970 through 1982, the best-performing listed individual stocks belonged to industry groups with a median strength rank of 61 out of**

200. This median industry-price rank of 61 was measured just before each stock's big price increases began.

Why Track 200 Industry Categories?

Why do we divide securities into 200 industry groups rather than the 82 groups categorized by S&P? In our modern economy there are many new segments to every industry. We call them subgroups.

For example, in the 1970 market, if economic research told you to look for an improvement in housing and a big turn in the building cycle, what stocks would have been included in your definition of the building group? Many institutions used Armstrong Corporation, Georgia Pacific, U.S. Gypsum, Johns Manville, and the like.

Rather than one building group, there were actually 10 different sub-segments to the building industry in the 1971 bull market. That means 10 different ways you could have played the building boom.

You could have invested in gypsum stocks, the lumber and plywood group, the plumbing group (Masco), home builders (Kaufman & Broad), mobile homes or low-cost housing, building material retailers and wholesalers (Standard Brands Paint, Scotty's Home Builders), the mortgage insurance group (MGIC), the air-conditioning group, the carpet industry, and the related cousin group of home furnishings and furniture.

Guess where the traditional building stocks were during 1971? That's right; they were buried deep in the back of Volume II (the weakest section) of the institutional database service all year, while newer subgroup sectors of the building industry in Volume I (the front half) of the service advanced over 200%!

In the 1978 to 1981 market sequence, the computer industry was one of the leading groups. Traditionally oriented money managers then considered the industry to consist of IBM, Burroughs, Sperry Rand, and the like. However, these were only large mainframe computer manufacturers. They failed to perform during that cycle, while the many subdivisions of the computer industry had unbelievable performance.

You could have selected the minicomputer group (Prime Computer), the microcomputer family (small home computers, such as Commodore International), the graphics group (which included cad-cam manufacturers like Computervision), word processing companies (Wang Labs), the peripheral group, the computer software industry (Cullinane Database), or the time-sharing industry. These winners increased five to ten times in price.

Industries of the Future or Past?

There will be many new subgroups in the future, imaginative applications most of us haven't thought of yet. As this endless stream of ingenious offshoots of the original mainframe industry multiply every year or two, exciting new subgroups to monitor will be added to our database. Change and new technology are occurring in the United States at an accelerating pace. Automation is also the way we keep track of it.

After all, we are in the computer, communications, and space age. New inventions and technologies will spawn thousands of new and superior products and services. Space research should be promoted.

Industries of the future can create gigantic opportunities for everyone. Industries of the past, while at times quite interesting, may present less dazzling possibilities.

Here are a few older industries whose greatest growth was possibly in the past (unless, of course, major changes occur).

1. Steel
2. Copper
3. Aluminum
4. Gold
5. Silver
6. Oil
7. Textile
8. Chemical
9. Paper
10. Railroad
11. Railroad equipment
12. Utilities
13. Tobacco
14. Airlines
15. Old-line department stores

Industries of the future might include:

1. Computer, computer-related services, and software
2. Laser

3. Electronics

4. Communications

5. New concepts in retailing

6. Space exploration and research

7. Medical and drug

8. Special services

A Stock's Weakness Can Spill Over to the Group

Displaying and monitoring stocks by industry groups can also help get you out of weakening investments faster! After a stretch of success, if one or two important stocks in a group break seriously, their weakness will usually wash over into the remaining issues in that field, sooner or later.

Weakness in several principal building stocks was the paramount indication in February 1973 that Kaufman & Broad and MGIC were vulnerable and should be sold, even though Kaufman & Broad and MGIC had to that date resisted the failure of sister stocks.

At that time there was unanimous agreement by fundamental research firms that MGIC had a 50% annual increase in earnings locked in for the next two years, and it would merrily continue its course, unaffected by the building cycle. The analysts were very wrong, as MGIC later collapsed along with the rest of the deteriorating group.

In February 1973, ITT traded between $50 and $60 while every other stock in the conglomerate classification to which ITT belonged had been in long declines. The two central points overlooked by four leading research firms that recommended ITT in 1973 were:

1. ITT was in a very weak group.

2. For the prior 20 months, ITT had been in a steady downtrend in relative price strength even though the stock's price had held up.

Oil and Oil Service Stocks Top in 1980–1981

This same "wash-over effect" within groups was seen in 1980–1981 after a long period of advance in oil and oil service stocks, when our early warning criteria caused us to put stocks like Standard Oil of Indiana, Schlumberger, Gulf Oil, and Mobil on the sell or avoid side in late 1980.

A few months later, we recognized we had turned negative on almost the entire oil sector and that we had seen the top in Schlumberger, which was the most outstanding of all the oil service companies. One simply had to conclude that, in time, the weakness would wash over into the complete oil service industry.

Therefore, we put equities like Hughes Tool, Western Co. of North America, Rowan Companies, Varco International, and N L Industries on the sell side even though the stocks were making new price highs and showed quarterly earnings escalating in some cases 100% or more. These moves baffled many experienced professionals on Wall Street and at large institutions.

However, we had documented and studied the historical precedence of how groups topped in the past. Our actions were based on sound principles and facts that had worked over decades, rather than on personal opinions of analysts or one-sided information from company officials.

Within a few months all of these stocks began substantial declines as professional money managers slowly realized that once the price of oil had topped and the major oil stocks were under liquidation, it would be only a matter of time before oil drilling activity would be cut back.

This single decision to advise clients to sell oil and oil service stocks from November 1980 to June 1981 was perhaps one of our more valuable calls. We even told a Houston seminar audience at The Galleria Plaza Hotel in October 1980 that the entire oil sector had topped. Seventy-five percent of those in attendance owned petroleum stocks. They probably didn't believe a word we said.

We were not aware at the time, or even in the several months following, of any other New York Stock Exchange firm that had taken a negative stand across the board on the energy and related drilling-and-service sector. In fact, the exact opposite occurred.

In the July 1982 issue of the *Institutional Investor* magazine, 10 energy analysts at eight of the largest and most respected brokerage firms took a highly positive view and advised purchasing these securities, as they appeared cheap because they had had their first correction from their price peak.

This is just another example of how opinions, even if they come from the very highest places, are frequently wrong when it comes to making or preserving money in the stock market. The behavior of markets is usually right. Analysts that do not understand this are destined to cause some substantial losses for their clients. Decisions like the above are one of the reasons why we were able to become a leading research and strategy input to some of the better institutional investors in the country.

Has the Stock Market Really Changed?

Many inexperienced investors somehow think the market today is very different. Some maintain it is more volatile. Others believe because it is dominated by institutions, many of the old methods don't work anymore.

Still others feel that with so much information available, everything is known and already discounted in the price of stocks. Stocks, as a result, are efficient, they feel, so attempts at stock selection are destined to fail. I was astonished to read as late as the early 1980s that some respected publications still repeated such academic nonsense.

Program trading is a recent development which can be disruptive and harmful and scares the public. For this reason, I think it should be restricted by the SEC or the Stock Exchange. (The 50-point rule helps.) The simultaneous execution and ganging up on a broad list of 150 blue chip stocks selected by a computer is unnerving and distorting.

However, my experience is that precious little has changed. The same old things happen in the market, cycle after cycle; it's just that the players are different. I'll give you an example to illustrate that what happened in 1973 and 1981, with weakness in certain stocks of a group spilling over and affecting the rest of the flock, happened years earlier in 1961.

The Bowling Boom Tops

Brunswick stock was a prominent performer in 1960 and 1961. Throughout Brunswick's tremendous move that began in 1958 until its peak in 1961, AMF, a stock that also made automatic pinspotters for bowling alleys, gyrated pretty much in unison with Brunswick. After Brunswick peaked in March 1961, it rallied back from $50 to $65. But for the first time, AMF did not recover with Brunswick. This was the subsurface tip-off that the move in Brunswick was not going to last, that the stock should be sold—the entire group had made a long-term top.

One practical rule is to avoid buying any stock unless there is confirmation of its strength and attractiveness by at least one other important stock in the same group. The few instances where this confirmation is missing should be in stocks you can classify as totally unique companies. Walt Disney should have been classified at points in the past as a unique entertainment company, rather than just a company in the unsteady movie group.

Through our building of historical models in the stock market, there are two other valuable concepts we've discovered. The first we named the "follow-on group effect."

The "Follow-On Group Effect"

When efficient new jet aircraft took to the skies in 1963 through 1965, airline stocks also flew. As a result of materially increased air travel, the hotel stocks had a tremendous bull market beginning in 1967. Loews and Hilton were big winners. A shortage of hotel space was the follow-on effect caused by the large increase in air travel.

When the price of oil grew dear in the late 1970s, oil companies began drilling like mad for the pricey substance. As a follow-on result, rising oil prices not only fueled a huge price surge in oil common stocks in 1979, but oil service stocks gushed the next year as oil companies aggressively stepped up exploration.

The roaring sales success of small- and medium-sized computer manufacturers during the 1978–1981 bull market created the "follow-on" demand for computer service, software, and peripheral products in the market resurgence of late 1982.

Use the Cousin Stock Theory

We labeled the second concept the "cousin stock theory." If a group is doing exceptionally well, there may be a distinctive supplier company that is also enjoying expanding sales.

In 1965, Boeing was selling many new jet airliners as a result of escalating airline demand. A cousin stock to Boeing was Monogram Industries which, of all things, supplied chemical toilets for all the new jets. Monogram earnings increased 200%, and this little gem had a 1000% advance.

In 1983, Fleetwood, a leading manufacturer of recreational vehicles, was a big winner in the stock market. Textone was a small "cousin stock" because it supplied vinyl-clad paneling and hollow-core cabinet doors to recreational vehicles and mobile home companies.

Basic Conditions Change in an Industry

Most industry group moves occur because of a substantial change in the conditions in an industry. For example, in 1953 aluminum and building stocks had a powerful bull market due to the pent-up demand for housing that was the follow-on aftermath of war. There was such a shortage of gypsum board that gypsum salespeople were offered new Cadillacs by some contractors just to let builders buy a carload of wallboard.

In 1965, the onrush of the Vietnam war, which was to cost $20 billion or more, created a solid demand for electronics. Companies such as Fairchild Camera advanced over 200% in price.

Scan Measures of an Industry's Relative Strength

Industry group-strength ratings are published by many services. On the next page is an example of group ratings which appear every week in the *Daily Graphs* service. A scan of this list each week will show you not only which groups are currently strongest, but which groups have just moved into the top 100. This could be an early indication of possible new group leadership when confirmed by other fundamental economic checks.

On August 14, 1970, the mobile home sector crossed into the top 100 groups and remained in the top 100 until February 12, 1971. The group returned to the top 100 on May 14, 1971, and fell into the bottom half on July 28, 1972. In the prior cycle, mobile homes were in the top 100 groups in December 1967 and dropped to the bottom half in 1969. The price advances of mobile home stocks were spellbinding during these positive periods.

Fidelity Funds of Boston also shows more than 25 industry mutual funds whose recent performance can be checked to spot the best-acting industry sectors.

Listed below are the leading industry groups of each bull market from 1953 through early 1994.

1953–1954	Aerospace, aluminums, building, paper, steels
1958	Bowling, electronics, publishing
1959	Vending machines
1960	Foods, savings & loan, tobacco
1963	Airlines
1965	Aerospace, color television, semiconductors
1967	Computers, conglomerates, hotels
1968	Mobile homes
1970	Building, coal, oil service, restaurants, retailing
1971	Mobile homes
1973	Gold, silver
1974	Coal
1975	Catalog showrooms, oil
1976	Hospitals, pollution, nursing homes, oil
1978	Electronics, oil, small computers
1979	Oil, oil service, small computers
1980	Small computers

1982   Apparel, autos, building, discount supermarkets, military electronics, mobile homes, retail apparel, toys

1984–1987   Generic drugs, foods, confectionery and bakery, supermarkets, cable TV, computer software

1988–1990   Shoes, sugar, cable TV, computer software, jewelry stores, telecommunications, outpatient healthcare

1990–1994   Medical products, biotech, HMOs, computer peripheral/LAN, restaurants, gaming, banks, oil and gas exploration, semiconductors, telecommunications, generic drugs, cable TV

You can purchase a 35-year wall chart from *Investor's Business Daily* that shows all the leading groups as they occurred in the market and the three or four individual stocks that lead each group. *Investor's Business Daily* also publishes wall charts covering 50 years of news events and key economic and market indicators.

TOP 50 INDUSTRY GROUPS

INDUSTRY	THIS WEEK	LAST WEEK	4 WEEKS AGO	8 WEEKS AGO	3 MONTHS AGO
CABLE TV	1	1	4	16	17
UTILITY-TELEPHONE	2	4	24	74	90
FOOD-CONFECTIONERY	3	5	51	54	120
TOBACCO	4	6	36	49	122
MACHINERY-FARM	5	3	3	5	14
STEEL-PIPE & TUBES	6	7	1	6	19
RETAIL-CONVENIENCE STRS	7	19	9	21	33
UTILITY-ELECTRIC POWER	8	12	128	182	188
FERTILIZERS	9	2	13	4	25
SOAP & CLNG PREPARATNS	10	10	77	81	98
CONGLOMERATE	11	13	41	55	48
FINANCE-CONSUMER LOANS	12	21	48	122	111
PUBLISHING-PERIODICALS	13	16	39	32	11
PAPER-BUSINESS FORMS	14	31	74	95	132
BANKS-MIDWEST	15	22	47	102	104
FOOD-MISC PREPARATION	16	17	94	71	69
AUTO MFRS-FOREIGN	17	9	5	38	45
IRON ORES	18	8	6	10	61
COPPER MINING & MILLING	19	43	2	1	2
RETAIL-SUPERMARKETS	20	18	17	26	23
PUBLISHING-NEWSPAPERS	21	11	22	22	22
UTILITY-WATER SUPPLY	22	38	163	169	172
BANKS-WEST	23	26	46	111	129
TRANSPORTATION-RAIL	24	15	43	35	36
BEVERAGES-BREWERS	25	20	93	91	139
CONTAINERS-METAL	26	32	52	63	88
CONTAINERS-PAPER/PLASTIC	27	55	61	86	145
RETAIL-CATALOG SHOWROOMS	28	29	29	20	15
GLASS PRODUCTS	29	40	38	15	28
SCHOOLS	30	24	16	43	51
FINANCE-PUBLIC TD INV FD	31	25	110	123	124
INSURANCE-PROP & CASUALY	32	46	98	173	157
MACHINERY-CONST/MINING	33	39	25	23	58
RETAIL-SHOE STORES	34	89	122	64	42
FOOD-FLOUR & GRAIN	35	48	33	33	60
UTILITY-GAS DISTRIBUTION	36	42	137	165	162
BLDG PROD-AIR COND/HEAT	37	61	10	17	59
FINANCE-SBIC&COMMRCL	38	65	108	108	158
FOOD-CANNED	39	64	164	138	123
ADVERTISING	40	33	31	59	75
COSMETICS & TOILETRIES	41	34	45	36	38
CHEMICALS-FIBERS	42	109	20	92	53
BROADCASTING-RADIO/TV	43	30	53	52	44
RUBBER&PLASTIC PRODUCTS	44	37	30	24	32
RETAIL-DRUG STORES	45	80	132	149	133
INSURANCE-MULTI LINE	46	70	95	155	147
INSURANCE-LIFE	47	50	106	130	153
FOOD-BAKERY PRODUCTS	48	27	7	30	64
LEASING COMPANIES	49	51	50	131	116
BANKS-NRTHEAST&FOREIGN	50	67	111	135	141

Weekly industry group ratings

The Importance of Tracking Thousands of OTCs

Early tip-offs of groups that will emerge as leaders in a new bull market cycle can, at times, be found by observing unusual strength in one or two over-the-counter issues and relating that strength to similar power in a listed stock of the same group.

Initial strength in only one listed stock is not sufficient to attract attention to a category, but confirmation by one or two kindred over-the-counter companies can quickly steer you to a new industry recovery in development. To do this, it is necessary to actively follow several thousand stock charts. Many institutional investors only closely study several hundred companies. (See Centex Builders, OTC, March-September 1970, and Kaufman & Broad, NYSE, April-September 1970.)

1. Centex Corporation's relative strength in the prior year was strong and made a new high three months before the stock's price did.

2. Note accelerating earnings, + 50%, during the June 1970 quarter.

3. In March-September 1970, the stock was selling near an all-time high at the bottom of a bear market.

4. A strong Centex (OTC) base coincided with the base in Kaufman & Broad (NYSE).

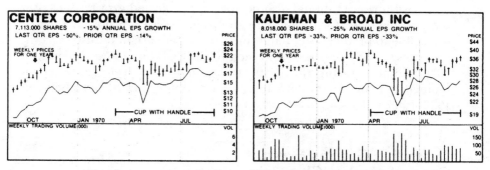

Simultaneous strength of two different stocks in an industry

Picking 1982's Leading Groups

In July 1982, we sent a wall chart to institutional accounts. It displayed 16 defense electronic stocks, because we deduced from analysis of the 7000-stock database that this would be one of the leading groups in the next bull market. Numerous OTC stocks such as Electrospace Systems and Atlantic Research helped us arrive at this early conclusion.

While economic indicators are generally not effective in helping predict moves in the stock market, there are, on occasion, some extremely profitable exceptions when you analyze specific industries. The unprecedented move in oil service stocks in 1980 was clearly forecast by industry employment statistics.

67% of Winners Are Part of Group Moves

Analyzing the most impressive stocks from 1953 through 1993 proved that two out of three of the big market winners were part of group advances. The importance of being on top of your job each week and being aware of new group movements should not be ignored.

In addition to narrow industry categories, there are broad general economic sector groupings, such as basic industry cyclical stocks, consumer goods and services, transportation, finance, and high-technology stocks. In database research we also pay attention to areas of the country where corporations are located. In our Datagraph rating of companies as far back as 1971, we assigned extra points for those headquartered in Dallas, Texas, and other key growth or technology centers in the United States, such as Santa Clara County and Los Angeles.

Shrewd investors should also be aware of projected growth rates over the next few years for various age groups in America. From such data it is possible to predict potential future growth for certain industries.

Because of the upsurge of women in the workplace and the gush of baby boomers during the 1980s, the women's apparel group, led by Limited Inc. and Dress Barn Inc., soared straight out of sight between 1982–1983 and 1986.

Defensive Groups Flash General Market Clues

It is also important for market buffs to know the defensive stock groups. Prime defensive industries are gold, silver, tobacco, foods, grocery chains, and electric and telephone utilities. If you see increased buying begin in a number of these stocks after a couple of years of a bull market, you may be witnessing an indication that many of the bull market groups could be near a top. Prolonged weakness in the Utility Average could also forecast increasing interest rates and a bear market ahead.

When analyzing industries, we have found some to be so small that signs of strength in the group might not be relevant. For example, if only two small, light-trading companies make up a sector, it may not be enough to call a group. On the other hand, there are industries with too many companies, such as the chemical industry. This excessive supply does not add to their attractiveness unless some extremely unusual changes occur in their industry conditions.

Is Your Stock in the Top Half of Its Own Group?

The institutional service arranges companies within an industry in order of their current week's computerized Datagraph rating. Quality stocks in the top half of their own group are better investments in almost all cases than are stocks in the bottom half of the same group.

Because every graph measures the same crucial investment factors on a comparable basis, a manager or analyst can quickly screen every alternative in a group by comparing 120 basic factors of one stock to another. In 15 minutes, an experienced professional can pinpoint the two or three equities in a group which appear worthy of further fundamental research. The remaining stocks that do not measure up should be eliminated from additional consideration.

An institution could save its research department a great deal of time and money if it checks extensive data such as this first to determine the stocks that have the best chance of gaining greater market acceptance.

This suggestion alone might save millions in needless research expenses and substantially increase efficiency and performance of pension fund portfolios. This, in particular, could be a boon to some state and educational funds, which really need the money but have, in the past, sometimes operated under antiquated methods and rules and, as a result, achieved relatively undistinguished results.

Before concluding this section, you must know that the gold group moved into the top half of all 200 industries on February 22, 1973. Anyone ferreting out such information received the first crystal clear warning of the worst market upheaval that has occurred since 1929.

So, if you want to produce superior results in the stock market, **you can't ignore the market strength or weakness of the 200 industry groups and subgroups.**

19

Improving Management of Pension and Institutional Portfolios

If you own a mutual fund or your employer has a company pension fund, it is quarterbacked by an institutional money manager and you, as an individual investor, have a vested interest in knowing that he or she is doing the job professionally.

Today's markets are dominated by institutional investors. That's perhaps good, because investing in the market can be a full-time business. Below is a list of institutional investors that, according to CDA Investment Technologies, Inc., of Rockville, MD, performed substantially better than average during the 5-year period that ended April 30, 1990. Professional

5 Years Ended 4/30/90

	Annualized rate of return
Bank pooled funds	
NCNB	31.0%
Sun Bank, N.A.	24.4%
Bank One, Indianapolis, N.A.	22.6%
Fidelity Management	21.5%
State Street Bank & Trust Co.	21.2%
Mutual funds	
Financial Strategical Portfolios-Health Sciences	24.0%
20th Century Gift Trust	22.9%
Hartwell Emerging Growth	20.9%
AIM Constellation	20.7%
Vanguard Special Portfolio-Health Care	20.7%

investors do not panic as easily on the downside as the public on occasion might. In fact, institutional buying support is commonly seen at prices on the way down.

Institutions also manage immense sums. For example, the California State Teacher's Retirement System and Public Employees' Retirement System's flow of new money to be invested is approximately $600 million per month. The total new monies being pumped into pension funds overall could increase by as much as 15% per year in the future.

Almost all institutional purchasing is 100% cash, with no borrowed, or margin, money used, so this builds a far sounder foundation for your securities than if more speculative margin accounts ruled our stock markets. (In 1929, the public was heavily involved in the stock market, speculating with 10% cash and 90% margin.) There is so much competition and evaluation of performance records today that the best professional investment managers are probably more proficient than 20 years ago.

The problems the stock market encountered from 1969 to 1982 were caused by economic mistakes and bad policy decisions made by our top politicians in Washington, D.C., not by institutional or public investors. The stock market is like a giant mirror that merely reflects basic conditions, political management, and psychology in the country.

Having managed individual accounts, pension funds, mutual funds, having supervised research analysts and dealt closely with many top institutional money managers, I have a few observations about some of the more difficult or debatable areas of professional money management.

I certainly am not perfect, and I've made my grand share of mistakes over the years; that's how all of us learn and, hopefully, become wiser. Maybe my having "hands on" experience with all sides of the street through many economic cycles will make a few of these attempts at constructive suggestions valuable.

If you are an individual investor, extra insight into the subject of the world's institutional money managers should be helpful because they are the enormous force behind 80% of the important price moves in the market. After all, institutions represent the "I" in our C-A-N S-L-I-M formula, and they exert far greater influence upon stock prices than specialists do.

The First Datagraph Books

Those initial 600-page research books were possible for us to produce because of our daily database on the stock market and a new piece of equipment known as a high-speed microfilm plotter.

At the time, this costly computer machinery was so new no one knew how to get a picture of graphs out of it. Once this barrier was cracked, it was possible to turn out complex updated graphs at the rate of one a second, in an automated process.

Today, a single institutional Datagraph displays 94 fundamental and 26 technical essential facts about a company. The same 120 variables are available for every company in the database. This means an analyst can compare any company to any other company either in the same industry or in the entire database.

Interpreting Dome Petroleum's Datagraph

The Datagraph of Dome Petroleum on the facing page has been marked up to highlight a few of the ways to interpret and use this graphic display of fundamental information. We recommended Dome to institutions in November 1977, at $48. Fund managers didn't like the idea or the company's nonconservative accounting, so we bought the stock ourselves. Dome Petroleum became one of our biggest winners of the decade. The case studies you are seeing are real live examples of how it is actually done.

The Pic'n'Save Story

Another stock we recommended in July 1977 that no institution would originally buy was Pic'n'Save. Most felt the company was too small because it only traded 500 shares a day. So we began purchasing it several months later. We had historical models of K-Mart when it traded only 1000 shares a day in 1962 and Jack Eckerd Drug in April 1967 when it traded 500 a day.

Both of these retailers grew into tremendous winners after they were discovered. Average daily trading volume of these issues, as a result, steadily increased. Historical precedence was on our side.

I've always thought of finding an outstanding stock and buying it every point on the way up. That is almost what happened with Pic'n'Save. We bought it every point or two on the way up for several years. I particularly liked the company because they provided a way for families of meager means to buy most of the necessities of life at exceptionally low prices.

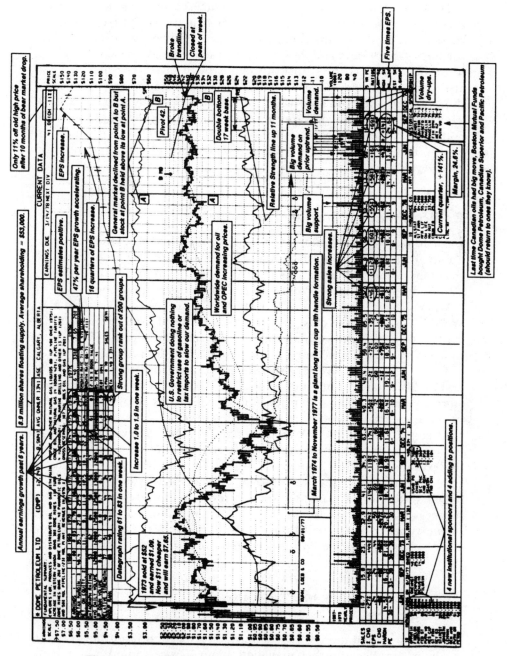

Thirty Positive factors on Dome Petroleum in November 1977

233

This little, unknown company headquartered in Carson, California, turned in a steady and remarkable performance for seven or eight years. In fact, Pic'n'Save's pretax margins, return on equity, annual earnings growth rate, and debt-to-equity ratio were at that time superior to other, better-accepted institutional growth favorites which we had also recommended, such as Wal-Mart Stores. Our early purchases showed over a tenfold gain when the stock was finally sold. The stock was purchased on 285 different days and held for a period of $7\frac{1}{2}$ years. Sometimes it seemed that if it wasn't Chock Full O'Nuts (located in New York City), Wall Street was not too aware of the company and cared even less.

Radio Shack's Charles Tandy

I ran into this same phenomenon in 1967 when we first uncovered Tandy Corp. We convinced only two institutions to buy Tandy stock at that time. Among the reasons given for not buying were that Charles Tandy was just a promoter and the stock didn't pay a dividend.

When I met Tandy for the first time in his office in downtown Fort Worth, Texas, my conclusion was the opposite of Wall Street's initial verdict. Charles Tandy was a brilliant financial man who also happened to be an outstanding salesman (a combination seldom found).

Tandy had innovative incentives, departmental financial statements, and highly detailed computer reports on the sales of every item in every store by merchandise type, price, and category. His automated inventory and financial controls were almost unbelievable.

After the stock tripled, Wall Street analysts began acknowledging its existence, and a few research reports started coming out noting what an undervalued situation Tandy was. Isn't it strange how far some stocks have to go up before they begin to look cheap to everyone?

One of the secrets you, as a winning individual investor, should never forget is that you want to buy a stock when it **is not completely obvious to everyone.** In fact, you'll find few or no research reports available on the very best stock ideas. When several reports show up, it's time to sell.

The Size Problem in Portfolio Management

Many institutional money management organizations feel their key difficulty is size. Because they manage billions in assets, there never seem to be enough big capitalization stocks they can buy or sell easily.

Size is a realistic problem. It's easier to manage $10 million than $100 million and simpler to manage $100 million than $1 billion, and $1 billion is a piece of cake compared to running $10 billion, $20 billion, or $30 billion. The size handicap simply means it is hard to buy or get rid of a huge stock holding in a small- or medium-sized company.

I believe it is a mistake for institutions to restrict investments solely to large capitalization companies. There aren't enough outstanding large capitalization companies in the first place. Why buy a slow-performing stock just because you can easily acquire a lot of it?

From 1981 through 1987, during the Reagan administration, for the first time in history 3000 dynamic, up-and-coming companies had initial public offerings of stock. Many of these small- to medium-sized entrepreneurial concerns will become future market leaders.

Today's markets are more liquid, with the daily volume of many medium-sized stocks averaging 100,000 to 500,000 shares a day. In addition, significant crossing of blocks occurs between institutions.

Individual corporations seeking partly to relieve size problems can divide their money among a number of different money managers.

The institutional asset manager who professionally manages billions of dollars would best be advised to substantially broaden the universe of stocks considered for potential investment to the 4000 or so available. This is preferable to restricting activities to the same limited, approved list of only a few hundred large, well-known or legal list-type companies. The research department of one of the largest banks in the United States only follows 600 companies.

A sizable institution would likely be better off owning 500 companies of all sizes than 100 large, mature, slow-moving companies.

Size Is Not the Key Problem

Size is not the number one problem of institutions. By far the number one trouble is the investment philosophy and particular investment methods utilized by some money management operations.

Many institutions buy stocks based on someone's opinion about the supposed value of a company. Others buy stories. Still others follow economists' top-down predictions of the broad sectors that ought to do well. We believe working from the bottom up produces better results.

For many years institutions used the same standard names and rarely changed their stodgy approved lists. If an institution had 100 widely accepted names on its list, it might add four or five a year and no more.

Many decisions had to be approved by investment committees. Committees make pitifully poor decisions in the stock market!

Investment committees even had members who were not experienced money managers. This is, generally, questionable investment policy.

Ancient rules even today inhibit investment flexibility. For example, some institutions are restricted from buying stocks that do not pay a dividend. This limitation seems in the dark ages because many outstanding growth stocks deliberately do not pay a dividend so they can reinvest their profits to continue internally funding their above-average growth rate.

Other restrictions mandate that half or more of the portfolio be invested in bonds. Most bond portfolios have produced weak results over the long term. Some of these bond portfolios historically used misleading accounting that did not mark their portfolio to current market prices.

In these few situations, reporting of bond portfolio results is too infrequent and the true overall performance is unclear. Too much emphasis is on yield and not enough is on the increase or decrease in market value of the assets in the portfolio.

Bottom Buyers' Bliss

Many institutions buy stocks on the way down and might be categorized as bottom guessers. This is, in some instances, not the best way to produce a superior performance record. It can place decision makers in the position of buying a stock that is slowly deteriorating.

Some money management organizations use evaluation models to select and restrict their investments to stocks in the lower end of past P/E ranges.

While this approach definitely works for a few unusually capable conservative professionals, it is not the best selection method and over time does not produce truly superior results for the typical institution or individual investor. Several major midwestern banking organizations have continually lagged in performance due to utilizing this approach.

Undervalued-Stock Buyers
Usually Lag

A major insurance company in New York that relied heavily on the undervalued method lost a huge account in 1983 due to steady underperformance.

I have witnessed hundreds of institutions and every type of investment philosophy imaginable over the last quarter century, and most of those that concentrate on the undervalued theory of stock selection invariably lag in the results produced when compared to the better money managers today. Sometimes these undervalued situations get more undervalued or trail the market for a considerable time.

Comparing Growth versus Value Results

Over the previous **10 business cycles,** it has been my experience that the very best money managers produced average annual compounded total returns of 25% to 30% and that they were either growth-stock managers or the majority of their successful investments were in growth stocks.

The best undervalued type managers in the same period averaged 15% to 20%, with a few a little over 20%. Of course, the best were definitely in the minority, with the majority not doing this well. Up to now, most individual investors haven't prepared themselves well enough to average 20% or more per year, regardless of the method used.

Value Line Dumps the Undervalued System

The Value Line service, from the 1930s up to the early 1960s, rated stocks it followed as undervalued or overvalued. The company's results were mediocre until they dumped their system in the 1960s and began rating stocks based on earnings increases and relative market action. Since the switch, their performance has materially improved.

Years ago there was a relatively small number of fund managers available for corporations or individuals to choose from. But today there is a proliferation of outstanding professional money management teams using various successful systems.

Institutions frequently require a lengthy glowing report from their research analysts before they can buy a stock not on their approved list. Since the institutions already own a substantial number of companies which they insist their analysts continually follow and update, an analyst might be to a year or more (or never) in getting all the interesting new names onto an approved list and preparing reports on these ideas.

Superior performance comes from fresh ideas, *not* the same old overused stale names. This too little-too late method should be reappraised.

Overweighting and Underweighting to the S&P

Many institutions invest primarily in stocks in the S&P 500 and try to overweight or underweight positions in certain sectors. This practice assures they will never do much better or worse than the S&P average. An outstanding growth stock manager should be able to average about 1½ times the S&P index over a period of many years.

Weaknesses of the Industry-Analysts System

Another widely used and fairly ineffective practice followed both by research firms and most institutional investors' research departments is to have a huge number of analysts with their responsibilities for company coverage broken down by industries.

For example, the classical securities research department has an auto analyst, electronics analyst, oil analyst, retail analyst, drug analyst, and on and on. The problem with this method is its tremendous inefficiency and its tendency to perpetuate mediocrity in performance. What does an analyst assigned two or three out-of-favor groups do? Recommend to their money managers the least bad of all the poor stocks followed by the analyst.

On the other hand, is an oil analyst outstanding just because the oil group is the big performing group for the year and he or she picks two or three good winners? When the oil stocks boomed in 1979 and 1980, all of them doubled or tripled. The best ones shot up five times or more. The theory behind this method of dividing research is that a person can be an expert on a particular industry. In fact, Wall Street firms go so far as to hire a chemist from a chemical company to be their chemical analyst and a Detroit auto specialist to be their automotive analyst.

These individuals frequently know many of the nuts and bolts about their industry but in some cases have a dubious understanding of the stock market and what makes leading stocks go up and down. Of course, it is stocks and the stock market that determine how successful your investments will be. (Incidentally, do you know what makes a stock go up? A stock generally goes up because it has fewer buyers. They just happen to be bigger buyers.)

Firms also like to advertise they have more analysts, the largest department, or more top-ranked "all star" analysts. I would rather have five good analysts who are generalists than 30, 40, or 50 who are confined to limited specialties. And what are your chances of finding 30 or more analysts who are all outstanding at **making money in the stock market or at coming up with money-making ideas?**

Financial World's Startling Survey of Top Analysts

A *Financial World* magazine article dated November 1, 1980, found that analysts selected by *Institutional Investor* magazine as the best (all-star) analysts on Wall Street were overrated, overpaid, and materially underperformed the S&P averages.

As a group, the "superstar" industry analysts failed on two stock picks out of three to match either the market as a whole or their own industry averages. They also seldom provided sell recommendations, limiting most of their advice to buy or hold. Investment banking creates conflicts.

The *Financial World* study confirmed research we performed in the early 1970s. In that study, we found that only the minority of Wall Street recommendations were successful. We also concluded that in a period where many sell opinions would have been proper, only one out of every ten reports made sell suggestions.

One of the unsolved problems is that 80% of the research in Wall Street today is written on the wrong companies. Every industry analyst has to turn out a certain amount of product. Buy only a few industry groups lead a typical market cycle. There is insufficient front-end screening or control to determine which are the superior companies on which current reports should actually be written.

The Daily Pile of Research Reports

Most institutional money managers daily receive a stack of research reports a foot or so high. It's a great waste of time trudging through these trying to find a good stock to buy. If you are lucky you may spot one company out of twenty that is right to buy.

Database Power and Efficiency

With massive automation we rapidly screen through over 8000 companies in our database. If we become interested in the defense industry, we can call up 225 different corporations whose primary business is in the defense area, whereas the typical institution might look at the standard names followed on its approved list, such as Boeing, Raytheon, United Technologies, and two or three other big, well-known names.

With 120 comparable variables on each of the 225 companies stretching back for a number of years, as well as the ability to display these variables quickly on identical graphic displays, it is possible, in 20 minutes, to determine the five or ten companies in the entire group that possess outstanding characteristics worthy of more detailed research.

The remaining companies, because they showed deficiencies on many vital variables, need not even be researched because of the substandard characteristics uncovered in the initial screening. In other words, you can generally help tell an institution's analysts where they should spend their time more productively. Yet, few research departments are organized to take advantage of such advanced and disciplined procedures.

How well has this approach worked? In 1977, we introduced an institutional service called *New Stock Market Ideas and Past Leaders to Avoid*. It is published every week, and its documented 16-year performance record is shown on the following page (+ 7126%).

Buy selections outperformed *avoid* suggestions more than 20 to 1, and *buy* picks outran the S&P 500 stocks over tenfold. The compounding over the 16 years' time helps make a record like this possible.

We provide institutional investors with computerized quarterly reports showing the performance of every *buy* and *avoid* recommendation made in the *New Stock Market Ideas* service.

In our organization, all analysts are young MBAs who have had a few years of varied business experience before coming to us.

We like to send two analysts on all company visits. However, we do not call on many companies. Having a massive amount of factual data on every firm, we are able to discover a corporation beginning to improve or to get into trouble much earlier.

Also, this method has the advantage of not being gullibly dependent on whatever the company happens to tell analysts. We have no investment banking clients or market-making activities, and we do not manage money for others, so those areas of potential bias are nonexistent.

Between June 1983 and June 1984 we gave 385 sell recommendations to institutional investors who subscribed to our consulting service. In no case was it necessary for us to have inside information or talk to the company or its officers before providing sell suggestions.

It is naive to believe companies are going to tell you when they are starting to have problems. By using our own data and research, we also thoroughly discourage any reliance on tips, rumors, and inside information. We just don't need, want, or believe in the use of inside information.

NEW STOCK MARKET IDEAS (NSMI) LONG-TERM RECORD

1 IN PERFORMANCE WITH 5628 BUY RECOMMENDATIONS

MARCH 1994

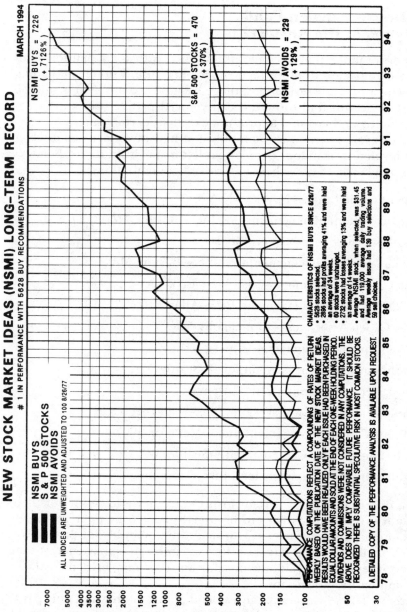

NSMI BUYS = 7226
(+ 7126%)

S&P 500 STOCKS = 470
(+ 370%)

NSMI AVOIDS = 229
(+ 129%)

▮ NSMI BUYS
▮ S & P 500 STOCKS
▮ NSMI AVOIDS

ALL INDICES ARE UNWEIGHTED AND ADJUSTED TO 100 8/26/77

CHARACTERISTICS OF NSMI BUYS SINCE 8/26/77
- 5628 stocks selected.
- 2896 stocks had profits averaging 41% and were held an average of 34 weeks.
- 60 stocks were unchanged.
- 2732 stocks had losses averaging 13% and were held an average of 14 weeks.
- Average NSMI stock, when selected, was $31.45 and had 119,000 average daily trading volume.
- Average weekly issue had 139 buy selections and 59 sell choices.

PERFORMANCE COMPUTATIONS REFLECT A COMPOUNDING OF RATES OF RETURN WEEKLY BASED ON THE PUBLICATION DATE OF THE NEW STOCK MARKET IDEAS. RESULTS WOULD HAVE BEEN REALIZED ONLY IF EACH ISSUE HAD BEEN PURCHASED IN EQUAL DOLLAR AMOUNTS AND SOLD AT THE END OF EACH ONE-WEEK HOLDING PERIOD. DIVIDENDS AND COMMISSIONS WERE NOT CONSIDERED IN ANY COMPUTATIONS. THE ABOVE DOES NOT IMPLY COMPARABLE FUTURE PERFORMANCE. IT SHOULD BE RECOGNIZED THERE IS SUBSTANTIAL SPECULATIVE RISK IN MOST COMMON STOCKS.

A DETAILED COPY OF THE PERFORMANCE ANALYSIS IS AVAILABLE UPON REQUEST.

Sixteen-year performance record of NSMI (or New Stock Market Ideas)

Is In-House Pension Fund Management the Answer?

A few corporations that become disillusioned with their pension fund performance decide to move their money in-house. I doubt that going in-house provides any serious advantage because the problem is still the same. How do you find those few experienced people who know what they are doing and are able to produce excellent performance?

Another growing trend is the number of new investment counseling groups formed by standout people that left major institutions. Below is only a small list of a few of these enterprising organizations.

Clement Capital, Inc.—New York, NY

Essex Investment Management Co., Inc.—Boston, MA

Friess Associates, Inc.—Greenville, DE

Hellman, Jordan Management Co., Inc.—Boston, MA

Husic Capital Management—San Francisco, CA

INVESCO Capital Management, Inc.—Atlanta, GA

Jundt/Capen Associates—Minneapolis, MN

Kailing Capital Management—Chicago, IL

Kunath, Karren, Rinne & Atkin, Inc.—Seattle, WA

Nelson, Benson & Zellmer, Inc.—Denver, CO

Nicholas-Applegate Capital Mgmt., Inc.—San Diego, CA

Northern Capital Management, Inc.—Madison, WI

Sirach/Flinn, Elvins Capital Mgmt.—Seattle, WA

Southeastern Asset Management, Inc.—Memphis, TN

On a different subject, certain institutions may allow some of their important investment policies to be overly dictated by their attorneys. For example, attorneys may say an institution should not pay up for research or they should pay cash for research. My experience is that some attorneys are so cautious or adamant they may prevent realistic and sound business decisions.

There are a few institutional investors that dictate they will only pay 6 or 7 cents a share for any order executions. These restrictive internal policies are sometimes set up by their attorney. They can always find some brokerage firms that will execute at the very cheapest prices, but they will probably lose access to the best research organizations. Once again, always buying the cheapest execution and the cheapest available research can substantially hurt your long-term performance.

On still another subject, many large money-management groups deal with entirely too many research firms. For one thing, there aren't that many strong research inputs, and dealing with 30 or 40 different firms dilutes the real value and impact of those few good ones. The confusion, doubt, and fear created by the conflicting advice given by several firms at critical junctures can be exceptionally expensive.

The 1982 and 1978 Full-Page Bullish Ads

Let me provide you with an example. We placed a full-page ad in *The Wall Street Journal* early in 1982 stating that the back of inflation had been broken and we believed the important stocks had already made their lows. In May 1982, we mailed out wall charts showing 20 consumer growth stocks and another wall chart on defense electronic issues we believed might be attractive for the bull market ahead.

In May 1982, we made a special point to go to New York and Chicago and contact several large institutions. In these meetings we stated a bullish posture and provided a list of names that should be purchased.

The stance we took was diametrically opposed to the position of most institutional research firms at that point and to the negative flood of news appearing daily in the national media.

Most firms were outright bearish, predicting another big down leg in the market and projecting that interest rates and inflation were going to soar back into new high ground under pressure of massive government borrowing that would crowd the private sector out of the marketplace.

The ill-founded fear and confusion created by these questionable judgments frightened large institutional investors so much they hesitated and could not fully capitalize on the fact that the two leading groups for the newly evolving bull market that was quickly to follow had already surfaced and had been identified.

It appeared professional managers had been bombarded with so much "expert" negative Wall Street input that they found it hard to believe these positive findings. By investing fully on margin in the summer of 1982, we internally produced the largest performance in the firm investment account in any year since the beginning of the firm. This account had a twenty-fold increase in profits from 1978 to 1991. Events such as this make us believe it is an advantage not to be headquartered in rumor-filled and emotion-packed Wall Street.

DON'T LET THE GLOOM BUGS FOOL YOU... INFLATION'S BACK IS BROKEN AND IT'S TIME TO INVEST FOR THE RECOVERY AHEAD

Now's the time for both corporations and individuals to grab on to President Reagan's powerful incentive programs and invest.
William O'Neil & Co. believes the stock market averages may be near their lows now. We also think the *best* individual stocks have seen their lows and will one by one find their way back to new high ground over the next 6 months.

It is very normal to have gloom, doubt and pessimism during the low point of a recession and the bottom of a bear market. However, we do not agree with Henry Kaufman's recent negative conclusion that inflation will move back toward old record levels when the economy recovers. We believe the backbone of excessive inflation has definitely been broken and will wind down more in the year ahead. There are a number of reasons for our optimistic outlook on inflation.

Long Term Trend Of Oil, Real Estate And Commodity Prices Has Broken
To begin with, oil prices, as well as oil company stocks, topped a year ago. OPEC should consider lowering prices; otherwise they may have to continue reducing production and income. The large oil price jumps of recent years caused widespread changes to other fuels, increased energy efficiency, lower overall demand and a loss of world oil markets. High prices also stimulated exploration and new production. The old law of supply and demand still works.

Gold, silver, diamonds and other inflation-hedge commodity prices have made major long term tops and are down substantially from their highs. And we do not agree with a well-known economist nor a prominent member of the House of Representatives who advocate the U.S. must return to the gold standard. This out-moded concept did not prevent government's financial mismanagement since 1965, and it can not now substitute for competence.

Real estate prices, after tremendous increases, have been coming down. In Southern California where building trends frequently lead other areas of the country, condominiums and homes became so overpriced that both prices and interest rates need to decline further before sales can pick up. The reason is simple. People can not make or qualify for monthly payments of $2,000 or more.

The auto giants' bad management decisions and high interest rates have caused them to permanently lose share of market. Their best hope is for both big labor and big management to reduce all costs and auto prices with no strings attached and try to regain part of their lost market. If they do not act together, the auto industry will likely be a declining U.S. industry in the future.

Airline fares have been too high and are being lowered to attract more customers.

The Consumer and Producer Price Indexes have fallen and the trend of money supply has been down for almost a year and a half. This should lead to lower inflation ahead.

Reasons Why Interest Rates Should Be Lowered
The Federal Reserve Board discount rate is now substantially higher than the inflation rate, and so are long term Bond yields.

A few years ago the discount rate was raised several times by abnormal amounts to protect the American dollar from attack. This problem no longer exists. Confidence in the U.S., its leadership and the dollar have materially improved.

Interest rates at the low point in each past recession have progressively been at higher levels. If this trend continues, we could have higher low points and higher high points for interest rates in each new business cycle. The Federal Reserve Board should consider lowering the rate over the next 6 months to a point slightly below the 10% low of the previous cycle, thus breaking the escalating trend.

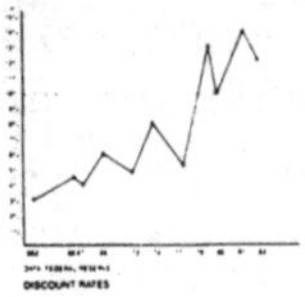

The Federal Reserve Board should probably not try to fight inflation all by itself. Tight money did not solve the inflationary problem in the recession in 1974, nor in 1977-78. While money supply is the primary determinant of the rate of inflation, it is not the sole cause as some people believe. Last year's decline in inflation was caused primarily by a leveling in oil prices and farm prices. Money supply policy, in no way, created good weather, good crops and an over-supply of oil.

Our government may also want to consider having money supply figures available monthly, rather than weekly since weekly guessing, over-reaction and public over-emphasis make sound interpretation of the major trend unlikely. The Fed may want to consider the possibility of better control of new sources of money supply.

For example, Money Market funds have no reserve requirements. What might occur if a run were to happen on Money Market funds? The high rates Money Market funds offer drain funds from other more productive areas and forces other agencies to raise their rates in order to try and compete.

Congress also has an important responsibility to cut spending and government inefficiency. Congress can also deregulate natural gas and include a windfall tax to help lessen the 100 billion dollar deficit.

Because of new tax incentives for saving there should be an increased pool of savings available as business begins to borrow in the recovering economy.

The auto industry and its supplier industries will not recover until interest rates decline further. Ten percent unemployment economically should be unacceptable and could be dangerous to the country as well as politically damaging.

High interest rates are hurting the world economy.

Why You Should Buy Common Stocks Now
Stocks are the only remaining area in the economy that appears greatly undervalued. Gold, real estate, diamonds, commodities have all had excessive increases and as a result seem over-priced with less potential for profit. The number of shareholders in America, after declining for many years, should increase significantly. The cause of this increase will be the substantially lower capital gains tax (20% vs. nearly 50% in recent years) and the new investor's retirement accounts with their flexibility and tax saving features.

Stocks on average are currently selling at 6 and 7 times annual earnings. Such low price earnings ratios have not occurred since the 6 P E at the bottom of the Dow Jones in 1974, the 7 P E in 1949 and the 5 P E in 1932. And as you know prices and P E's improved materially from these historical lows. We believe the decline in price earnings ratios that began in 1962 has ended and the future will show progressive upward reevaluation for stocks.

If channel lines are drawn along the tops and bottoms of the Dow Jones Industrial average since the early 1930's the Dow is once again sitting on its major long term bottom trendline.

The lower tax for all consumers, combined with lower inflation, will ease the pressure on consumer's discretionary income for the first time in many years. This should result in a resurgence in the better consumer growth stocks.

The William O'Neil & Co. Senior Growth Stock Index is performing stronger than general market indexes; and the Dow Jones Industrials failed to confirm the recent new lows in the transportation index.

Not only have we seen several brokerage house economists being very bearish, but a preponderance of public advisory services have been preaching total gloom and doom. This usually happens around market bottoms.

Odd lot short selling accelerated in January—another psychological sign of bottom market action. Those who expect a climax bottom with heavy selling will likely be disappointed since this phenomenon occurred mainly in past years when markets had greater public involvement. Institutions, which dominate our markets today, do not panic as readily along bear market lows. They tend to pull back from selling or actually buy on the way down.

What Areas Of The Market Seem Favorable Now?
We are in the midst of a revolutionary computer and communication age. The better, innovative leaders in this area should continue to do well.

As mentioned earlier, we believe there will be a resurgence in selected consumer growth stocks. As time passes, various defense electronic stocks should benefit from our planned defense build-up. Companies producing automated teller equipment should benefit from increased branch banking and automation. Selected drug and medical companies that show superior earnings per share increases should be favored. Speciality retailers plus entertainment companies with new products in areas such as video games seem to be succeeding. As the economy slowly recovers, other areas will emerge with improved and accelerating earnings.

Why Corporate America Should Be Investing Now
Big corporate America, in the past, has invested somewhat backwards and been slow to take innovative new risks. Traditionally, big business only expands at the end of a business cycle. It seems to us that the top of a cycle is the poorest time to invest in new plant capacity and automation, because interest rates and competition are at a peak. The shrewdest and cheapest time to invest is at the low point in a business cycle where prices will be the best and your bargaining power the greatest. Andrew Carnegie, an earlier industrial leader, used to say, "the first man gets the oyster, the second the shell."

The American people and in particular American businessmen and women, in our opinion, may have one of the best Presidents since Abraham Lincoln. They should get off the dime and take advantage of the tremendous tax incentives now available. President Reagan's incentive programs are broad and very workable. The sole cause of the current recession has been the Federal Reserve's tight money policy. The press, the country and many politicians may be making the mistake of continually underestimating Ronald Reagan's ability and leadership.

Big companies need to change in order to survive. All growth is built on change. They need new products and some of them need new management. Giants like Mobil, U.S. Steel and DuPont, trying to acquire other large companies for the most part is counterproductive only making a giant larger, less creative and less efficient. Few conglomerates know how to run more than one or two businesses correctly and the high prices paid for such acquisitions are questionable to say nothing of the poor utilization of billions of dollars of this nation's badly needed capital.

The Administration's recently announced council to study productivity is primarily staffed with big business representatives. The makeup of this group should be amended to include several leaders of small to medium-sized, innovative growth companies. These are the companies that have shown the greatest productivity in our country. Big business has been the least productive, least creative and least imaginative. Having a council loaded with big business leaders is a little like a council of losing football coaches meeting to tell everyone how to be No. 1.

How Many Truly Successful Pessimists Do You Know?
In summary, we see a psychological comparison to 1947-49. This was the time our troops returned home after World War II. The common thinking then was that bad times were ahead because there wouldn't be enough jobs to absorb those returning from war. The common fears turned out to be wrong as pent-up demand launched a new economic surge. Likewise, today we believe the common fears may turn out to be wrong. The economy will be stimulated with the strongest incentives in decades and the needs of mankind. We are also reminded of old Sewell Avery forever hoarding his money and completely missing his market. Springtime is only around the corner and it makes us think. How many truly successful pessimists do you know? So, don't let the gloom bugs fool you.

If you are an institutional or a corporate investor you may be interested to know that our latest January issue of *New Stock Market Ideas & Past Leaders To Avoid* lists 170 stocks as buy recommendations and only 38 stocks that should be avoided. Our advice to all Institutional consulting clients throughout the month of January was to buy specific growth stocks into the correction.

If you are an individual investor you may wish to examine our latest new service titled, *Long Term Values*. We introduced this investment service, which covers 4,000 securities, at the bottom of the market in October. This, along with our Daily Graphs Services have over 22,000 annual subscribers, and can be seen in full page ads in *Barron's* every week.

William O'Neil + Co.
INCORPORATED

February 1982 bull market ad

"NOW'S THE TIME TO GRAB THE BULL BY THE HORNS SO YOU DON'T END UP ON THE TAIL END."

William O'Neil + Company believes we are about to enter a new bull market that will be led by small to medium-sized growth companies. So we feel now is the time to begin buying to take maximum advantage of the coming phase.

We realize that most economists and investment firms are still pessimistic; or at best, guardedly optimistic about the direction of the market.

But back on December 5, 1976, when virtually all economists, Washington officials and the majority of investment firms were positive and optimistic about the market, we were quoted in a major article in *Business Week* as being bearish, and suggesting the sale of basic industry and senior growth stocks.

The events of that year have proved us to be correct. And we feel confident that the events of the coming year will prove our current calculations to be equally correct.

There are a number of reasons for our bullish outlook.

Looking back at the Crash of '29.

To begin with, the stock market holocaust of 1973-74 was more severe than generally recognized. While the Dow Jones corrected from 1067 to 570, the vast cross-section of the market experienced huge losses averaging 70% to 80% as measured by broad, unweighted market indexes.

We believe this magnitude of decline most closely resembled the 1929-32 collapse which was 89%. When we look at this earlier dislocation, we see that economic and market recoveries made immediately afterwards were slow and short-lived, followed by a downward correction of less serious magnitude in 1934. That was because the serious damage had already occurred and there were no longer the excess demands in the economy or the market. Rampant speculative consumer spending and business over-extension had ceased. This downward correction was then followed by a steady upward recovery.

Looking at the current situation, we followed the 1973-1974 collapse with a short recovery period in 1975-1976. Then, as we predicted in *Business Week*, there followed a downward correction in 1977 that has extended until the present. But as in the recovery period of the early 30's, we expect this current bear market to be milder than the one in 1973-74, and to end this year.

How high will the market go?

William O'Neil + Co. believes the Dow Jones Industrials could hit 1300 over the next 36 months.

This is based on the historical precedence that bull market cycles have recovered 85% to 90% from their low points. On this basis, a low this year anywhere in the 700-736 area would yield a Dow of 1300. And from a Dow level of approximately 750, we believe the risk/reward ratio is 7 to 1 in favor of buying stocks. This is calculated on our estimates that the maximum probable downside risk is 675 (−10%), and the maximum probable upside potential is 1300 (+550 DJIA points or over 70%).

The market is currently undervalued.

Another factor that supports our stand on a new bull market is that stocks are currently cheap and, for the most part, undervalued.

As an example, in 1961 IBM sold for 80 times its annual earnings, and paid a dividend yield of less than ½ of 1%. Today you can buy it for 12 times earnings, and get a 4.7% dividend to boot.

Furthermore, the price-earnings ratio of the Dow Industrials today is 8 times. The yield is approximately 6%. And the Dow sells below book value. These value levels have only been achieved at a few points in the last 30 years.

Finally, cash rich corporations are taking advantage of the values with large numbers of tender offers for companies.

Sources of demand in the new bull market.

We believe that there is a large potential demand for common stocks that are currently undervalued. The current conservative trend among many institutions has resulted in sizeable cash reserves which represent major potential buying power.

Similarly, individuals have invested in high yield areas that represent another large source of future demand, once interest rates decline.

Finally, foreign investors are an area of demand we expect to see in the future because the U.S. is still the strongest democratic country, and represents one of the world's soundest investment markets.

How to know when we reach the bottom.

There is still the question of when we will reach the bottom of the current bear market, and how it can be recognized. It has been the thesis of William O'Neil + Co. as expounded in a series of investment conferences given last September in New York, Boston, Chicago and San Francisco that the market would not bottom out until there was more fear. This fear would produce the necessary technical shakeout and additional pessimism.

We feel that fear has now occurred.

One index of it is the price of gold, which at near $200 has become a highly speculative and risky commodity.

Earlier this year the non-reappointment of Arthur Burns reinforced concern for the American dollar and our balance of payments deficit in light of our dependence on foreign oil supplies. We feel the new chairman, G. William Miller, will prove to be strong, sound and innovative. And we expect to see an energy program implemented to ease fears about our balance of payments deficit. Furthermore, we think a tax cut this year is inevitable. If this cut is tied directly to an immediate reduction in price and wage increases and to reducing interest rates, it will help arrest our inflationary spiral. And this will help reaffirm confidence in the American dollar.

We feel that once confidence in the dollar is regained, it will shake loose the potential sources of demand for stocks among institutions, foreign investors and eventually individual investors, particularly once the market passes 1100 on the Dow.

Why we say small to medium-sized growth firms will lead the next phase.

Many experts believe the bear market won't be over until secondary stocks break down. We believe this stand is similar to the one technicians took in 1976 when they predicted a third leg up to a 1200 Dow that never occurred.

We believe good secondary companies with continual increases in earnings are not going to break down, but will hold up and actually become leaders in the new bull market. We can look back to 1960 as a recent example of a recessionary year in which secondary stocks failed to break down, and subsequently provided market leadership.

We feel this will be true again in the next cycle, because in the past few cycles major institutions have concentrated heavily in the same high-priced, large capitalization, senior growth stocks that fulfilled "approved list" requirements. Today many of these companies are showing maturing or poor growth in earnings. At the same time, hundreds of smaller and medium-sized companies with innovative new products are showing outstanding growth records, and are selling at cheaper prices.

We believe that in the future more organizations, under pressure from ERISA to cover the "actuarial" requirements of their funds, will look for wider diversification and non-index stocks because these stocks will probably continue to outperform the indexes.

We can see the value in this diversification today when the S & P 500 is stronger than the Dow Jones Average. The NYSE Composite is stronger than the S & P. And the total market itself is stronger than the NYSE Composite. We can also see that the Transportation Index is stronger than the Industrials. And the OTC stocks are performing very well. The American Stock Exchange, overlooked the past few cycles, is near new highs for the year. And Barron's Low Priced Stock Index is equally powerful. Even the London Stock Exchange has displayed unusual strength, providing an advanced hint that our stock market's next major cycle will be up.

Which categories will be the leaders.

We expect to see many companies that have been overlooked since the 1973-74 credit crunch become prominent again because of their outstanding earnings records. We believe the leaders in the new bull market will be found among hospital and medical stocks, aerospace, airlines and airfreight, hotel stocks, computer peripheral companies, publishing, food franchisers, insurance companies, pollution-control companies, drug companies with new products, contact lens companies, Japanese stocks traded on our market, Canadian Oil companies, private aircraft and dozens of specialty companies with unique products.

Looking back at 1954-68.

If we look back at the bull market cycles from 1954 to 1968, we see that they were led by small to medium-sized companies that, at the time, had exciting new products to market.

1954: Reynolds and other aluminum companies with new light-weight metals. North American Aviation and the aerospace group with I.C.B.M. missiles.

1955: Schering Plough with new drugs.

1956: IBM (4 million shares then outstanding) with the computer age.

1958: MMM with scotch tape products. Polaroid with instant pictures. Rexall with tupperware. Thiokol and General Tire with rocket propellants. Texas Instruments and Fairchild Camera with transistors. Crown Cork & Seal with aerosol cans. American Photocopy with photocopy machines. AMF and Brunswick with automatic pinspotters for bowling.

1961: Great Western Financial and S&L's with higher interest for savers. Mead Johnson with Metrecal.

1963: Kresge with discount stores. Delta and Northwest Airlines with jet travel. Xerox with dry office copiers. Syntex with birth control pills.

1965: Baxter Labs with new hospital lab and test equipment. Simmonds Precision with space computers and electronics. Xtra with freight containerization. Motorola and Magnavox with color TV's.

1967: Duplan with double knit fabrics. McDonalds with fast food franchising. Digital Equipment with mini-computers. Hilton, Holiday Inns and Loews with follow-on effect of increased jet travel creating demand for more hotels.

1968: Champion Home Builders and Skyline with mobile homes for low cost housing.

Taking a stand on the new bull market.

At William O'Neil + Co. we believe strongly enough in the coming bull market to remove 50 companies from our Sell List. And our Research Analysts have in the last 60 days visited 40 new companies which are included in the 150 names on our Buy List.

On top of that, we recently purchased our third seat on the NYSE.

But we're also putting our mouth where our money is by running this ad and taking a strong stand on the coming bull market. So if we're wrong we stand to lose more than just our money.

We still expect economic news to continue to be poor in the near future. We could continue to see disappointing automobile sales, housing slowing, etc.

But remember that the market started down when people were optimistic, and it will start back up when most people are pessimistic. The market will discount and look ahead 8 to 9 months. By the time economists decide whether or not we are in a recession, the new bull market will be underway. And the biggest profits from any bull market are usually made by those who recognize it first. So those who fail to grab the bull by the horns will wind up on the tail end.

Wall Street Journal
March 29, 1978

□° William O'Neil + Co., Inc.
Publishers of Datagraphs Institutional Research, Member New York Stock Exchange.

March 1978 bull market ad

The savvy individual investor has a gigantic advantage in not having to listen to 50 different strongly held opinions. Perhaps the common-sense lesson you, the private investor, can learn from this example is that majority opinions seldom work in the stock market and stocks seem to require a wall of worry, doubt, and disbelief to climb. Fear is probably the strongest emotion in most of us.

We generally do not attempt to call every short-term or intermediate correction, as sometimes this could be a little foolish and shortsighted for the institutional investor. Primary concentration is on recognizing and acting upon the early stage of a new bull market and on the early beginning phase of each new bear market. This focus includes searching for the market sectors and groups that should be bought and those that should be avoided.

In March 1978, we entered our first full-page ad in *The Wall Street Journal* predicting a new bull market in small- to medium-sized growth stocks. This ad was written weeks ahead of time and we waited to run it until we felt the time was right. This "just right" time happened to be when the market was making new lows and caught investors by surprise.

Our only reason for placing the ad was to document in print exactly what our position was at that juncture so there could be no question with institutional investors later on.

The time when an institutional research firm can be of inestimable value is at these extremely difficult turning points, where many people are petrified with fears or carried away with excessive fundamental stories, information, and overconfidence.

If you don't think fear and emotion can ride high among professional investors, it can. I remember meeting with a group of the top three or four money managers of one important bank at the bottom of the market in 1974. They were about as totally shell-shocked, demoralized, and confused as anyone could possibly be. (They deserved to be; the ordinary stock in the market was off 75%.)

I recall seeing another prime manager about that same time who was thoroughly worn out and actually suffering from market sickness, judging from the peculiar color of his face.

In that period, one of the top mutual fund managers in Boston looked as if he had been run over by a freight train! Of course, all of that is preferable to what happened in 1929, when a few people jumped out of office buildings.

While we no longer place full-page ads in the *Journal* or *Barron's* for obvious reasons, we do have more than 600 of the leading institutional accounts in the United States and around the world that receive our confidential market memos when we feel a major market change could be in process.

The following is verbatim the last memo written before the current edition of this book was published. It projects a moderately bearish 1994 with most growth stocks topping. Sometimes these memos are right and sometimes they are not. This one gave institutions ten weeks of rally to sell into before the market topped in late January 1994. Of course, almost all institutions either were unsure, argued with the conclusions, or just found it impossible to reduce commitments and hold cash when the market was strong and going up. Institutions had less cash in April 1994 than they had in November 1993.

TO: Institutional Clients
FR: William O'Neil
RE: November 19, 1993 Market Memo

For the past four weeks, we have continued to add a large number of this year's growth leaders to the sell/avoid side in our New Stock Market Ideas and Big Cap service. We believe a bear market has started in these stocks. Examples included companies like Best Buy, Promus, Int'l Game Technology, Cabletron, Countrywide Credit, Dial Page, Glenayre, Newbridge, Nextel, Qualcomm, Tellabs, etc. These stocks are different from the Philip Morris, Novell, Nike, and Waste Management names added to the avoid category earlier this year. The recent changes cover a broad area in the high tech and gambling sectors, the two leading groups of the year. If you combine this with noticeable weakness in the banks, insurance and utilities stocks, the breadth of the distribution that has taken place is significant.

Here are a few other pertinent facts: the general market (S&P and DJIA) on Tuesday, Wednesday, and Thursday, November 2–4, came under abnormal liquidation on heavy volume. Likewise, the daily breadth suffered its sharpest two-day drop in two years and was unable to rally back. The IBD Mutual Fund Index also had its sharpest two-day break, as did the NASDAQ average. We believe that the NASDAQ and AMEX average had a speculative price climax on heavy volume four weeks earlier and has since been in a topping process. On Wednesday, November 17, the relative price strength line on the NASDAQ Composite shown in *Investor's Business Daily* broke below its support low of four weeks ago on 360 million shares.

Laggard stocks have been up in recent weeks and the bond market has been down. Last month was an all-time record for new issues and both Zacks and Value Line introduced major new investment services for the public. Both the DJIA and the S&P 500 have shown wedging patterns with no ability to follow through. Interest has revived in gold as a place to hide, even though the fundamentals are not powerful. Finally, the market on a yield and PE basis has been in overvalued territory for some time now. On a worldwide perspective, Europe and Japan still do not have strong economies.

We do not believe this is just another short-term correction and do not believe a stock like Intel is a value simply because it sells for nine times earnings. We expect an earnings slow-down over the next several quarters for Intel. Furthermore, we see a number of market leaders that are topping and expect the next three months and much of 1994 to be a some-what more difficult year.

Many of President Clinton's proposals appear to us to be unsound, particularly in the healthcare area. Our estimate is that 10 years from now, more than $1 trillion in new taxes will be needed to fund his enormous new program. Price controls along with government management could lead to other difficulties. There also seems to be a credibility problem with the President. The Administration says they've decided against price controls, everyone will get to choose his or her own doctor, the system will be better and we'll save more money. Most of his statements are mis-representations of the facts contained in his plan submitted to Congress.

Our suggestion is to reduce your portfolio volatility and reduce portfo-lio concentration in aggressive stocks and groups. We do not, however, expect any bear market correction that might occur to be of a substantial nature (when compared to historical bear markets). Perhaps 15% might be a reasonable guesstimate, because America is in an entrepreneurial phase with hundreds of emerging new companies and new technologies that will cushion any adjustment. We are also in a low interest rate, low inflationary environment with the economy showing a degree of pick-up.

How High-Techs Topped

At the opposite end of the pole. I remember a high-tech seminar given in 1983 in San Francisco that was attended by a crowd of 2000 highly educated, ebullient, and self-confident analysts and portfolio managers. Everyone was there. That marked the exact top for high-tech stocks.

Over the years there have also been some funny situations. We gave a presentation to a bank in another large city. The bank brought in all of its analysts. Close to 20 people were sitting around an impressive table in the board room. Not one analyst or portfolio manager asked any questions during or after the entire presentation. It was the strangest situation I've ever seen, and I've never seen it since. Needless to say, this institution con-sistently performed in the lower quartiles when compared to its more alive and venturesome competitors. It's important to communicate.

Years ago, one medium-sized bank for which we did consulting work insisted we give them recommendations only from the stocks they car-ried on their limited approved list. After consulting with them each month for three months and telling them that there was nothing on their approved list which met our qualifications for buying, we had to honorably part company. A few months later we learned that key offi-cials in that trust department were relieved of their jobs due to their laggard performance for the past several years.

A poor practice followed by some large money-management organiza-tions with relatively unrewarding performance is to fire the head of the investment department and trot outside for a successor who invests in pretty much the same way. Naturally, this does not solve the problem of deficient investment methods and philosophy that continues to be perpetuated.

Security Pacific Bank in Los Angeles was an exception to this rule. In July 1981, it made a change in its top investment management, but it brought in an individual with a completely different approach and superior investment philosophy, as well as an outstanding performance record. The results were dramatic and were accomplished almost overnight. In 1982, Security Pacific's Fund G was ranked number one in the country.

At still another midwestern institution we provided consulting recommendations but they were of doubtful value because the institution was wedded to the cast-in-concrete belief that any potential investment must be screened to see if it passed an undervalued model.

Clearly the best investments rarely show up on any undervalued model. There is no way this institution will ever produce a first-rate result until it changes its philosophy and throws out its undervalued model. This is exceedingly hard for large organizations to do. It's perhaps like attacking deep-seated religious habits and asking a Baptist to become a Catholic or vice-versa.

Penny Wise and Performance Foolish

Some corporations place entirely too much emphasis on saving management fees, particularly when they have giant funds to be managed. Usually an actuary convinces them of the tremendous dollars their pension fund can save by shaving the management fee just one-eighth of 1%.

If companies have billions of dollars to be managed, they should increase the management fees and incentives so the money managers can hire the best money-makers available in the marketplace. The better money managers will earn the extra one-quarter or one-half of 1%, 10 or 20 times over. The last thing you ever want is cheap advice in the stock market. If you were going to have open heart surgery, would you select the doctor who would do it for the absolutely cheapest fee?

Modern Portfolio Theory Not Recommended

As discussed earlier, modern portfolio theory, a strictly theoretical approach that emanated from statisticians in the academic world, acquired a following with a number of institutions in the 1970s.

This effort has proven to be almost a complete waste of time, since its theories were built on assumptions that were not true. One of the reasons that it gained acceptance was many institutions did not understand the market as well as they should have and were, therefore, susceptible to the seemingly plausible application of statistical formulas by college professors.

Of course, most of the university professors who devised these new answers to the stock market had very limited understanding of, or real success with, the stock market. Every study we have conducted and virtually every organization utilizing these statistical methods has shown the concept to be inferior to that used by today's more successful money-management organizations.

All the random-walk theories, to me, are like the experts who years ago claimed a baseball didn't curve, that it was just an optical illusion.

The only thing that can be said about these overeducated, sheltered experts is that they certainly never had to stand at home plate and have a pitcher fire a pitch right at their head before curving a foot and a half over the outside edge of the plate where it was impossible to hit. Actual experience quickly unravels a lot of academic theories.

A few of these academicians have taken jobs on Wall Street. Coming from a world of poorly conceived dividend discount models, it will be interesting to observe how they fare in the real world.

Modern portfolio theory should not be used by institutional investors; it should not be taught in business schools, and it should not be forced upon young analysts studying to pass CFA examinations. It is, in my view, a tremendous misuse of valuable time.

How to Select and Measure Money Managers Properly

Here are a few tips for corporations and organizations that want to farm out their funds to money managers.

In general, managers should be given a complete cycle before you compare and evaluate their performance for purposes of changing managers—from the peak of one bull market period to the peak of another cycle or the trough of one cycle to the trough of another. This will usually cover a three- or four-year period and will allow all managers to go through both an up market and a down market.

At the end of this period, the bottom 20% or so of the managers in total overall performance should then be replaced. Thereafter, every year or two the bottom 5% or 10% of managers over the immediately prior **three- or four-year period** should be eliminated.

This avoids hasty decisions based on disappointing performance over a short period of a few quarters or in any one year. Given time, this process will automatically lead to a positively outstanding group of proven money managers. And it should stay that way, because you'll have a sound, longer-term, self-correcting mechanism, and you won't need to pay outside consultants to tell you when they think you should suddenly replace managers.

In your selection of managers, consideration could be given to their latest three- to five-year performance statistics as well as to a more recent period. Diversification should be considered among the types, styles, and locations of managers. The search should be widespread and not limited to one consultant's narrow, captive universe or stable of managers.

The corporate or pension fund client with money to be managed has to also be especially careful not to interfere at critical junctures—for example, deciding at some time that a greater proportion of their hired managers' portfolios should be either in stocks or bonds or that under-valued stocks should be emphasized.

Clients can intercede by attempting to direct where commissions should go or by directing that executions be given to whoever will provide the cheapest executions. The latter, while a well-meaning attempt to save money, commonly results in forcing upon a money manager someone that provides poorer executions or no research input of real value. This handicap costs the portfolio money as it pays $\frac{1}{8}$, $\frac{1}{4}$, or $\frac{1}{2}$ point or more on trades being executed by more inexperienced people. Meddling corporate sponsors usually think they are saving money.

Another practice that should be seriously curtailed is that of a corporate plan sponsor dictating that portions of the commissions from execution of fund orders be directed to a third party who will then largely rebate them to the corporation. This siphons off incentive dollars that should be used to pay for the best research, execution, and market ideas available to the fund's money manager. A fund will positively never be able to buy the "best market brains" at the cheapest price.

State and Educational Funds Could Do Better

The investment methods used by some state and educational funds could be improved. Some employ fairly deficient methods of stock selection. Once these so-so investment decisions are made, the decision makers tend to ride through the years with losing investments.

Taxpayers normally have to ante up when these funds have mediocre performance. In some cases, states might be better off turning their investment portfolio over to several professional money managers rather than having it run by state employees.

Is an Index Fund the Way to Go?

One last thought about the indexing of equity portfolios. A key fallacy of index funds is the bold assumption that a pension fund's basic objective should be to match some general market index. This is a dangerous and false conclusion.

For example, if we were to go through another 1929, and the general market indexes were to decline 90% in value, no intelligent trustee could possibly believe his or her fund's objective should be to lose 90% of its value. Positively no one would be happy just because they achieved their target of matching the market indexes' disastrous performance.

I actually saw a version of this happen in 1974. I was called in to evaluate a fund that lost exactly 50% of its assets because it was managed by an organization that specialized in and promoted index funds. The irony of the situation was that the corporation was furious at such horrendous losses, but of course this sort of bad performance by an index fund was hushed up and never allowed to be publicized in the press. It was an embarrassment to the company.

I have also seen several index funds that failed to keep up with the index they were supposed to match. Once this occurred, the master planners went back to the drawing board and came up with new versions of indexing which injected more human judgment into formulas. This human analysis and personal analytical opinion contradicted the broad assumption that index funds began with in the first place.

My answer to the whole thing is simple. Why should anyone expect the majority of thousands of money managers to do any better than an average or mediocre job, any more than the majority of musicians, ball players, doctors, teachers, artists, or carpenters perform better than average? The truth of the matter is that the typical person in many fields might be a slightly subpar performer.

The answer in money management is the same as in other occupations—to get above-average results, you have to go out of your way to find the small minority of managers who are above average in their profession.

To say this is impossible and just can't be done is narrow-minded and foolhardy. To say that stocks are a random walk and you can't select securities successfully because all information is already known and totally discounted is also simpleminded, academic nonsense.

Value Line's rating system since 1965 is ample evidence that stocks can be selected which materially outperform the market. Our top Datagraph-rated stocks have substantially outperformed market averages over the 30 years from 1964 through 1993.

Professor Marc Reinganum of the University of Iowa, during a University of Chicago sabbatical produced an independent research study entitled "Selecting Superior Securities." He selected nine variables comparable to those discussed in this book and achieved a 1984–1985 research result 36.7 percentage points greater than the S&P 500.

The stock market is neither efficient nor a random walk simply because there are too many poorly conceived opinions, too many incorrect interpretations, and too many emotions such as pride, doubt, fear, and hope. Sometimes there are just shallow or bad judgments, numerous complex variables, and fast-changing events which analysts do not properly weight even when they possess all relevant information, which is the exception rather than the rule. And finally, there are just too many poor fundamental and technical research reports always recommending mediocre-acting stocks or stocks off in price. Sell recommendations are few and far between at the beginning of each bear market because everything is always a buy on the way down.

One of the nation's largest retailers indexed part of its pension fund because its fund was so huge and unwieldy to manage. The other part they managed internally. I'll end this chapter with a fascinating story about this retailer that illustrates how large older companies react to new opportunities compared to how fast-growing entrepreneurially-managed companies react.

The head of investments for this large retailer was visiting with me in Los Angeles. I took him out to Colton, California and showed him the first Price Club warehouse store that had just opened in the Los Angeles area. I said, "Dave, this is what your company should be doing." He replied that it looked a little like one of their warehouses in Chicago. At a later board meeting, I'm told he presented the idea to top management and was laughed out of the place.

Several months later, Sam Walton flew out to San Diego, talked to Saul Price and went through one of their stores. That night when he returned to Bentonville, Arkansas, his architects were up all night drawing plans for the first SAM's warehouse stores for Wal-Mart.

I know we were pleased with Price Co. since we discovered it early on and held their stock for $3\frac{1}{2}$ years while it was performing well during the early 1980s. Institutional investors might do well to emphasize entrepreneurially-run companies that are in business less than 15 years.

20

18 Common Mistakes Most Investors Make

Knute Rockne, the famous Notre Dame football coach, used to say, "The way to succeed is to build up your weaknesses until they become your strengths." The reason the rank and file either lose money or achieve embarrassing results is because they simply make too many mistakes.

Over a period of 35 years, I have dealt with or known thousands of individual risk takers, all the way from green beginners and amateurs to the most knowledgeable and successful professionals. Following are the mistakes I have noticed made most frequently by individual investors who were not too successful.

1. Most investors never get past the starting gate because they do not use good selection criteria. They do not know what to look for to find a successful stock. Therefore, they buy fourth-rate "nothing-to-write-home-about" stocks that are not acting particularly well in the marketplace and are not real market leaders.

2. A good way to ensure miserable results is to buy on the way down in price; a declining stock seems a real bargain because it's cheaper than it was a few months earlier. For example, an acquaintance of mine bought International Harvester at $19 in March 1981 because it was down in price sharply and seemed a great bargain. This was his first investment, and he made the classic tyro's mistake. He bought a stock near its low for the year. As it turned out, the company was in serious trouble and was headed, at the time, for possible bankruptcy.

3. An even worse habit is to average down in your buying, rather than up. If you buy a stock at $40 and then buy more at $30 and average out your cost at $35, you are following up your losers and mistakes by

putting good money after bad. This amateur strategy can produce serious losses and weigh you down with a few big losers.

4. The public loves to buy cheap stocks selling at low prices per share. They incorrectly feel it's wiser to buy more shares of stock in round lots of 100 or 1000 shares, and this makes them feel better, perhaps more important. You would be better off buying 30 or 50 shares of higher-priced, sounder companies. You must think in terms of the number of dollars you are investing, not the number of shares you can buy. By the best merchandise available, not the poorest. The appeal of a $2, $5, or $10 stock seems irresistible. But most stocks selling for $10 or lower are there because the companies have either been inferior in the past or have had something wrong with them recently. Stocks are like anything else. You can't buy the best quality at the cheapest price!

It usually costs more in commissions and markups to buy low-priced stock, and your risk is greater, since cheap stocks can drop 15% to 20% faster than most higher-priced stocks. Professionals and institutions will not normally buy the $5 and $10 stocks, so you have a much poorer-grade following and support for these low-quality securities. As discussed earlier, institutional sponsorship is one of the ingredients needed to help propel a stock higher in price.

5. First-time speculators want to make a killing in the market. They want too much, too fast, without doing the necessary study and preparation or acquiring the essential methods and skills. They are looking for an easy way to make a quick buck without spending any time or effort really learning what they are doing.

6. Mainstream America delights in buying on tips, rumors, stories, and advisory service recommendations. In other words, they are willing to risk their hard earned money on what someone else says, rather than on knowing for sure what they are doing themselves. Most rumors are false, and even if a tip is correct, the stock ironically will, in many cases, go down in price.

7. Investors buy second-rate stocks because of dividends or low price-earnings ratios. Dividends are not as important as earnings per share; in fact the more a company pays in dividends, the weaker the company may be because it may have to pay high interest rates to replenish internally needed funds that were paid out in the form of dividends. An investor can lose the amount of a dividend in one or two days' fluctuation in the price of the stock. A low P/E, of course, is probably low because the company's past record is inferior.

8. People buy company names they are familiar with, names they know. Just because you used to work for General Motors doesn't make

General Motors necessarily a good stock to buy. Many of the best investments will be newer names you won't know very well but could and should know if you would do a little studying and research.

9. Most investors are not able to find good information and advice. Many, if they had sound advice, would not recognize or follow it. The average friend, stockbroker, or advisory service could be a source of losing advice. It is always the exceedingly small minority of your friends, brokers, or advisory services that are successful enough in the market themselves to merit your consideration. Outstanding stockbrokers or advisory services are no more frequent than are outstanding doctors, lawyers, or baseball players. Only one out of nine baseball players that sign professional contracts ever make it to the big leagues. And, of course, the majority of ball players that graduate from college are not even good enough to sign a professional contract.

10. Over 98% of the masses are afraid to buy a stock that is beginning to go into new high ground, pricewise. It just seems too high to them. Personal feelings and opinions are far less accurate than markets.

11. The majority of unskilled investors stubbornly hold onto their losses when the losses are small and reasonable. They could get out cheaply, but being emotionally involved and human, they keep waiting and hoping until their loss gets much bigger and costs them dearly.

12. In a similar vein, investors cash in small, easy-to-take profits and hold their losers. This tactic is exactly the opposite of correct investment procedure. Investors will sell a stock with a profit before they will sell one with a loss.

13. Individual investors worry too much about taxes and commissions. Your key objective should be to first make a net profit. Excessive worrying about taxes usually leads to unsound investments in the hope of achieving a tax shelter. At other times in the past, investors lost a good profit by holding on too long, trying to get a long-term capital gain. Some investors, even erroneously, convince themselves they can't sell because of taxes—strong ego, weak judgment.

Commission costs of buying or selling stocks, especially through a discount broker, are a relatively minor factor, compared to more important aspects such as making the right decisions in the first place and taking action when needed. One of the great advantages of owning stock over real estate is the substantially lower commission and instant marketability and liquidity. This enables you to protect yourself quickly at a low cost or to take advantage of highly profitable new trends as they continually evolve.

14. The multitude speculates in options too much because they think it is a way to get rich quick. When they buy options, they incorrectly

concentrate entirely in shorter-term, lower-priced options that involve greater volatility and risk rather than in longer-term options. The limited time period works against short-term option holders. Many options speculators also write what is referred to as "naked options," which are nothing but taking a great risk for a potentially small reward and, therefore, a relatively unsound investment procedure.

15. Novice investors like to put price limits on their buy-and-sell orders. They rarely place market orders. This procedure is poor because the investor is quibbling for eighths and quarters of a point, rather than emphasizing the more important and larger overall movement. Limit orders eventually result in your completely missing the market and not getting out of stocks that should be sold to avoid substantial losses.

16. Some investors have trouble making decisions to buy or sell. In other words, they vacillate and can't make up their minds. They are unsure because they really don't know what they are doing. They do not have a plan, a set of principles, or rules, to guide them and, therefore, are uncertain of what they should be doing.

17. Most investors cannot look at stocks objectively. They are always hoping and having favorites, and they rely on their hopes and personal opinions rather than paying attention to the opinion of the marketplace, which is more frequently right.

18. Investors are usually influenced by things that are not really crucial, such as stock splits, increased dividends, news announcements, and brokerage firm or advisory recommendations.

If you hunger to become a winning investor, read the above items over very carefully several times and be totally honest with yourself. How many of the habits mentioned above describe your investment beliefs and practices? As Rockne would say, "These are the weaknesses which you must systematically work on until you can change and build them up into your strong points."

Poor principles and poor methods will yield poor results. Sound principles and sound methods will, in time, create sound results.

My parting advice to you is: Have courage, be positive, and don't ever give up. Great opportunities occur every year in America. Get yourself prepared and go for it. You'll find that little acorns can grow into giant oaks. Anything is possible with persistence and hard work. It can be done, and your own determination to succeed is the most important element.

Index

About the Author

William J. O'Neil is one of Wall Street's most seasoned and successful veterans. At age 30, he bought his own seat on the Big Board with profits made in the stock market and founded William O'Neil and Co., Inc., a leading investment research organization now based in Los Angeles. The firm's current clients are 600 of the top institutional investment managers in the world. Mr. O'Neil created the New USA Mutual Fund, whose assets are over $200 million—and is also the founder of Investor's Business Daily, the fastest-growing national competitor of The Wall Street Journal.

Get All The Information
Every Business Day —
With *Investor's Business Daily!*

Now that you've read the book, *"How To Make Money In Stocks,"* it's time to use your knowledge to make money in the stock market. Investor's Business Daily can help.

With *Investor's Business Daily*, you get:

- *"Actionable" market data and research in easy-to-use tables, charts and graphs that can make your investment decisions that much better.*
- *"Smarter" stock tables that help you use the C-A-N S-L-I-M method to select stocks.*
- *More, improved business news every day, including "The New America," featuring profiles of fast-growing, innovative companies; "News For You," with features that can show you how to improve your personal and professional life; and "The Economy," with all the pertinent facts executives need to make decisions.*
- *All of this ... every business day.*

And best of all, you get **TWO WEEKS FREE** — with no obligations or commitment. To start your subscription, just complete and send in the postpaid form below. Then you'll be on your way to being more informed about business — *every business day*.

FOLD HERE

✔ **Yes,** I want 2 weeks of Investor's Business Daily FREE!

(Please Print)

Name _____

           Last   First   M

Address _____

City _____ State _____ Zip Code _____

Home Phone (_____) _____

Business Phone(_____) _____

RETURN THIS CARD TODAY TO GET STARTED
ON YOUR TRIAL SUBSCRIPTION!!

For faster service, call **1-800-831-2525.**

(Subscribers within the last 4 months not eligible. This offer valid in the U.S.A. only.)

CUT HERE

FOLD OVER FLAP, TAPE AND MAIL